POLICING THE POLICE

VOLUME 2

Contents

Preface   vii

INTRODUCTION: Peter Hain   1

Section 1

THE POLITICS OF POLICING AND THE POLICING OF
POLITICS: Martin Kettle   9
    Sir Robert Mark Speaks Out – 11, *The Royal Commission Debate*
    – 21, *Law and Order Campaign* – 27, *Police Chiefs and their*
    rank-and-file – 31, *Police and the Army* – 33, *Police Leadership*
    and Politics – 35, *The Special Branch* – 52, *Conclusion* – 58,
    Notes – 60

Section 2

SOCIETY UNDER SURVEILLANCE: Duncan Campbell   65

    The Police National Computer – 72, *Personal Files on the PNC* –
    83, *Security and Secrecy* – 93, *'C' Department: National*
    Intelligence Computer – 96, *Northern Ireland: Society under*
    control – 109, *Collators: Local Intelligence Gathering* – 117,
    Thames Valley Collator Project – 120, *Command and*
    Control/Management Information – 131, *Society and Privacy* –
    140, *Notes* – 146

Section 3

THE SPECIAL PATROL GROUP: Joanna Rollo   153

    Prologue – 153, *Solving the 'Worst of All Crimes'* – 165, *Economic*

Crisis and Industrial Struggle – 167, *The Third Force* – 171, *The SPG Comes of Age* – 173, *Death of Kevin Gately* – 179, *Grunwick* – 181, *Lewisham* – 184, *The SPG and the Black Community* – 186, *Regional Versions of the SPG* – 194, *Riot Control* – 197, *Conclusion* – 199, *Epilogue* – 202, *Notes* – 206

Index   213
Contributors   216

Preface

This second volume of *Policing the Police* is divided into three parts. First, Martin Kettle looks at the politics of modern policing; then Duncan Campbell reveals the alarming extent to which society is being kept under surveillance by the use of sophisticated technology; finally, Joanna Rollo examines the Special Patrol Group and its responsibility for Blair Peach's death in Southall in April 1979.

The first volume* concentrated on the police complaints system and the Prevention of Terrorism Act, sharing with this book the objective of providing an alternative analysis of modern policing to the conventional wisdom dominating media coverage and public attitudes.

I am particularly grateful to Bill Swainson of John Calder (Publishers) Ltd. and to our agent, Tessa Sayle, for their effort and persistence over the book; thanks also to Sam and Jake who must imagine sometimes that their father (when at home) is more interested in playing with his typewriter than with them ...

Peter Hain, September 1979

---

* Peter Hain (ed.), Derek Humphry and Brian Rose-Smith, *Policing the Police*, Volume 1 (John Calder, 1979).

Are the police becoming a law unto themselves? And are they assuming an independent political role? These were the main questions posed in the first volume of *Policing the Police*, and this second volume attempts to answer them more thoroughly.

In particular, we focus on the issue of control: both the control function performed by the police and the lack of democratic control of the Force. Martin Kettle identifies two key elements in the politics of modern policing: *centralization* and *specialization*. Operationally and organizationally, the police are becoming increasingly centralized; whilst the manner in which different sections of the Force now specialize in particular areas, often employing sophisticated methods, contrasts with the traditional notion of generalized policing which required police officers to be sensitive to the wider public they served in many different ways. Both these elements are accentuating the problem of police accountability and encouraging the Force's tendency to operate as an independent political agency with its own political objectives, albeit ones which conform to the British police's historic function of defending the capitalist system.[1] Duncan Campbell adds a third crucial element: *surveillance technology*. Growing police dependence upon computer networks, and the collection of files on literally millions of people, is placing the whole of society under surveillance in a way which makes easy clichés about Orwell's *1984* look all too uncomfortably prophetic. And he develops the concept of 'pre-emptive policing' which he shows is quite different from conventional detective work and poses an enormous threat to civil liberty.

All three of these elements – centralization, specialization and surveillance technology – are sharply exhibited in the Special Patrol Group of the Metropolitan Police which Joanna Rollo analyzes. She also discusses a fourth element – *professional elitism* – which, with the other three, contributes more towards a clearer understanding of the role of modern policing than is often suggested.

For this book, above all, seeks to expose the myth of impartiality that surrounds public perception of the police's function in society: the common view that they stand in the middle, playing referee and holding the ring for decent upright citizens to go about their lawful business in freedom and security. That they stand at the interface between the capitalist state and the people is not denied. Indeed, once that is accepted, the bias of their wider role is more readily comprehensible. Nor is it denied that individual police officers and police units often perform honourable and even heroic tasks which leave many individuals and whole communities severely in their debt. What this book seeks to show is that, notwithstanding individual acts of bravery or whole areas of public service performed by the police, the general direction of the Force and the ideology by which it operates threatens a society purporting both to be democratic and to protect the rights of each citizen impartially. In short, it is the system and ideology of modern policing which this book criticizes rather than the failings of individual officers.

Where the police as individuals particularly invite attack however is in their failure to acknowledge legitimate criticism or even to accept that such criticism is permissible. This is shown successively by each of the contributors to the book and was exemplified in the typical police response to the first volume. Rather than attempting to counter the evidence and arguments assembled in the first volume, police spokesmen were generally dismissive in terms – 'It's that Hain again!' said the Police Federation's official magazine[2] – which make it impossible to engage in debate at a level that rises above the mere exchange of slogans. This unwillingness to enter into serious public debate becomes pernicious in the case of police malpractice, and can be part of an official cover-up, as Joanna Rollo demonstrates has occurred over the activities of the Special Patrol Group in general and its responsibility for Blair Peach's death in particular. It may also mask bureaucratic dishonesty, as Duncan Campbell shows has been repeatedly the case in the gradual extension of computerized policing and surveillance which has largely been done without prior Parliamentary approval. Lack of Parliamentary control of the police is indeed an issue repeatedly identified by all three contributors. For example, Martin Kettle shows how police chiefs since the time of Robert Mark have been able to ignore Parliament almost with impunity; whilst Joanna Rollo demonstrates that the evolution of the Special Patrol Group from confronting high crime to its present overtly political role as the guardian of public order, has never been sanctioned or even questioned by Parliament.

Yet, in the context of deepening economic recession, growing unemployment and political crisis, the police will inevitably be called upon to pursue with still greater vigour their traditional function of controlling political and industrial dissent. The curbs on 'secondary picketing' and other limitations on trade union rights supported by the Conservatives could thrust the police into even greater confrontation with trade unionists than occurred over the Saltley, Shrewsbury or Grunwick cases.

In such circumstances, where policeman is put up starkly against worker, the police will be unable to escape being portrayed as the state's political shock troops. Joanna Rollo's analysis of the Special Patrol Group as a 'third force' between civilian policing and military intervention shows how far this process has gone already. As Martin Kettle also emphasizes, there appears to be a blurring of the distinct roles traditionally performed by the police and the armed forces. A combination of external political circumstances and the internal organizational and technological developments described in the book, is encouraging the Force to adopt a quasi-military role. Yet – partly because those who approve this development frequently invoke an alibi of terrorist outbreaks or violent crime as an excuse for infringements of liberty – there has so far been no substantial public concern voiced about this remorseless shift in police activity.

The situation is exacerbated by a potent mixture of the urban crisis and the plight of the black community. Faced with institutionalized racism on all fronts – the system of immigration controls and employment discrimination being just two key examples – black people are becoming increasingly distanced from what they see as a hostile white power structure. In turn, the response of that structure has been to increase its capacity for social control of Blacks rather than to remove the causes of racism.

One strategy has been through such measures as the urban aid programme and the sponsoring of community development projects. These were explicitly born out of the fear in the late 1960s of black unrest, which had expressed itself so violently in American cities, appearing in Britain.[3] It was hoped that, through this strategy, the poor in general and Blacks in particular would be involved in self-help projects and public participation schemes that would encourage their identification with and absorption into the social system – without tackling the maldistribution of resources, wealth and power that placed them at the bottom of society.[4] This can be termed the 'soft' strategy of social control whereby dissent and unrest is co-opted rather than the causes for it removed. In the context of policing, it expressed itself, for example, in local police proposals to curb vandalism by setting up neighbourhood councils – which, it was envisaged, would encourage neighbourly self-policing and self-disciplining of delinquents.[5] Belated moves to put local constables 'back on the beat' were also part of that. So, too, in areas with a high black population, were the creation of new police community liaison officers who were charged with building links with Blacks and with improving the image of the Force. Special drives in the 1970s to recruit black policemen were another component of this 'soft' strategy: it is often said of the police force that it is an agency for the recruitment of working class people to police the working class, and this principle is now being applied to Blacks. It is therefore necessary to underline that this strategy of community involvement has been a method of social control, rather than an act of benevolence toward the citizen. It has been a mechanism by which a bridge could be built between the police and an increasingly distant and restless community, especially in poor (and often black) localities.

The other face of this overall mechanism of social control is the 'hard' one, against which the 'soft' one pales into virtual insignificance. It is the heavy-handed crackdown on dissidents; aggression towards trade unionists; ubiquitous computerized surveillance; the Special Patrol Group; and, notwithstanding the paraphernalia of community bridge-building, it is a growing intolerance towards the individual.

The 'hard' approach also expresses itself in systematic racism. The police in practice if not in theory favour racist groups at the expense of anti-racist groups,[6] whilst a detailed study by the Institute of Race Relations has documented the systematic hostility of the Force towards black people.[7] The study is, first, a devastating indictment of the failure of the police to protect black people from race violence. Meticulously assessing evidence from all over the country, the IRR shows how the police are 'unwilling' to afford protection; that they consistently refuse to acknowledge the racial dimension of attacks on black people; that they delay reaching the scene of attacks or homes under siege; that they are unwilling to investigate seriously and sympathetically racial assaults, let alone to prosecute attackers; and that all this is compounded by misguided advice to victims, and hostility to complainants, often resulting in treating black victims as the aggressors.

As disturbing is the abuse of police powers which the IRR study catalogues. Blacks are stopped and searched quite arbitrarily; they are arrested with unnecessary violence; and their homes or premises are entered at will. Not content with this, the police harass black youth (with the 'sus' law, amongst other methods) and drag in for detention black witnesses, bystanders and even those who wish merely to assert their rights.

However, none of this can be put down simply to racist attitudes of police officers on the spot. The general stance of the police toward the black community is aggressive because Blacks are perceived as a threat to social stability. Being at the very bottom of the class structure, and thereby suffering disproportionately from unemployment, poverty, bad housing and so forth, black people may be a convenient servant class for the state, but they also present it with a problem. With public expenditure cuts reducing the state's capacity to neutralize black dissatisfaction, the police's intervention becomes more crucial. Furthermore, the predicament of the black community is simply a microcosm of the situation facing the working class as a whole, as its living standards are steadily cut. It follows that police tactics against Blacks today could be applied on a more generalized basis tomorrow.

If we are prepared, therefore, to accept that the police role in society must be analyzed politically in terms of a social 'control function' rather than a 'referee function', it becomes possible to make more sense of modern policing. The distinction between 'soft' and 'hard' strategies of policing, which are nevertheless components of the same control function, can also help with a more precise understanding of police activities. For unless we are clear about the *political* purpose of the Police Force we shall be unable to formulate an effective political defence of the very civil liberties and democratic values which the police are so consistently undermining.

NOTES

1. See Tony Bunyan, *The History and Practice of the Political Police in Britain* (Quartet, 1977).
2. *Police*, vol. 11, No. 2 (March 1979), p. 36.
3. See Phil Read, *The Urban Aid Programme and the role of local authorities* (MA Thesis, University of Sussex, 1974), and J. Edwards and R. Batley, *Politics of Positive Discrimination* (Tavistock, 1978).
4. This is demonstrated in several publications produced by the Community Development Projects sponsored by the Home Office from 1969 onwards. See for instance *Gilding the Ghetto* (CDP Inter-Project Editorial Team, February 1977).
5. See Keith MacDonald, 'A police state in Britain?', *New Society*, 8 January 1976, pp. 50-1, and also my forthcoming book on public participation and neighbourhood councils, to be published by Maurice Temple Smith.
6. For example, see *Policing the Police*, Volume 1, pp. 6-7.
7. Institute of Race Relations, *Police Against Black People*, Evidence submitted to the Royal Commission on Criminal Procedure (1979), available from 247-9 Pentonville Road, N.1.

Section 1

THE POLITICS OF POLICING
AND THE POLICING OF POLITICS

I think that from a police point of view that my task in the future, in the ten to fifteen years from now, the period during which I shall continue to serve, that basic crime as such – theft, burglary, even violent crime – will not be the predominant police feature. What will be the matter of greatest concern to me will be the covert and ultimately overt attempts to overthrow democracy, to subvert the authority of the state, and, in fact, to involve themselves in acts of sedition designed to destroy our parliamentary system and the democratic government in this country.

James Anderton, Chief Constable of Greater Manchester, BBC-1's *Question Time*, 16 October 1979.

The Politics of Policing
and the Policing of Politics
Martin Kettle

The idea that policing and politics do not mix is obviously an illusion but it is an illusion which is deeply embedded in contemporary political life.

The Police Force as a whole has to take hundreds of decisions – not to mention the *ad hoc* decisions of individual officers in particular circumstances – which have a 'political' dimension. These decisions illustrate and are influenced by individual and collective police attitudes – attitudes which cover subjects such as the family, sexual behaviour, individual and group lifestyles, race relations, industrial relations, reading matter and political beliefs. Nor are such decisions confined to the more obvious circumstances, like demonstrations. They apply equally in a host of individual encounters between one officer and one citizen. Politics is involved in the way the police do their job.

The way a police force is administered also involves political choices. Decisions about priorities are particularly significant. Is it, for example, more important to spend limited resources on crime prevention projects among young people or on acquiring riot equipment and guns? The political consequences of such decisions can be momentous. Again, it is a political matter as to who makes these choices. Should it be the police themselves alone, or on the advice of local and national government, or should elected bodies make these decisions for the police to obey? Control of the police force involves politics.

These are two areas where there is an inescapable interplay between policing and politics. But the relationship goes much further. If there is a proposal to change a law – whether it be one which the police will have to enforce, or one which directly affects the running of the Police Force, or whether it affects criminal or judicial procedure – there is a certainty that the police will have a distinct interest in the shape of that law.

Take the issue of whether a suspected person should have to answer police questions, for example. It is in the interests of the police that the criminal interrogation process should penalize the suspect who stays silent. In this way, the police can get the suspect to talk and maybe provide evidence that could help get a conviction. But it may be in the suspect's interest not to talk. In that way, an innocent person might avoid incriminating himself. The interests of society are different again. Society both wants criminals to be caught and wants innocent people to have protection against wrongful arrest. So society has an interest which is not necessarily the same as the police's interest. In the legislative process, therefore, the police will have to press for the adoption of their point of view. This is an indisputably political act – whether it takes place in secret or in public and whether it is a response or an initiative.

Finally, the police may choose to affect the climate of opinion in which they do their job or may press for changes. If they want the courts to come down harder on some groups of offenders then it may make sense for a respected policeman to make an outspoken attack on permissiveness and liberalism in the hope that this may rally general support for the police's point of view. And if he can tar his opponents with the label 'anti-police', so much the better.

Each of these examples of the meeting of politics and policing occurs regularly in Britain today. Yet we – or, more particularly, the major political parties – still pretend that it does not and that policing properly shelters within political purdah. This partly explains why, in the absence of public debate, the police have begun to assert, through their own political activity, their wish to control policing and, in the light of their own political judgments, to extend the territorial boundaries of policing. Far from merely resisting or mitigating the rare outside attempts to police them – notably over the handling of complaints and the tape-recording of interrogations[1] – they have successfully introduced controversial operational changes and launched their own campaigns for new laws.

The object of this section is to trace some of the main themes in this process, as well as to examine some of the political assumptions which underlie it – assumptions which derive in large part from the police's methods of work. The process has not been coordinated but it has gradually involved all levels in the Police Force. Although it began with and is rightly associated with a few senior officers best in a position to obtain publicity and change policy, it has also involved the police staff organizations. The most important – because it is the largest – is the Police Federation, representing all police up to and including chief inspector rank. But the process also encompasses the Superintendents' Association – which represents both superintendents and chief superintendents – and the important Association of Chief Police Officers (ACPO), which covers all superior ranks including the chief constables. In the past fifteen years, all these bodies have begun to break free of the restrictions still formally placed on them by statute.

Sir Robert Mark Speaks Out

The man who is rightly most associated with this wide-ranging change is Sir Robert Mark, Metropolitan Police Commissioner between 1972 and 1977. As the head of the country's largest force – the Met employs one fifth of the total Police Force in England and Wales – the Commissioner would in any event be regarded as the first among equals. His job makes him even more special. Unlike the chief constables – who are appointed by local police authorities (committees composed of councillors and magistrates) – the Commissioner is appointed on the Home Secretary's recommendation. The Home Secretary – not the Greater London Council – is the police authority for the capital. As a result, though the Metropolitan Commissioner is formally answerable to Parliament through the Home Secretary, in practice he retains a wide degree of independence and initiative in the way he polices his community as well as the traditional operational autonomy of all police chiefs.

Robert Mark's reputation as a liberal owes much to the circumstances of his appointment to the Met and the consolidation of his position within it. He was put into the Met on the personal decision of a liberal Home Secretary, Roy Jenkins, in 1967. For Mark was the Home Office's weapon to bring the Met to heel and in the execution of this task he rightly appeared as a force for necessary change. He is best known for his fight against corruption and his overhauling of London's CID – the firm within a firm. Even so, his record as 'one of the great reforming administrators of the age' has tended to cloud the fact that Mark was and is a man of very definite right wing views.

It is conventional constitutional wisdom and police wisdom that the police are the servants of the community as a whole. Mark has put it like this:

> We discharge the communal will, not that of any government minister, mayor or other public official, or that of any political party, while remaining fully accountable to the community for what we do or fail to do.[2]

It is not the least important aspect of his career that Mark has subtly transformed this doctrine. Whereas it was traditionally the justification for police *inaction* in political affairs, Mark turned it into a justification for *action*. In his view, as the representatives of the community, the police in general and Robert Mark in particular became an alternative sounding-board for public opinion to politicians who were, by definition, *party* politicians. In 1976, Mark justified his campaigns for changes in the law in the following terms:

> It is important also to understand that no one but the police sees collectively the failure of the criminal process. We alone know the numbers of crimes not followed by prosecution of the offender, of crimes committed on bail, of acquittals of those who are only too obviously not innocent. We alone experience the collective effect of the difference between the theory of criminal justice and its defects in practice, which undermines its efficiency and lessens public confidence in it. In Britain the police are coming to realize that the public interest requires us to gather and make known information of this kind to the public itself rather than those who have vested interests in the making or practice of law.[3]

His recent autobiography showed the extent of Mark's contempt for the conventional institutions of liberal democracy. Writing about the 1976 Police Act – which introduced a form of independent scrutiny of complaints against the police which he bitterly opposed – Mark states:

> When the Prime Minister told the House that the Police Bill was the will of Parliament, he tactfully omitted to mention that if every member of the House was compelled to sit an examination paper consisting of ten simple questions about the working of the police disciplinary system and the pass mark was set as low as 20 per cent, not 5 per cent of them would be likely to pass. So much for the will of Parliament![4]

But Mark's own views, so he appears to believe, are or were untainted by bias or party. Sometimes he clearly believed that his position fully entitled him to defy the elected government in public.

When the Wilson government planned, in 1974, to introduce a statutory right for pickets to stop vehicles he told the Home Office that 'if there was any danger of this proposal reaching the Statute book I would declare in *The Times* that this was an unjustifiable infringement of individual liberty'.[5]

The impartiality of his political views was shown most clearly during the recent general election, when he published an article in *Security Gazette*. It received front-page treatment in several papers. Mark made a controversial comparison:

Not only do the unions enjoy a high degree of immunity from the law; in any critical situation in which the law does not support them the Government of the day – their partner or their puppet according to your view – declares its intention to change the law in their favour. This is not unlike the way in which the National Socialist German Workers Party achieved unrestricted control of the German State between 1930 and 1938.[6]

Mark's use of the comparison is highly instructive. It does not merely show us his very deep hostility to trade unionism – a view he is, after all, absolutely entitled to hold. It also shows us something of the political terms in which Mark sees himself and within which he saw himself operating as a policeman.

Elsewhere in the article he specifies 'one or two unpleasant truths'.

The first is that socialism is changing the nature of our society irreversibly. The original laudable intention to eradicate poverty and to achieve equality of opportunity has given way to a deliberate policy of egalitarianism, primarily by fiscal means, by high taxation, and secondly by the erosion of freedom of choice – in education and the health services for example.

This deep hostility to the Labour Party and the trade unions spills over into his attitude to the Conservatives. 'I am dismayed by the apparent lack of any really attractive or convincing alternative'. And what is the reason for the dismay? It is the stance of James Prior – from May 1979 the Employment Minister but, at the time Mark wrote, still Shadow Minister.

Older readers may remember the first words from Churchill which warmed our hearts in 1940. They were a reference to Hitler as 'This Nazi guttersnipe'. We had been waiting to hear this for years. It may not have been diplomatic or gentlemanly but it was what we all felt. Poor Neville Chamberlain's references to Herr Hitler and Signor Mussolini caused as much dismay then as the Shadow Employment Minister's respectful touching of his forelock to the trade unions on television causes now.

Since his retirement Mark has given vent to a number of other clear political opinions and instincts. He has written in his autobiography of his approval of Grunwick boss George Ward who 'courageously and successfully stood firm against politically motivated violence'. He described the assassinated right-wing campaigner, Ross McWhirter, as 'a notable upholder of freedom for the individual', whilst labelling the more left-wing National Council for Civil Liberties 'a small self-appointed political pressure group with a misleading title ... usually trying to usurp the function of the democratically appointed agencies for the achievement of political change'. And even though Sir Leslie Scarman called the Third World pressure group, Liberation, 'a responsible organization' whose leaders were 'dedicated to the principle of peaceful protest', Robert Mark believes Liberation to be 'not a whit less odious than the National Front'. And where does Mark see the police in all this? Significantly, no longer as an instrument of society's will, but as a distinct and positive force of its own – standing against part of society.

> The police are ... very much on their own in attempting to preserve order in an increasingly turbulent society in which Socialist philosophy has changed from raising the standards of the poor and deprived to reducing the standards of the wealthy, the skilled and the deserving to the lowest common denominator.[7]

Mark supplied the levels of organizational ability, political determination and public relations flair that were required to liberate the police from their traditionally introspective – often secretive – approach to their work, what he describes as their 'unnatural reticence in matters of public interest'. It is clear from his autobiography that Mark also has little respect for what he calls the 'limited intellectual capacity' of the traditional police officer (indeed he gives as his reason for joining the force in 1937 the belief that as an academic *manqué* he would be assured of a successful career in an essentially 'artisan service'). With his own example as a self-assured publicist to guide him, one of Mark's early reforms at the Met was to transform relations with the media. 'The police have everything to gain by opening their doors to the press', he wrote.[8]

In his first Annual Report as Commissioner, Mark set out his plans.

He reported on his meeting with national editors at Scotland Yard in September 1972:

> I explained my view that the ability to improve the situation lay to a large extent with the Force itself. Many police officers found some difficulty in accepting that the press had an important part to play in reporting on the affairs of the Force and there was a strong tendency to play safe and withhold information unnecessarily. To try to correct this I said that it had been resolved to delegate authority to disclose information to the news media to a lower level; to insist on a greatly improved flow of information from the Force to the Press Bureau; to demonstrate an increased willingness to provide facilities for feature articles; to place much greater emphasis on the role of the press in the training programme, both for recruits and for serving officers; and to train a large number of police officers at all levels in the technique of television and radio interviews.[9]

Not only did this mean more publicity. It could also mean better publicity, which the police (the Met in particular) badly needed in the wake of successive corruption revelations. Mark's proudest and most daring achievement in this line was to allow *Sunday Times* reporter Philip Knightley free range in the new complaints department, A10, to research an authoritative and influential article on Mark's clean-out of corrupt policemen. The fruits of the new closeness between Mark's Scotland Yard and the media were soon obvious. In his report for 1974, Mark was able to state that 'our more open and co-operative attitude towards the news media appears already to have brought a handsome return in terms of public knowledge and understanding of our aims and activities.' He continued:

> the force owes a debt of gratitude to the press, television and radio for the highly responsible and generally sympathetic way in which they have handled the vast majority of the many thousands of news items and features produced on police matters during the two years since our new policy was introduced.[10]

The new openness had its limits, however. In 1972, Mark introduced a new system of press cards. Hitherto, a journalist's credentials had simply been his union membership card. Now Mark began to issue his own cards. In a circular of 1973 he told the Force that the Met press card would benefit the journalists because it carried 'a significance which is readily recognized and accepted by all members of the Force'. It was understood that no applications for Met cards would be refused. As a result, 'special facilities cannot be accorded to non-holders'. With the passing of time, the Met card system has become more exclusive. They are no longer issued automatically and in 1978 Scotland Yard told the London freelance branch of the National Union of Journalists that while the cards were issued to nominated journalists from newspapers 'involved in news gathering', freelance or magazine journalists did not have that entitlement.[11]

A similar process occurred in broadcasting. In July 1979, *The Leveller* magazine revealed that the Met had won exceptional editorial privileges from the BBC. A year previously, the Met's director of information, Deputy Assistant Commissioner Peter Nievens, had complained to BBC news and current affairs planners about 'the Metropolitan policemen's disillusion with the BBC'. The police, said Nievens, felt that 'over the years there had been an absence of any real partnership'. Negotiations followed, culminating in an agreement reached in March 1979. Under this arrangement, the BBC agreed that in 'cases which the Metropolitan Police consider delicate, affecting privacy, *sub judice*, national security and such areas' the BBC and Scotland Yard would reach prior joint agreement about the scope, subject matter and facilities for such programmes, to be confirmed in an exchange of letters. The agreement put the police in a unique position to preview and control broadcasting about their work – a right which is not given to others. Finalized under Sir David McNee's regime, the arrangement carried forward the policies initiated by his predecessor as Commissioner.

Having improved his channels of communication with the public, Mark set about using them not only to provide information but also to put forward his views on policing, the law and the administration of justice. He himself views this as a natural progression:

> The post war years have seen a gradual change in our role from mere law enforcement to participants in the role of social welfare and even more importantly to that of contributors in the moulding of public opinion and legislation.[12]

This statement underestimates the fact that Mark virtually created – certainly moulded – this change in a most deliberate and remarkably clear-sighted fashion. And nowhere has this contribution been more sustained or concentrated than over questions of criminal law procedure.

In 1965 – while he was Chief Constable of Leicester – Mark wrote that 'the criminal trial is less a test of guilt or innocence than a competition ... a kind of show jumping contest in which the rider for the prosecution must clear every obstacle to succeed.'[13] In a lecture in the same year, he called for four major changes in legal procedure: majority verdicts in jury trials, pre-trial disclosure of defence alibis; abolition of the caution against self-incrimination, and the introduction of a requirement on an accused to enter the witness box. In 1967, Parliament passed a Criminal Justice Act which enacted the first two of Mark's four proposals.

By the time Mark became Met Commissioner, a report had been published which gave major support to his other two proposals. This was the eleventh report of the Criminal Law Revision Committee, published in 1972 – the most important manifesto of proposed restrictions on the procedural protection of the suspect in recent times. The Committee was chaired by Lord Justice Edmund Davies – more recently notable for his committee of inquiry into police pay and conditions – and contained a number of very senior lawyers such as Lord Justice Lawton, Lord Justice James, Judge Griffith-Jones, Professor Rupert Cross, Professor Glanville Williams and the then Director of Public Prosecutions, Sir Norman Skelhorn.

The report dealt with problems of evidence. Its proposals were centred on the principle that a person should be forced to give evidence in a court. The committee therefore proposed the abolition of the two 'rights to silence'. Then – as now – a person suspected of committing an offence does not have to answer the police questions. A policeman must advise the suspect:

> You are not obliged to say anything unless you wish to do so but what you say may be put in writing and given in evidence.

If the suspect chooses to remain silent at that time he may do so and no adverse consequences to him will follow. Similarly a person accused of an offence is not obliged to make any statement or give any evidence during his trial. Once more, no adverse consequences attach to this choice.

The Criminal Law Revision Committee recognized that there is no direct means of forcing a person to speak in either circumstance. Instead they proposed to make the consequences of silence unattractive. Any suspect or accused who decided to stay silent would be liable to have this lack of co-operation with the police or the court held against him. In certain circumstances a judge and jury would be able to draw 'adverse inferences' from a person's silence. In other words, your silence would be held against you – though it couldn't be used as evidence of actual guilt.

The hostile reaction which the report received was a great disappointment to the police. Mark's response was characteristic. In January 1973 he was invited to give that year's Dimbleby Memorial Lecture on BBC television. It was delivered in November. Mark writes in his autobiography:

> From my point of view it could not have come at a better time. Public ignorance about the policing of Great Britain is appalling and the Metropolitan force, after so many shocks, was in some doubt about its role.[14]

Mark used this opportunity – 'never again in my life would I be able to talk to so large an audience' – to counterattack on criminal procedure. His central point was the reiteration of his frustrations with the failings, as he saw them, of the jury trial system.[15]

> What we know about trials in higher courts doesn't justify any complacency. Indeed, there is one fact I can mention which should be enough in itself to demand some kind of inquiry. This is the rate of acquittals. Of all the people who plead not guilty and are tried by jury, about half are acquitted. You may perhaps say to yourselves, 'Well, why not? Perhaps they really were innocent. How do the police know they were guilty?' But things are not quite so simple. For one thing, the English criminal trial never decides whether the accused is innocent. The only question is whether, in accordance with the rules of evidence, the prosecution has proved that he is guilty – and this is not at all the same thing.

To Mark, the rules of evidence were engineered to favour the defence:

> It is, of course, right that in a serious criminal case the burden of proof should be upon the prosecution. But in trying to discharge that burden the prosecution has to act within a complicated framework of rules which were designed to give every advantage to the defence. The prosecution has to give the defence advance notice of the whole of its case, but the accused, unless he wants to raise an alibi, can keep his a secret until the actual trial. When the police interrogate a suspect or charge him they have to keep reminding him that he need not say anything. If he has a criminal record the jury are not ordinarily allowed to know about it. Most of these rules are very old. They date from a time when, incredible as it may seem,

an accused person was not allowed to give evidence in his own defence, when most accused were ignorant or illiterate. There was no legal aid and, perhaps most important, if someone was convicted he would most likely be hanged or transported. Under these conditions it is not surprising that the judges who made the rules were concerned to give the accused every possible protection. But it is, to say the least, arguable that the same rules were not suited to the trial of an experienced criminal, using skilled legal assistance, in the late twentieth century.

In fact – as Sir Henry Fisher was to point out in his inquiry into the Confait murder case in 1977 – both the Criminal Law Revision Committee and Sir Robert Mark were wrong to portray criminal procedure as if it only affected the 'experienced criminal'. The picture was as over-simplified as the lecture's later – more notorious – attack on crooked defence lawyers who are 'more harmful to society than the cheats they represent'. However, Mark was defiantly proud of such tactics. Indeed he went very close to admitting that it was a calculated smear against defences as a whole:

> Of course, I speak in general terms. I would like to be more specific but for obvious reasons I cannot. I am conscious too that people who make general accusations can be said to be willing to wound and yet afraid to strike. This does not mean that such general accusations ought not to be made.[16]

The calculated provocation of Mark's Dimbleby lecture was a turning point not only in Mark's campaign for the introduction of specific changes in the criminal procedure system – changes like the abolition of the rights to silence or the introduction of wider pre-trial disclosure of the defence case. It also marked the coming of age of a politically assertive police force in this country. As he himself reminds us, it was 'the first occasion on which a senior policeman has publicly voiced at length comment about the reality of criminal justice.'[17]

Towards the end of the lecture, Mark made a threat. 'Unwillingness to make the law more effective will inevitably provoke demands for harsher punishments and will increase the pressures on the police to use more arbitrary methods.'

The suggestion that the police could and would make their own rules – whatever anyone else said – was highlighted during the lengthy investigations into the police's handling of the Confait murder case. The Confait murder took place in London only four days after Mark took over as Commissioner.[18] A special inquiry published in 1977 by a former High Court judge – Sir Henry Fisher – found major police abuses of existing evidence gathering methods.

When the police attempt to gather evidence by questioning a suspect, they are supposed to follow the procedures – which include the caution quoted earlier – set out in the *Judges' Rules and Administrative Directions to the Police*, a document originally drawn up in 1912 and last fully revised in 1964. The Rules cover questioning and the taking of statements and confessions. The Administrative Directions cover record keeping of details of an interrogation, the 'comfort and refreshment' of the suspect, the questioning of juveniles and the mentally handicapped and 'facilities for the defence' – that is, when and whether a suspect may see a lawyer or be informed of his rights.

The Rules are not statutory. In the words of one leading authority, they represent 'a code of practice which the police are expected to follow and, inevitably, supply the standard, observance of which is expected of the police.'[19] As a result, they are unenforceable at law. There is no obligation upon a court to exclude evidence which is gathered through breaches of the Rules. And even if there were, the Rules embody such extensive police discretion that in many cases the police could not be prevented from ignoring them. As the Legal Action Group – a body of radical lawyers – has said:

> Unlawful behaviour by police officers is not discouraged under the present system because there is no effective procedure for review of their actions or, where the procedures exist, no adequate sanctions against breach of the law.

It may seem that such conclusions are veering towards the generalized accusations for which Robert Mark was earlier criticized. The answer lies in Sir Henry Fisher's report on the Confait case. Fisher found that individual police officers on the case were unaware of – or misunderstood – the rights set out in the Judges' Rules. But he went even further than these specific censures. He examined one of the Administrative Directions, number seven, which reads:

Facilities for defence

(a) A person in custody should be supplied on request with writing materials.

Provided that no hindrance is reasonably likely to be caused to the processes of investigation or the administration of justice:

(i)   he should be allowed to speak on the telephone to his solicitor or to his friends;

(ii) his letters should be sent by post or otherwise with the least possible delay;

(iii) telegrams should be sent at once, at his own expense.

(b) Persons in custody should not only be informed orally of the rights and facilities available to them, but in addition notices describing them should be displayed at convenient and conspicuous places at police stations and the attention of persons in custody should be drawn to these notices.

Fisher concluded that 'the very existence' of this administrative direction was 'unknown to counsel and to senior police officers who gave evidence before me.' And in a statement which presumably applied to each of the more than 300,000 arrests which take place in London each year, he said 'in the Metropolitan Police District it is not observed.'

From their very different viewpoints, Fisher and Mark both found the existing rules of criminal procedure inadequate and in need of more detailed inquiry. Mark had hinted at a study of 'the whole system of criminal justice' in his Dimbleby lecture. Fisher suggested that reform of the Judges' Rules could only be made in the light of a wider investigation – 'something like a royal commission' which would have the task of analyzing criminal procedure with the object of achieving 'balance between police effectiveness and individual rights.' The result of this suggestion was the setting up, in June 1977, of the Royal Commission on Criminal Procedure.

Mark had by this time resigned, to be succeeded as Commissioner by David McNee, Chief Constable of Strathclyde – the first man ever to be given the Met job without any experience of working within it. But Mark's lessons had been learned and the Royal Commission provided the opportunity for several police leaders and representative bodies to outstrip his proposals for reform of criminal evidence.

The Royal Commission Debate

Nevertheless, the setting up of the Royal Commission did not, provoke general police acclaim. The Police Federation's national chairman, Constable Jim Jardine, called it 'a sure way of postponing the problem for two or three years.' The Superintendents Association said 'when the Royal Commission was announced it was greeted by police officers nationwide with almost universal pessimism'. The police feared the Commission would be a device for foisting liberal measures on them. 'It was seen,' said the Association, 'as an attack on the limited powers already possessed by police.'

When proposals calling for strengthening of suspects' rights were submitted to the Commission, Jim Jardine responded:

> Some of the evidence submitted to that Royal Commission makes us wonder what kind of a world its authors are living in. It is certainly not the world peopled by the criminals our members deal with. The latest daftness came from, of all people, the TUC. They want the powers of the police to be cut. A lot of people seem to have a similar idea about the powers of the TUC.[20]

In their own submission of evidence the Federation had hit out at another of their traditional bogies – again in the name of the public at large.

> Much of the discussion on this subject is pitched at an academic level. Police officers deal in the realities of crime. With respect to academic theorists, it may well be that the police view of these matters is closer to the general wishes of the community.

The Superintendents Association would not have been surprised by such proposals either. In their own evidence to the Commission, the Association expressed their deep suspicion of reformers and, yet again identified their own views with 'public opinion'.

> One feature of present day life is the far reaching change achieved by relatively small bodies of people, often contrary to or ignorant of public opinion. That these groups perform a useful service by drawing attention to certain shortcomings is self-evident in a democratic society, but it is not always apparent that their motives are purely altruistic, or whether they have public opinion on their side ... The fears of the Police Service are that only the Police and, on track record, a minority of the legal profession, will speak for law and order in the enforcement sense. On the other side will be ranged the big guns of every minority group and sociological agency – many with doubtful motives – propounding the theory of a violent and unfeeling Police Service whose only aim is to inconvenience or convict as many innocent persons as possible.

Sir David McNee may privately have shared some of these suspicions. But, if so, he put a brave face on it and, in his first annual report for 1977 as Commissioner, gave it a welcome. He added a clear warning.

Whilst I acknowledge and defend the need to maintain a proper balance between the rights and liberties of the suspect on the one hand and the powers conferred on the police for the effective discharge of their responsibilities on the other, I am firmly of the opinion that the task of the police is being made unwarrantably difficult by certain restraints of criminal procedure ... Before well-meaning people approvingly cite procedures in other countries for the protection of persons charged with crime they must ask themselves if the resulting quality of life in those countries is what we would wish here.

Scotland Yard set up a working party under the chairmanship of the Metropolitan Police Solicitor to prepare its evidence. Members of the Metropolitan force were encouraged to submit their views to the working party. The results of their work were leaked in *The Times* in August 1978 – Robert Mark would never have allowed such a propaganda coup to be given to his adversaries. This highly significant set of proposals is popularly associated with Sir David McNee alone, but it is worth emphasizing that it is also Scotland Yard's evidence generally, and was prepared after extensive soundings and consultations.

The 'philosophy' – his own term for it – behind Sir David McNee's evidence to the Royal Commission on Criminal Procedure[21] is that since the police are finding it convenient to abuse existing procedures, their actions should be legitimized, for – whatever anyone else is going to rule – this is the way they intend to proceed anyway. The introductory memorandum to the first part of his evidence spells this out.

In the past, the police in England and Wales have been dealing with a population which, in the main, was ignorant of its civil rights.

But, it continues, because Parliament chose not to give the police what they wanted – or as McNee puts it 'Because Parliament had become very reluctant to face up to the necessity of giving the police adequate powers to deal with crime' – the police have relied upon such ignorance in their methods of investigation.

This 'requirement to use stealth or force illegally' is an embarrassment to the police but it does not mean that they therefore cease to use such methods. Indeed McNee explains that they intend to go on using them. The problem is that 'the general public is becoming far more conscious of its rights and more apathetic about its responsibilities'. As a result, the public are taking more legal actions and making more complaints against the police. McNee accepts that his real difficulty is not that the police are breaking the rules but that they are no longer able to get away with it.

> The days when they could expect to bluff their way into obtaining consent to take body samples, or enter premises, are numbered.

McNee's answer therefore is simple. Regularize the position 'in the interests of the public' – not, presumably, that meddlesome, litigious, complaining public that won't put up with police abuses any more, but some other public of whose collective opinion the police claim unique knowledge.

If indeed McNee's proposals are so essential and if – as on his own admission they are – they are only the power that the police have been using for some years anyway, then there has been extensive police illegality in London for a long time. His main proposals are wholesale, not marginal, changes. While they incorporate Mark's proposals for the abolition of the rights of silence, they range much further.

McNee wants restrictions on policy powers of search to be lifted. Powers of search are, admittedly, haphazard and uneven but, under his plans, once a search warrant for premises was granted the police would be able to seize any property whether or not it related to the offence or putative offence specified in the warrant. Indeed it appears from his proposals that such a search warrant for evidence could be obtained in the investigation of any type of criminal offence and not merely the present specific list of offences.

The police would get easier access to a person's bank account under McNee's proposals. An officer would have to explain to a magistrate 'the nature of his enquiry, the relevance of the bank accounts in question and the information he hoped to be able to obtain from an inspection', following which a disclosure order could be made to the bank. Powers of search without warrant in a public place would also be widened. The police would be entitled to look for 'any article which has been or is intended to be used to cause injury to the person or damage to property' in spite of the notorious breadth of such definitions and the difficulty or proving intention. They would get the right to search 'if by reason of a person's presence at a particular location an officer believes that such search may assist in the prevention of a serious crime or danger to the public.'

In each of these cases the proposals shift the exercise of police powers to an earlier, less specific and more speculative stage in the process of criminal evidence gathering. Two further proposals in McNee's package particularly emphasize this rationale.

The first would empower a senior police officer – not a magistrate – to authorize general road block searches of motor vehicles and their passengers. McNee would give him this power where the officer 'considers that the stopping and searching may prove a fruitful source of the discovery or prevention of criminal offences.'

In the second case, McNee proposes that a senior police officer would be able to apply to a judge to order the compulsory fingerprinting of 'every person or category of person living or working in the area described in such application.' The yardstick proposed by McNee is that the fingerprinting 'would be likely to be of significant assistance to a police investigation into a specific crime or series of crimes involving death or serious bodily harm.' And since the fingerprinting would be compulsory, McNee proposes the creation of a new arrestable criminal offence of failing to comply with such an order.

In considering reform of the police's power to arrest, McNee has similarly come down in favour of uniform codification and alignment of existing *ad hoc* and specific statutory powers of arrest to provide a general power to arrest on reasonable suspicion of the commission of any imprisonable offence. As in the case of search powers, the desirable intention to achieve overall consistency is harnessed to the less desirable intention to bring to bear more serious police powers at an earlier stage of the case. A general power of arrest or reasonable suspicion in all such cases enables the police to detain a person 'at or near the starting point of an investigation of which the obtaining of *prima facie* proof is the end.'[22]

It obviously suits the police best if someone whom they suspect of committing an offence can always be taken to the police station. McNee suggests that it favours the suspect, too. 'The suspect is given the opportunity whether in writing or verbally of offering an explanation for his actions or behaviour which give rise to the officer's suspicions or the opportunity of making an admission of guilt.' And, of course, 'the legitimate questioning of a suspect which is part of the investigation of the offence, is more conveniently carried out at the police station than elsewhere.' But his own tacit admissions of breaches of the rules and those exposed by the Fisher Report take the gilt off this proposal.

McNee does not propose a power to detain a person, merely to question him. There still has to be that 'reasonable suspicion' before the police have the legal right to detain. But he does propose to extend the time available for questioning a person who has been detained. At present, an arrested person is supposed to be bailed or brought before a magistrates court within 24 hours of arrest. McNee wants to extend the period to 72 hours, with the opportunity to get further extensions of up to 72 hours, with the approval of a single magistrate. The justification offered for this proposal is not only that questioning takes time but also 'the other equally urgent police work that has to be carried on unrelated to that particular investigation.'

While a suspect is in this extended custody, McNee wants the pressures on him to talk to be increased. Like Mark and the Criminal Law Revision Committee before him, he seeks the weakening of the Judges' Rules by the abolition of the existing caution in which the suspect is granted a right to silence. In its place he proposes that a suspect should be told the reasons why he is under suspicion and that if he does not answer the police's questions 'the Court will be told of your failure to answer and your evidence may be less likely to be believed.'

Under such rules, the importance of legal advice to the suspect is increased – but McNee's proposals would not extend access to lawyers beyond existing provisions. And just in case you are tempted to think this a little unfair, McNee – again like Mark – even contrives to suggest that a lawyer's job *as such* is contrary to the public interest. It is a sublime piece of sophistry.

> The lawyer is duty bound to advise his client, subject to his client's instructions, to refuse to answer any police questions which might reveal the truth if that truth indicates that his client was responsible for a criminal offence ... The police officer is duty bound to attempt to discover the truth whether that truth discloses the innocence or the guilt of the suspect. It follows that the duty of the lawyer to his client on the one hand and the duty of an investigating officer and the interests of the public that those responsible for crime be brought to justice on the other hand are diametrically opposed.

The only form of supervision proposed by McNee in this system of questioning to prevent false admissions or statements is 'action taken by senior officers'. No concession on tape-recording – that would be impracticable and of dubious value. No separation of the decision to prosecute from the investigation; the police would continue themselves to bring cases to court. Internal controls are all that is envisaged: the police should police the police. Freedom from outside supervision and increased police powers go hand in hand.

On the other side, McNee recommends absolutely no extension or further safeguard to a suspect's existing rights. He goes to some lengths to explain that existing disciplinary, civil and criminal procedures offer ample opportunity for the complainant to obtain redress. The Metropolitan Commissioner clearly concurs with the uncompromising words of ACPO (of which he is a member) in their evidence to the Royal Commission. 'No further safeguards to the rights of suspects need be given.'

McNee's proposals have dominated public perception of the work of the Royal Commission. They have strongly influenced the proposals emerging from the rest of the police. They are undoubtedly the most influential set of recommendations received by the commission, and the most detailed modern manifesto of police intentions in the exercise of their principal task, the enforcement of the criminal law.

The Law and Order Campaign

A tradition of campaigning by the country's senior policemen is not Mark's only legacy in this field. It was undoubtedly Mark's influence and initiative which encouraged the Police Federation to launch its 'law and order campaign' at the end of 1975. As a Federation representative put it in 1976:

> In recent years, Sir Robert Mark has spelt out the increasing frustration of the police service in very forceful and forthright terms. What he has been saying in public police officers have been feeling in their hearts for years.[23]

Police Federation campaigning about police powers and law, wasn't previously completely unknown. In 1965 they had published *The Problem*, a manifesto of changes in police pay, equipment and management. It was described by the authorities as 'unprecedented' and henceforth the Federation was more regularly consulted by government over a wide range of policing issues. But the law and order campaign went both further and wider. Robert Reiner calls it a 'crucial turning point' in the emergence of the British police as 'an overtly political force'.[24]

Once again, the police view was depicted as the public view. The aim of the campaign was 'to harness the public's growing concern about the state of crime and public order in Britain into a programme for positive action.' The programme consisted of publicizing the growth of crime, the growth of violence, the effectiveness (i.e. the ineffectiveness) of the criminal law, present sentencing policy, and weaknesses in criminal procedure. It also drew attention to

> the attitude of some people and some bodies in public life towards the rule of law, instancing the sympathy shown to law breakers whose crimes have allegedly 'Political' overtones. The need for the 'silent majority' to assert itself in order that politicians and judges fully understand the true feelings of the public.

The Federation aimed at copying what it saw as the successful tactics of 'pressure groups, often representing a minority view, able to secure major changes in the law'. Federation representatives were encouraged to take on speaking engagements, and lobby elected representatives at local and parliamentary level. The objects of the campaign were explained thus:

> In appealing to the silent majority to make its true feelings known, the Police Federation is not trying to mobilize the 'hang 'em and flog 'em' brigade, but we have noticed how many major changes have been accomplished in the cause of penal reform and the liberal society, sometimes in the teeth of the reality of public opinion. One can instance the long and, eventually, successful campaign to abolish capital punishment. Other examples have been homosexual law reform and the Obscene Publications Act. It is neither here nor there whether the police have a collective view about such matters. What is remarkable is the way in which articulate but, frankly, unrepresentative groups appear capable of securing changes in the law from a parliament which remains impervious to the widest expression of genuine public feeling.[25]

A major prestige event in the campaign was the Federation's seminar, 'The Challenge of Crime' held at Emmanuel College, Cambridge, in April 1976 and attended by 'politicians, church leaders, magistrates and trade unionists, leaders of voluntary bodies and members of the police service.' Among the speakers were Enoch Powell and Mr Justice Melford Stevenson. Though they shared the platform with people such as John Alderson and Arthur Davidson, the choice of Powell in particular seemed remarkably ill-advised and provocative and duly drew criticism. To this, the Federation replied that 'an organization must be free to hold what meetings it wishes and invite which speakers it wants, without having to submit them to the Community Relations Commission for prior approval.'[26]

The Federation's then Chairman, Leslie Male, explained the reasons for the campaign. He said that the police had been 'the silent service for too long', conditioned to the belief that 'we are not supposed to have any interest in the outcome of the trial.' Such views were 'based upon the principle that the police were impartial and completely disinterested spectators of the trial procedure.' But, said Male, 'The reality was, and is, different.'

The law and order campaign of 1975 and 1976 was transcended by the crisis of 1977 and 1978 over police pay and demands for police unionization with the right to strike. In 1978, however, with the Labour government's acceptance of the Edmund-Davies Committee's police pay awards, the campaign began again. In February 1978, the Federation announced that it intended to make 'law and order' an issue in the forthcoming general election. Federation chairman James Jardine called on all major political parties to state their solutions to the problem.

The revived campaign centred on two issues: the rise in violent crime and the drop in police recruitment. It criticized all branches of the legal system for failing to give adequate support to an under strength police force. Once again the Federation criticized parents for failing to assert their authority to prevent the rise in juvenile crime. Jardine attacked the 'well-meaning but totally misguided experts' who have 'neutralized' justice in Britain. And his efforts won the support of the Conservative shadow Home Secretary William Whitelaw who called for 'unstinting backing' for the police and for 'the widest range of penalties so that the punishment fits the crime.'

Before and during the election of 1979 the Federation continued its campaign. At Halifax, during the election campaign, Jardine made a major speech which closely paralleled the main demands in the Conservative manifesto. He called – as the Federation had done for some years – for the repeal of the Children and Young Persons Act; reform, though not repeal, of this law was the major Conservative manifesto pledge. He called for the reintroduction of the death penalty; a free vote on hanging was another Conservative pledge. He attacked the Labour government's Bail Act.

On 20 April 1979, just under a fortnight before polling day the Federation published an advertisement in every national daily newspaper – except the *Financial Times* which took it as a letter to the editor. The advertisement took the form of an open letter to all candidates from James Jardine, under the banner headline 'LAW & ORDER'. The letter outlines the Federation's policies – tougher penalties, more secure accommodation for convicted juveniles and 'the duty of Government and politicians to uphold the rule of law and to support the police in efforts to apply it.'

The Federation has always denied links with the Conservative Party. It has attempted to adopt a non-party image. Jardine told a meeting of West Midlands Conservatives in 1978 'My presence here does not, of course, imply any connection with a political party.' In line with this principle the Federation has traditionally avoided particular party ties in its parliamentary lobbying work. It appoints a 'parliamentary adviser' whose job is both to represent the Federation's case in relevant Westminster debates and to suggest lobbying tactics to the police. The practice has always been that the parliamentary adviser is a member of the opposition party. The first holder of the job was the former Prime Minister, James Callaghan. Subsequently he gave way to Conservative Eldon Griffiths who in turn gave way to Labour's Alf Morris.

When there is a change of government, the adviser changes too. Until 1979. During the last period of Labour Government, the adviser was once more Conservative MP Eldon Griffiths. This was, of course, the period of the law and order campaign and on the election of the Conservative government in May 1979, the Federation decided to break with their past practice. By an unanimous vote, the Joint Central Committee of the Federation re-appointed Griffiths. In a statement they explained why:

> The Committee felt that his very close links with the Federation, his vast experience, and his commitment to the policies which the Police Federation has been putting forward on law and order, ought to be retained. The Government's mandate includes several major reforms which coincide with our policies and no one in the House would be better qualified to put forward our views.[27]

There really can be little doubt that the Police Federation now openly adopts a right-wing viewpoint and that, as a consequence, it has abandoned the attempt to maintain an all-party or non-party approach to campaigning. According to Robert Reiner, this is reflected in the party allegiances of individual officers as revealed in an unpublished dissertation by one policeman. This officer found that 80 per cent of a sample group described themselves as Conservatives, with the remainder evenly divided between Labour, Liberal and 'don't know'. Of the sample, 80 per cent had voted in all recent elections. However, 64 per cent agreed with the proposition that the police should remain politically neutral in all times – off as well as on duty.[28]

Police Chiefs and their Rank-and-File

Although the police chiefs, like Mark and McNee, and the rank and file, in the form of the Federation, have all campaigned for similar demands, and though these campaigns and these demands can be seen as two sides of the same coin – the politicization of the police – they do not necessarily see eye to eye, and their objectives have important differences.

Mark, for instance, despises the Federation. This is something which no serving chief constable or commissioner could or should say, but Mark made his views very clear quite shortly after his retirement. They were obviously affected by the Federation's tactics during the lobbying over the Police Bill in 1976. Their activity, he says 'was a powerfully disrupting factor which put an end to any hope of achieving an effective, inexpensive and generally acceptable solution.'

Mark resented this 'disrupting' by the Federation because he feared that it undermined the authority of chief officers in general – and of Robert Mark in particular – to give a clear, uncontradicted (and public) 'police view' of the issues. And as a meritocrat, Mark did not take kindly to the lower ranks cutting in on his well-laid schemes to convince his fellow 'experts'. In his autobiography he writes:

> The unwillingness of police chiefs to make their views public means that the staff associations, the Police Federation and the Superintendents Association, rush gladly into the breach and express views to the Press or on radio or television on matters which they have no experience or knowledge and for which they have no responsibility. Much harm has been done in recent years to the police image by irresponsible and ill-informed comment by police spokesmen whose only real concern is with the negotiation of pay and conditions of service and who, in many cases, have not had any practical experience of police work for many years. Thus issues like complaints, bail, terrorism and the death penalty are discussed in public by those who are in fact the least qualified or competent to express an informed view whilst the chief officers remain silent for fear of departing from a tradition of questionable value.[29]

This is a key difference between say, Mark and the Federation. Mark — and some other police chiefs — are politicians. They already hold power and their campaigns are designed to force decision and policy makers to make politically realizable changes. The Federation — by contrast — is tilting at windmills, forever launching grand schemes which have no real chance of fulfilment. Enoch Powell saw this in his speech to the Federation's Cambridge seminar in 1976 already referred to, when he pointed out the difficulties in the Federation's attempts to get 'the silent majority to assert itself'. This, said Powell, is escapism.

> You are really saying, 'We must find a way to do the impossible.' You are saying that the answer is to do that which is inherently contradictory, to make the silent majority speak.

As we have already seen, rank and file policemen and Federation representatives do not reciprocate Mark's hostility. Nevertheless, the Federation is not entirely happy with the general phenomenon of political police chiefs. An editorial in *Police* in March 1979 voiced an interesting fear:

> The danger of chief officers pontificating on the true nature of the police role is that the police service itself will begin to question that role.

But this is precisely the process in which — for all the fundamentalist talk — the Federation is an active participant. The law and order campaign may be perceived by its authors as simply a reassertion of neutral, incontrovertible social truths. But it is also, willy-nilly, a contribution to a process of debate and questioning. It may be that the Federation — rather like someone who blows on a flame intending to put it out only to make it burn more strongly — has succeeded in raising far more questions about policing than it has answered.

Robert Mark tried to plan things better than that. Mark's campaigns and statements were intended to achieve specific results. These intended results were occasionally long-term, as in the case of his Dimbleby lecture. He could hardly have expected to win the changes he wanted in criminal procedure overnight. But he could try to stir things up so that the Criminal Law Revision Committee's proposals did not simply sink into oblivion. More often, though, his campaigns had limited objectives (like his opposition to the Police Bill in 1976) or were responses to the initiatives of others (like his views on policing public demonstrations which were drawn together as a result of the setting up of the Scarman Inquiry into the events in Red Lion Square in 1974).

Police and the Army

A notable example of Mark's calculated venturing into the political arena came over the use of troops in support of the civil power. As an issue, this was put on Mark's desk early in 1974 when, according to his autobiography, he learned of the possibility of a missile attack being made on aircraft at Heathrow airport. He decided that a deterrent operation involving the army was required.

The use of the army in support of the civil power is too complex a legal question to cover here in any detail.[30] Politically, it has traditionally been a highly sensitive subject. Governments have been extremely reluctant to involve the military overtly in keeping the civil peace, principally because the army is an ultimate sanction. It is an armed force and governments do not seek to use or threaten to use arms against the population unless they have to. Nor is there any tradition, in either theory or practice, of a community sanction or basis for the use of the armed forces. They are the arm of government itself and the most direct expression of State power.

The British government began to rethink the legal and practical procedures for the use of troops in civil life in 1970. The Ministry of Defence conducted a review on which Mark, among others, represented the Home Office. Work on the review took Mark around the world to America, Japan, Hong Kong, Singapore, Cyprus, Italy, France, Germany and Ulster. So, when the occasion arose at Heathrow in 1974, Mark was well-versed in the issues involved. Although he describes the way the decision to call in the army was taken in a somewhat low key manner, the significance of the incident is considerable.

> I tried to reach the Home Secretary and the Permanent Under-Secretary, but without success. I had no better luck with the Minister of Defence. There was nothing for it but to cross the Rubicon. I asked the GSOI of London District to get the GOC's agreement to move troops into Heathrow by first light on the following morning and he readily agreed. During the night we managed to find the Home Secretary who gave us his blessing.[31]

The significance of the affair was Mark's willingness to take the decision himself, without the approval of any political leader. The procedure for the use of troops, as set out by Mark, is that

> permission of the Home Secretary is sought by the chief officer of police to invoke military aid and the Minister of Defence, in consultation with the Home Secretary, who will have considered the views of the chief officer of police, will decide whether to authorize the ultimate sanction of force by such troops as he may make available. Such assistance was formerly sought by police.[32]

This procedure places the decision to use troops in the hands of police chiefs and ministers. It is a significant shift from the procedure which existed prior to the re-think of the early 1970s. Under the old system, requests for military assistance might come from a variety of sources – a magistrate, a mayor, or the chief officer of police. But all had one thing in common, their status as a justice of the peace. The JP basis has now been removed, and with it the vestiges of local control. Now the system is centralized and more weight than ever attaches to the police. And as the Heathrow episode showed, the police force felt entitled to ignore the new procedures.

In March 1976, Mark delivered a speech at Leicester University in which he outlined the procedures – though without making it clear that they had been changed. His speech was, in effect, a public confirmation of a *fait accompli*. It also discussed the circumstances under which troops might be called on in industrial disputes in a franker manner than any conventional political leader has ever done. Mark recognized that this was 'a subject about which needless secrecy or reserve is more likely to provoke than allay social disquiet and on which I think a little plain speaking is overdue.' This became a self-fulfilling prophecy. The lecture, he said later, 'put an end to the speculative nonsense which had caused public unrest in the preceding twelve months.'

In 1978, Mark wrote a report on policing in Australia in which he made clear that he regarded this as a political legitimation process. He explained once more the circumstances in which the armed forces may be called on:

> In Great Britain they have moved dustbins and manned fire engines without objection by the trade unions ... not even the most eloquent radical can pretend that they undermine the position of trade unions or threaten civil liberty when employed in that way.

And he concluded, in a passage which is of great value for understanding his approach:

> In Britain, this philosophy is not concealed. Every Member of Parliament is aware of it. It has been the subject of a public lecture which scarcely caused a ripple of adverse comment, largely because clarification of the position alleviated public unease.[33]

The whole episode illustrates the Markian method. First, perceive the problem – that troops may be needed to counter terrorism or to break a strike. Second, devise your own solution – make new arrangements for calling in the troops. Third, employ your own solution – call in the troops to Heathrow. Fourth, do it again, maybe in slightly different circumstances. Fifth, make it public – make a speech telling people what you have done. The problem is solved. Secret and important changes have been accomplished without any public discussion.

Police Leadership and Politics

Mark said in a lecture in 1974 that 'the maintenance of order during political demonstrations has always been the most sensitive problem of the Metropolitan Police.' The control of marches and crowds is, inevitably, a particularly important issue in the capital city. The original instructions to the Met in 1829 included responsibility for maintaining public order and the early 1830s 'provided endless opportunities for the police to perfect techniques of crowd control'.[34]

Every year, the Commissioner's annual report contains a chapter on public order. It lists the major demonstrations and public meetings for which the police have been mobilized. However, every year without fail this section of the report also engages in political analysis.

The tradition predates Mark. His predecessor, Sir John Waldron wrote of events in 1970, for instance:

> The number of people involved in individual demonstrations was not large, at the most several thousands, but a minority of determined militants was invariably there, making use of the event to pursue their own aims and presenting a threat to public order. Whilst most organizers are genuine in their beliefs, it is unfortunate that some participants judge the success of their protests by the amount of disorder they create.[35]

This is a very typical example. It contains characteristic examples of police analysis of demonstrations: the suggestion that demonstrations are always liable to be violent; that there is always a sinister group of manipulators present; that this group uses demonstrations for some, generally unspecified, destructive objective; that the majority of demonstrators are slightly naive.

Mark's first report – an extremely interesting document in several respects – came back to the subject:

> Public order is a matter of constant concern. Not only is it difficult to maintain the nice balance between freedom and restriction – preserving the rights of ordinary citizens as well as the right to demonstrate – but there is the continual interference with police duty rosters and entitlement to time off and the constant strain on the tolerance of police officers in dealing with those who seek to achieve political objectives by coercion and force.[36]

Mark, too, liked to go beyond the mere reporting of events. Of a protest against Margaret Thatcher's attacks on student union autonomy in 1972, he wrote: 'the subject aroused a genuine interest among students generally as opposed to the usual minority involved at demonstrations unconnected with student affairs.' In 1973, when the Special Patrol Group killed two men at India House, he wrote:

> Subsequent protest marches, culminating in an open air memorial service in Hyde Park, were in a low key and the absence of any general condemnation of the police response showed the widespread public acceptance of the need for firm action in this type of situation.[37]

By far the most serious public order event which took place during Mark's period as Commissioner was the riot in Red Lion Square in June 1974, during which Kevin Gately died. The subsequent Scarman Inquiry investigated not only the specific events of that day, but also the state of the law relating to public order. Mark responded to the inquiry with proposals for amendments to the law. The most important was that:

> No person shall organize, arrange or advertise any public procession unless, within seven clear days before the holding of the said procession, notice has been given to the Superintendent of Police for the district or districts in which the same is to be held, of the proposed route, purpose and arrangements for the control of the said procession and the numbers expected to take part therein, provided that the period of seven days may be reduced to one of twenty-four hours if notice is given to the chief of

police of the matters herein before referred to and he consents to the holding of the said procession.[38]

The object of the proposal was to penalize the organizers of marches which take place without the necessary details being given with the necessary notice. Scarman rejected the proposal. He said 'I do not think the need for it has been established; and it does present really insuperable difficulty for the urgently called demonstration.' To Scarman, to give notice was 'a largely unnecessary requirement'; the police normally know about marches in advance as it is, and they are normally consulted by the organizers. He added, significantly, that 'in the present instance (Red Lion Square) the police did fail to make proper use of the notice that they had.' It certainly seems that Mark's desire to impose notice conditions on demonstrations arose from a wider wish to reduce the amount of police public order work rather than from any particular lessons of Red Lion Square. In short, the police wanted to restrict the right to demonstrate.

Mark made further proposals to Scarman. He wanted to make it an offence to disobey a police constable when taking part in a public procession. Scarman held that this 'goes too far'. Mark also wanted to give a constable the right to direct 'that any article which in his opinion is likely to provoke a breach of the peace may not be carried or worn by any person taking part in the said procession'. Scarman turned this down too, saying it would 'cause trouble rather than lead to the maintenance of peace'.

It is perhaps significant that the central police proposal for the containment of demonstrations – the seven days notice clause – reappeared in 1978 and 1979. A number of local authorities attempted (with mixed success) to acquire such powers through the recondite parliamentary private bill procedure. What both Scarman and a 1977 Home Office review rejected has now been adopted by Parliament for the West Midlands. Further notice provisions seem likely, at the time of writing, to be applied in other local authority areas. And though Labour's Home Secretary in 1978, Merlyn Rees, saw 'no reason for this requirement in London', William Whitelaw has declared himself 'more open-minded'. It may well be that Scarman's rejection of Mark's ideas was only a temporary setback for the police.

Certainly the post-Red Lion Square period saw no decrease in police attention to public order issues. Far from it. The police tendency to look for a conspiratorial motive behind demonstrations continued. It was undoubtedly stimulated by the deliberate attack on the police in Red Lion Square by the International Marxist Group. However, subsequent police suspicion of anti-racist and anti-National Front movements went much deeper. In June 1976, an Asian student, Gurdip Singh Chagger was murdered in Southall. According to Mark, the crime was not racially motivated. Police reluctance to see the racial dimension in this and subsequent killings has been striking. The community anxiety which followed the Chagger murder simply exasperated Mark. 'This racial unrest was stimulated and manipulated for their own ends by extremist elements including the International Socialists and the International Marxist Group', said his 1976 Report.

McNee has strongly continued this approach. His first annual report highlighted public order in a manner which reveals a lot about the police and little about the reality of the political campaigns he describes. Discussing the Grunwick dispute he wrote that the decision to begin the mass picket was taken by 'the strike committee, prompted by the Socialist Workers Party.' This was clearly not true. Similarly, he writes that 'The final trial of strength came on 7th November when a "day of reckoning" was organized. This attracted 7,000 to 8,000 supporters, many of them militant students, who made violent attacks on police cordons.' The singling out of militant students seems designed as a crude smear job on the picketers. After all, no other group is mentioned.

In the same report, McNee describes an anti-National Front march in Haringey in April 1977 as 'a counter-demonstration organized by the Socialist Workers Party, the International Marxist Group, the Communist Party of England and others'. What is most notable here is the word 'others'. These 'others' included the Labour Party (the Labour mayor of Haringey and many Labour councillors and ordinary Labour supporters were prominent in this demonstration) and even anti-racist Conservative councillors. But they don't appear worthy of a mention. McNee's purpose is to try to discredit certain forms of public political protest by pretending that they are in the grip of groups which can be portrayed as sinister manipulators – a trend he has continued in his public analyses of the Southall disturbances of April 1979.

His most recent annual report contains a further, charming example of his capacity for smelling rats:

On 30th April the Anti-Nazi League organized a march from Trafalgar Square to Victoria Park in East London where a rally was held accompanied by performances of 'pop' music. It was advertised as 'Rock

Against Racism' and attracted 60,000 people. Among the many teenagers attending the rally was an element of those described as 'punk rockers' who had not hitherto been regarded as opponents of the extreme right ... The significance of the occasion was the alliance of so many apparently non-politically-minded youths with political activists by the introduction of popular music.[39]

This event obviously taxed the Yard's top conspiracy theorists. It didn't conform to any of their stereotypes. It might help David McNee to read a recent police text book, which tells its readers that audiences at pop festivals 'composed largely of young people, can sometimes be seen as almost intoxicated with the deafening and rhythmic music, into a state bordering upon hysteria.'[40] It shouldn't prove impossible to construct a theory involving extreme political elements cynically hypnotizing young people through the medium of 'intoxicating' pop music.

McNee's attitude to public order policing is to deploy ever larger numbers of men. ever more highly trained and ever more highly equipped to ensure that the right to demonstrate is maintained. He has been quick to emphasize the cost and size of the operations. In 1977, his report stressed the operational burden caused by 'the problems of providing the massive presence that was required for the maintenance of public order at scenes of mass picketing and political marches.' It carried on the tradition established by Mark after Red Lion Square of publishing in an appendix details of injuries to police officers as a result of being assaulted on duty. The vast majority of serious cases came at demonstrations.

The statistics in these appendices are shocking, as they are meant to be, but they give a false impression. Public order in no way accounts for the largest number of working days lost in the Met. In 1978, for instance, 56,246 days were lost through injury on duty. Of these, 2,170 of these were lost due to injuries received while controlling crowds (this of course includes football crowds), a decrease of 38 per cent from 1977. By contrast, 8,067 were due to motor cycle accidents when the injured officer was riding (an increase of 29 per cent) and 6,556 were due to accidents when the injured officer was in a car (an increase of 4 per cent). The largest of all categories was the 11,326 days lost due to assaults by prisoners. And a further 50,545 days were lost through injury off duty. Over three times as many police working days were lost through injury sustained playing sports as through

injury sustained in controlling crowds. All such injury figures are
always too high, but to single out the dangers of public order work is
simply to deceive the public about the real dangers of policing.

In his latest report, Sir David McNee has gone further in his
questioning of the right to demonstrate:

> It is the citizens of London who suffer. They should know the burden that
> the policing of public order events imposes upon them and be aware of the
> serious reduction in the policing of other areas that is thereby involved.[41]

And later he states

> It falls to the Metropolitan police to supervise these occasions and to the
> taxpayer and the London ratepayer to finance the police operations ...
> The burden placed by these events on the men of the Metropolitan Police
> Force is also heavy. Police officers for the most part are diverted from
> normal employment elsewhere in the Metropolitan Police District to
> maintain public order at demonstrations and marches. Often their hours
> of duty are extended and rest days withdrawn. At these times the
> everyday workload of police duties is left to those officers remaining
> behind on divisions to cope with as best they can. Despite these costs,
> personal and financial, the police are required to fulfil their public order
> responsibilities to ensure that peace is maintained.[42]

Under the heading 'Court Proceedings' – a very inappropriate
heading – we find in the 1978 report for the first time a table showing
the financial cost of selected police public order operations during the
year. The 23 events listed are said to have cost £2,454,000 – ranging
from the £591,000 of the Notting Hill Carnival (here classed as a
'demonstration') to £51,000 on an Anti-Nazi League march in East
London. No breakdown of these costs is given. It is not clear how
much if any, of the expenditure is taken up in wages and overhead
costs which would be paid in any event. Only 'political' public order
events are listed. No other aspect of Metropolitan police work is
treated in this manner. In the year in question over £300 million was
spent in the Met but only the amount spent on this part of public order
work – less than one per cent of total expenditure – is highlighted.

So McNee is continuing and developing the Mark tradition of
making good use of public order issues to capture general support for
the police. He is also continuing Mark's habit of resentment of
criticism – in public, at least, for McNee had a reputation as a good
listener, when he came to the Yard. This impatience has become
particularly marked since the Southall disturbances of April 1979.

Speaking in Canada in August 1979 he not only made the usual attack on extremists feeding off social unrest but extended it to those who 'with apparent good intent' – a quintessential police phrase – undermined the maintenance of law by 'injudicious criticism'. And he continued

> It is particularly irritating when the criticism comes from church leaders who should be concerned more with their spiritual role and from certain politicians who perhaps ought to concentrate more on the eradiction of inner-city deprivation.[43]

It seems clear that McNee would like to be rid of the public order section of his work, or at least that he would love it to disappear. In 1978 he became the first Commissioner for fifteen years to seek and obtain a ban on processions in London under section 3(3) of the Public Order Act 1936. The ban was provoked by the prospect of National Front demonstrations and anti-Nazi counter-demonstrations during a parliamentary by-election in Ilford North. But McNee's ban went far further, to cover all marches in any part of London for a period of two months. The sweeping nature of the ban obscured the fact that there were alternatives open to the Commissioner – he could have limited the ban to a specific area (e.g. a borough) to a shorter period and even to a specific group or groups (e.g. the National Front). For instance, in September 1961 an order of this type was issued, banning for 24 hours any procession organized by the Committee of 100 in Central London.

A different type of ban employed by McNee came to light in March 1979. Organizers of the London Labour Party's May Day rally and march discovered that Scotland Yard had begun to operate a ban – under the Metropolitan Police Act 1839 – on all demonstrations along Oxford Street except on Sundays and bank holidays. This unilateral ban was made in October 1978 and removed the right of processions along a well-established traditional route through London's West End shopping district.

But bans offer only short term relief to the police. They provide brief illusory periods in which the questions of public order can be forgotten. In the long term no such escapism is possible, which is why the likelihood must be that the police will continue to seek changes in public order law along the lines proposed by Mark. An indication of this strategy was given by ACPO in September 1977 when they stated that 'the police can no longer prevent public disorder in the streets' and called for 'a new Public Order Act giving the police power to control marches and demonstrations, similar to police powers in Ulster.' In Northern Ireland a three day notice provision exists and the Northern Ireland Secretary has powers to restrict to one the number of processions allowed in one place at once time. The law in Northern Ireland also penalizes participants in unauthorized processions, not merely the organizers.

At the same time the police undoubtedly feel that public order issues are useful in rallying public support. A front-page photo of a policeman injured in a demonstration can be very useful cover for getting the changes the police want in several fields. So can the impression that enormous amounts of police time and money are being expended on the protection of the rights of extremists. For the Federation, on the other hand, the issue appears simpler. They are now opposed to any demonstrations which seem likely to lead to a breach of the peace. They want more vigorous use of the power to ban processions and less reverence for what they regard the 'abstract' right to demonstrate. According to a post-General Election article in the Federation's journal:

> What is this right of assembly that transcends, apparently, the question of whether it is reasonable to order police officers to run the gauntlet at enormous personal risk to themselves? Is it so paramount that any chief officer has the right to insist that officers under his orders shall be exposed to danger, in pursuit of an abstract belief that every blow sustained by those officers is in defence of freedom.[44]

None of the police chiefs has made a more ostentatious attempt to delegitimate public demonstrations in this way than James Anderton, Chief Constable of Greater Manchester since 1976. His most spectacular operations have – like McNee's – been concerned with protecting National Front marches. Three times – at Hyde in October 1977, at Hyde again in January 1978 and at Bolton in February 1978 – he deployed almost 5,000 police, co-ordinated by closed circuit television and helicopter surveillance in operations designed to keep opponents apart. The scale of such operations was unprecedented outside London.

The first Hyde mobilization was especially significant. In September 1977, Anderton sought and obtained a ban on all processions in the borough of Tameside under the Public Order Act. The object was to prevent both a National Front march and an opposition counter march. When the Front's National Activities Organizer, Martin Webster, threatened to defy the ban, Anderton – by his own admission – 'connived' with Webster to allow this one-man breach of the ban. The sight of Webster's march through Hyde guarded by hundreds of police, has become the classic image of the police policy of enforcing the National Front's right to demonstrate. But it was also valuable ammunition in Anderton's characteristic pugnacious attempts to win changes in the law.

Shortly after the Hyde mobilization, Anderton said:

> I would ask those who argue against me and seek to simplify the affair, to reflect upon the spreading violence of politics and the growing politics of violence. Our present legislation will not do!

Later, in the same speech, he said:

> The effect of street confrontations between opposing political groups is that impossible demands are made on the police who are subjected to an unfair test of their ability to keep the peace. Any visible defeat of the police as the primary force for law and order is a blow to democracy and a triumph for anarchy. The inevitable question, therefore, is posed – Is it not reasonable to use such laws as we have, or create new law, to avoid conflicts of this sort and the apparent damage to the invincibility of the police?[45]

Anderton's view of the Public Order Act is that it places the police, against their will and interest, in the position of taking political decisions. He has called for the abolition of the necessity for the police to apply for a ban. Under his proposals, when violence is anticipated, the chief constable will merely supply a 'statutory declaration' of the facts to the local authority – who would then take all the decisions. This would remove the possible imputation of partiality by the police. And he is very keen on notice provisions too. In 1977 he suggested a 14-day rule.

No British police chief has ever allowed himself to become so controversial a public figure as Anderton. He is always willing to talk to the press and frequently gives major lectures on a wide range of subjects. He sees himself as 'an obstinate and irrevocable moralist' and his job as part of a moral crusade. His targets have included 'social nonconformists, malingerers, idlers, parasites, spongers, frauds, cheats and unrepentant criminals.' He has described himself as 'shattered by the double standards and hypocrisy in public life, among politicians and other public figures. They are wavering when strong, reassuring voices are needed.'

In 1978 he delivered an outspoken attack on white-collar crime:

> The public generally appears quite indifferent to white collar crime and unethical professional and business tactics ... The countless millions of unreported crimes forming the hidden or unseen part of the 'crime iceberg', no matter how harmful to society, do not prick the conscience of the majority of the public.[46]

And he concluded:

> If we do not establish the right sort of community morality is it any wonder that weak people fail so often and use the evidence of wholesale corruption around them to justify their own misdeeds.

Anderton's policing has reflected his own view of that 'community morality'. He has denounced people who 'openly hanker after total debauchery and lewdness'. He has suggested 'cleansing television and the theatre of their harmful influences'. In his first year as Chief Constable, the number of searches made under the Obscene Publications Act quintupled. His men have been deployed on a major clamp-down on after hours drinking and other breaches of the licensing laws. Anderton's justification is that he is merely enforcing the law. But at the same time he has pursued a 'soft' policy of not prosecuting certain types of motoring offence, which rather contradicts the impression that he has no discretion in enforcement.

He has gone further. His public speeches and comments have not been confined to matters of morality. Some have been more conventionally political. In April 1978 he said that 'our progress along the road to understanding has been hindered rather than helped by some race relations laws.' He has advocated what he describes as 'reasonable measure of restraint', such as the compulsory carrying of identity cards with the bearer's fingerprint. He has speculated that detention for 'political subversives' may be needed in 'the not too distant future'.

Anderton likes to think of himself as 'the beginning of a new generation of policemen'. It can, of course, be dangerous to accept such remarks uncritically, but there is some substance to his claim. In 1966 the number of police forces in England and Wales was reduced from 117 to 49 and subsequent reorganizations have brought it down to 43. One consequence of this re-organization has been to thrust the fewer chief constables into greater prominence. As Critchley writes:

This was a foreseeable – and foreseen – result of the change to fewer and larger forces. At the same time the change has provided the opportunity for greater cohesion among chief constables, under the machinery of the central conference and elsewhere, in policy-making. Theoretically, at least, it would seem that they are able to speak with greater authority than ever before – both locally and nationally. And this trend can only have been reinforced by the abolition or dismemberment of many police authorities with the consequent lack of experience.[47]

The operation of this 'theoretical authority' has obviously been uneven. The Association of Chief Police Officers has for instance, more potential influence than it sometimes bothers to wield. Nor should it be assumed that what ACPO says today, the Home Office will inevitably say tomorrow.

Nevertheless ACPO has developed for itself a central role in government policy assessment and planning. In 1975 – along with Robert Mark – it helped lobby against the Labour government's proposed changes in picketing law. In 1979 it set up a specialist committee to produce recommendations for government both on picketing law and on the reform of public order legislation generally. The effect of ACPO's increased activity on these issues, as on police spending, complaints and police powers, must necessarily be to homogenize the political impact of the chief constables. While a few chiefs, notably the Metropolitan Commissioner, will continue to wield the individual influence that goes with the seniority of their office, most now make their influence effective collectively. They retain individual autonomy at the local level but when it comes to changes in policy or the law they tend to work through ACPO. One effect of this is that disagreement between senior officers is less publicly apparent. A limited doctrine of collective responsibility discourages individual chief constables from criticising the ACPO line.

Most of the chief constables appear to favour some degree of greater operational centralization. The redoubtable James Anderton has called for a 'non-political national department or council to oversee and co-ordinate a total war on crime, avoiding the present disordered and fragmented system, and providing a means for maximum collaboration between law enforcement agencies and related disciplines.' The very organization of the chief constables within ACPO helps them to encourage such moves. In 1974 it was an ACPO working party that proposed the centralization of police intelligence within a three-tier system focused on a national criminal records and intelligence bureau. One or two chief constables have publicly supported the idea of a national, centrally controlled police force administered on a regional basis – even though that was rejected by the Royal Commission on the police in 1962. The latest to take up this question is Albert Laugharne, chief constable of Lancashire. In an address to the 1979 joint conference of local authorities and ACPO, Laugharne argued powerfully that local discretion is outmoded:

> Such is the pervasive nature of crime and the need for national security that the resources sometimes must be used in ways which are not solely, or even mainly, for the benefit of the ratepayers who initially provide them.[48]

Laugharne suggests three ingenious arguments for centralization. First, an increased and uneven rating system places the police at unjustifiable financial and political risk: 'If there are financial changes in respect of police the local authority argument that he who partially pays the piper should at least have some call to the tune, might soon fall away.' Other police chiefs have begun to doubt the stability of their relations with local authorities. Robert Bunyard of Essex wrote in 1978 of a police authority

> If it is basically non party-political, then it can aid the police to retain the politically-neutral role that has been the strength of the British police for so long. Unfortunately, such neutrality may be in danger due to the growth of party politics in local government.[49]

Laugharne's second reason is the growth – in spite of the defeat in 1979 of government devolution proposals for Wales and Scotland – of 'regional culture' in Britain. This, he claims, was brought home by 'the difficulties posed for police and many other institutions during the strikes earlier this year.' Presumably – though this is not made quite clear – he means that the local government workers' strikes in the 'winter of discontent' of 1978-9 threw up too many administrative and command anomalies for the police's liking.

And finally, Laugharne looks to the other members of the EEC as models of a 'changing view of the "police state" ' – nationally administered but still subservient to the will of the majority. He states:

> It seems that the term 'police state' first entered common English usage in the 1930s, with specific reference to the totalitarian methods of government in National Socialist Germany, and it is not unnatural, therefore, that we should ascribe a sinister, if historically inaccurate,

meaning to it. But, as we come closer to Europe and as modern problems of law and order escalate, the suspicion in people's minds that any change in police organization is somehow a step towards the terrors of dictatorship, is itself changing.

Whilst he is anxious to retain the local and personal connections which are indisputably of value to the police in their relations with the community, Laugharne believes that the police have to accept that they have grown apart from the community and are no longer simply a part of it. His argument is that the police are, and must be, a disciplined, command structure whose principal function is not law enforcement *per se* but the protection of the state. As his speech puts it – in an argument that owes much to Dr A.L. Goodhart's dissenting memorandum to the 1962 Royal Commission and, perversely, to the pessimistic last chapter of T.A. Critchley's revised history of the police:

> Major police operations, such as those arising from racial and political disturbances, the pursuit of terrorists and violent criminals – indeed, almost every aspect of modern policing – have shaken out of the policeman's mind any old idea he may have had that he should for historical reasons be part of a flabby organization. He knows that he will be able to meet many of his new problems only under a cohesive command system which is able to react quickly to changing circumstances. He is realizing, too, that the widening of his aims, and the introduction of new police powers, following the exacerbations of modern problems, make it unsafe for him to hold too firmly to the view that he is just, to quote an old saying, 'a person paid to perform, as a matter of duty, acts which if he were so minded he might have done voluntarily.' There is a widening gap between powers of citizens under the criminal law and powers of policemen.

Although the historical tendency within the police is towards centralization, there remain many tenacious connections which anchor policing within local areas. Whether these are eventually severed is open to speculation. Laugharne, for one, believes that they will be. Several key aspects of specialized training and police practice are already effectively centralized and there is little doubt that others will be soon. The change from thirty years ago implicit in such developments should not be underestimated. According to Robert Mark, the cumulative effect of these trends is 'the emergence of the British police as a unified service having a stabilizing and reassuring influence in an inevitably changing and uncertain society.'[50]

However, for the moment at least, chief constables still retain a large amount of their traditional operational autonomy and individual style. If we look at the annual reports of the chief constables, this uneven pattern becomes very obvious. Well over half of them remain very conventional annual reports, without a whisper or suggestion of pontification or political opinion. This is especially true of the Scottish reports, which rigidly contain no more than basic details of police activity under traditional headings. The most controversial remark in the 1978 annual report of the Chief Constable of Dumfries and Galloway force, for instance, is this:

> While it is gratifying to note a slight decrease in almost all aspects of crime, including the more serious ones of theft by housebreaking, theft, fraud and reset I am concerned by the significant increase in the theft and non-recovery of bicycles.

Several of the remaining reports adhere to this traditional formula, whilst allowing pauses for the occasional political observation. One example comes in Kent's latest report where Chief Constable Barry Pain – who was also secretary of ACPO's working party on evidence to the Royal Commission on Criminal Procedure – says that some of ACPO's proposals 'caused comment from organizations whose main interest is not the well-being of society'. Leicestershire's report devotes a paragraph to public order which mentions 'the rash of industrial disputes that broke out during the year' and ends 'The cult of violence is not, in my view, a passing phase.'

This is a small harvest, but the chief constables are absolutely determined to retain their freedom of choice over what they put in their reports. Merseyside's chief constable, Kenneth Oxford, was reported in 1979 to have had a bitter wrangle with some local council members of his police authority over whether he should submit his report to them for vetting before publication. The 1978 annual autumn conference of ACPO expressed concern at the possible growth of such attempts to put the chief constables in harness to the local authorities.

Annual reports prepared by public controversialists like Mark, McNee and Anderton contain more sustained political comment. So too do the reports of the Chief Inspector of Constabulary. Many examples have already been quoted from the two Metropolitan Commissioners' reports. The Greater Manchester chief constable has gone further – by extending comments upon particular events into general speculations. Anderton's report for 1977 contained a

particularly notable example under the heading 'Freedom in Society'.
It said:

> The future is still uncertain. Far too many established and worthwhile
> values have gone, and too much initiative is in the hands of hotheads and
> unruly and criminally disruptive elements in society. People speak glibly
> about social change as though it is always for the better when more and
> more evidence points to a steady loss of responsibility and discipline in
> community life. Unless present trends are halted and the public order
> pendulum swings back, we are surely heading for a situation in which
> stricter measures of social control may have to be applied to stabilize
> society and secure our democratic system. I am not looking for Utopia for
> I doubt it is attainable. But it cannot be unreasonable to hope for a society
> in which more discipline, good sense, courtesy, respect and kindness are
> predominant once again.

> Crime, public disorder, violence and vandalism are like bursting boils on
> the skin of life. They will remain until such time as we rid ourselves of the
> poison which causes them. We must make sure that good triumphs over
> evil otherwise the present crime wave will continue to take its relentless
> toll of helpless and innocent victims. Police measures and other social
> controls will always be necessary but the burden of them will be lessened
> commensurate with the genuine desire of people to regularize their affairs
> for the common good.

However, the police chief who in many ways has gone furthest of all
down the campaigning road is John Alderson, chief constable of
Devon and Cornwall, a former Met man and commandant of the
Police College at Bramshill. Alderson is frequently depicted both as
the thinking person's chief constable and as Britain's most liberal
police chief. He owes both labels to his policies of 'preventive
community policing'. Alderson's method emphasizes the social work
aspect of policing. Its principal target is juvenile crime. By harnessing
the work of youth leaders, community groups, social services and
police and by evolving a common strategy, he has tried to encourage
social action – setting up youth projects, and voluntary schemes as
well as influencing planning, transport and housing policies – all aimed
at reducing the chances of crime in the neighbourhoods.

Some of the articles written about Alderson might give the
impression that his strategy ends there. Far from it. This is only the
'primary preventive' stage. The secondary and tertiary preventive
stages are integral to his philosophy. The secondary stage requires the
police and the security industry to provide 'a climate of security' by

means of visible beat patrolling and guarding work. The tertiary stage consists of detection of crime and prosecution of suspects. The difference in style is immediately obvious in Devon and Cornwall's chief constable's annual reports. Alderson's 1978 report spelled out his approach in great detail. It was even titled *Policing with the Community*. It begins with an article by Alderson, setting out at some length his views on the meaning of crime, changes in public morality, and the functions of the police. Elsewhere there are copies of press comments on his policies and a major section on public relations. The appearance and emphasis of the document are completely different to those of other annual reports. Alderson even puts the statistics – which dominate most reports – into yellow pages at the back. But what precedes it is a good deal more readable than the telephone directory.

Alderson is an active propagandist. You can get a free booklet containing two of his more important speeches from the force headquarters – a unique piece of public relations. In a TV interview in November 1978 at the same time that police bodies were deluging the Royal Commission on Criminal Procedure with demands for extra powers – Alderson publicly warned that an increase in police powers might spark a violent backlash. During the 1979 election he made a remarkable attack on hawkish law and order philosophy. His speech, to a security and safety conference – developed the themes in the booklet. He attacked the 'considerable social deception' of those who offer 'simple panaceas' on crime. He called the view that harsh punishment of offenders will reduce crime 'patently false' and described the belief that the crime rate would be cut by concentrating spending on police, courts and prisons as 'almost completely misplaced.' He denounced 'people who have never taken the slightest interest in the behaviour of young people or who have never attended a juvenile court or visited a community home' but who 'speak with the greatest gravitas and authority about this particular sea of troubles'. If children grow up in an acquisitive society, he said, it should not be a matter of astonishment that they sometimes turn to acquisitive crime. And those who do so are not only the petty thieves; they have 'counterparts growing up in respectable neighbourhoods elsewhere who will perpetuate the big frauds, the corrupt practices and dubious business deals behind facades of decency.'[51]

By complete chance, this speech was made in London on the same day that another example of his different approach was unveiled in

Plymouth. Only days after the Southall disturbances and the death of Blair Peach, Devon police allowed anti-National Front protesters to enter a hall in which NF leader John Tyndall was due to speak that evening. The hall was filled with protesters by the time Tyndall and his followers arrived. Unable to get into the hall they abandoned their meeting. The encounter passed off with virtually no violence. It was a clear refutation of the strategy of mass guarding of the National Front which McNee and Anderton had presented to the public as their inevitable and inescapable duty.

Alderson has also developed a major attack on what Robert Mark called 'fire-brigade policing'. In a paper delivered at the Cranfield Institute of Technology in 1978 to a European crime prevention conference he put it thus, in terms not unlike those of Albert Laugharne quoted earlier; but with a very different conclusion.

> The concept of the constable as a citizen in uniform appointed to keep the peace is the keystone of a unique and valuable concept of policing. But social pressures tend more and more to seduce police thinking and public awareness away from this towards a quasi-military reactive concept ...

> The modern generation of officers are beginning to see themselves as mobile responders to incidents. Technology is seductive. The car, the radio and the computer dominate the police scene. The era of preventive police is phasing out in favour of a responsive or reactive police.[52]

By counterposing his community preventive policing to fire-brigade reactive policing Alderson has won himself many liberal admirers. But his approach, while it is 'idealistic and draws heavily on philosophy' appears to contain the seeds of new and different antagonisms. As we have seen, it does not seek to do away with traditional policing functions, but to supplement them. Alderson explains that this policing goes beyond 'omnipresence and high visibility'. His policing 'reaches out to penetrate the community in a multitude of ways ... It seeks to reinforce social discipline and mutual trust in communities'.[53] Above all, it harnesses the full resources of the state to enforce norms which, for all that they may be determined by constant democratic debate at all levels in the community are norms none the less. Though Alderson has frequently condemned old-style policing and concepts of law and order which are based on imaginary theories of consensus and homogeneity, it is not evident that his approach is ultimately free from such yardsticks either. As he puts it at the conclusion of one of his lectures, the task of social policing is 'to reinforce our control'.

The Special Branch

Such a range of political policemen will obviously carry out a varying programme of political policing. Political policing has been an integral part of the police function from the earliest days. The Special Branch was formed in 1883, a specialist group whose task was to gather information on political activities. The Special Branch of our own day still carries out this task in each force area. In the words of the *State Research Bulletin* it is 'the political arm of the police'.[54] The standard official definition of the Branch's work is

> The police officers employed on Special Branch duties are concerned mainly with criminal offences against the security of the State, with terrorist or subversive organizations, with certain protection duties, with keeping watch on seaports and airports, and with making enquiries about aliens.[55]

In the majority of these tasks there is an emphasis on intelligence gathering and monitoring. The emphasis is not that of the police as 'thief-takers' but the police as watchers. But who do the Special Branch watch? Many attempts have been made to answer this question. Much of the problem hinges upon the operational scope of the term 'subversive'.

The standard modern definition of this term was given by Lord Denning in his 1963 report on the Profumo case. He said that subversives were people who 'would contemplate the overthrow of government by unlawful means'. These words, as Robin Cook MP said in a rare parliamentary debate on the Special Branch in April 1978, 'are capable of clear, precise and narrow interpretation based on statute and common law.' The test imposed by Denning is stringent, but it has now been abandoned. In that same 1978 debate, the then Home Secretary, Merlyn Rees, made the first extended parliamentary defence of the Branch by a Secretary of State. In the course of his speech he reformulated the Denning definition in a significant way. Subversive activities, said Rees, were those which 'threaten the safety or wellbeing of the State, and are intended to undermine or overthrow parliamentary democracy by political, industrial or violent means.'[56]

Rees's definition replaces the 'overthrow of government' in Denning's definition with a series of much wider and less definable objects. These include activities which merely 'threaten' the 'safety or wellbeing' of the State — not just the government, and activities intended not only to overthrow but also to 'undermine' parliamentary democracy – again not just the government. The means are extended from Denning's 'unlawful' means to 'political, industrial or violent means'.

The Rees definition is both an admission of the wide scope of Special Branch work and a green light for it to continue. It endorses the police's practice of watching and monitoring political and industrial activity. As Rees himself put it on a previous occasion: 'The Special Branch collects information on those who I think cause problems for the State.'

Though this statement – for all the breadth of possibilities implied in causing 'problems' – contains the suggestion that the limits of surveillance are defined by the Home Secretary, this apparent safeguard is an illusion. In practice the limits are determined by the police, not by national government, and most certainly never by local government. The Chief Inspector of Constabulary, Sir Colin Woods, wrote in 1978 that Special Branch work is 'a normal part of police duty'. Merseyside's chief constable, Ken Oxford, has stressed that Branch work is 'operational police work'. As such it is work for which the police, not police authorities, are responsible.

Following the persistent questioning of one Member of Parliament – Labour MP Robin Cook – some aspects of the Special Branch's work and operation achieved a first parliamentary airing in 1977 and 1978. In the 1978 debate, Merlyn Rees disclosed for the first time the numbers of officers engaged in these duties – a total of 1,259 in England and Wales, 409 of whom were in the Metropolitan force. A total of about 300 civilian staff work with the Branch. Figures for Scotland were not given – they are not the Home Secretary's responsibility – but estimates by State Research suggest about 100. The Royal Ulster Constabulary has a Special Branch of 279.

It was obviously the impact of Cook's questioning which led in 1979 to many chief constables revealing some details of their Special Branch work in the annual reports for 1978. Whereas in the 1976 reports, only one force – Durham – revealed any details, by 1978, 23 out of 43 forces in England and Wales had decided to comment. Although the Home Office denies any prompting occurred, similarity of the form of words used by several of the 23 one to another and to the words of the Chief Inspector of Constabulary quoted above is too close for coincidence. Moreover, no Scottish police chief has been seized with a desire for candour – as we have just seen, Scotland's police force is not the Home Office's responsibility.

The theme of subversion recurs in several of these reports. Merseyside's Kenneth Oxford draws attention to the fact that 'the Branch maintains a close liaison with the Security Service' – MI5, at whose behest the Branch often works – 'the armed forces and all police forces throughout the United Kingdom, endeavouring at all times to keep in touch with the current climate in respect of terrorist activities.'[57] James Anderton of Greater Manchester – who is characteristically proud of his openness on the subject – says in his report:

> The work of the Branch is concerned with security matters, investigating or assisting in the investigation of 'offences against the State' and subversion. It operates as an intelligence gathering agency to counter terrorist activities and provides the Chief Constable with early warning of public order situations which may require the deployment of additional police strength in a particular area or situation.[58]

Warwickshire's Chief Constable refers to 'terrorist or criminally subversive groups'; West Yorkshire's refers to 'terrorist activities and subversive actions'; South Wales's to 'terrorist or subversive organizations'. The significance of this juxtaposition is obvious. As *State Research* has said, it conveniently brackets 'terrorism (implying violent means) and subversion (which by the official definition can be taken to include *all* political and trade union activity)'.[59]

As with so many of these questions, Robert Mark's autobiography provides further important leads. He explains that the Branch 'take a close interest in organizations exploiting the freedom of democracy in order to subvert it' and later spells out who he means.

> The simple truth is that fascists, communists, Trotskyites, anarchists *et al* are committed to the overthrow of democracy and to the principle that the end justifies the means. Democracy must therefore protect itself by keeping a careful eye upon them.[60]

In his report on policing in Australia, Mark was even more trenchant:

> Most democracies these days are more vulnerable to internal subversion than external attack. Their governments have a clear duty to prevent the exploitation of the freedom of democracy by those who seek to undermine it. It is essential that the police in a free society should take careful note of overt or clandestine activities which allow even the suspicion of subversion. Far from there being a need to justify a Special Branch, it

should be made clear that any government unwilling to establish and maintain one is failing in its duty to protect those freedoms regarded as essential to democracy. Opposition to Special Branches almost always comes from self-appointed political pressure groups whose newsworthiness encourages them to usurp the function of those who are democratically elected to guard and determine our civil liberties.[61]

Earlier in his report, Mark commented that 'during my brief stay in Australia, I have noticed that the term "Special Branch" tends to provoke an emotional, unthinking and ill-informed reaction from people who clearly have no conception of its role, its limitations or accountability.'

The reason for this reaction may not be hard to explain. In November 1977, the Prime Minister of the state of South Australia, Don Dunstan, appointed Judge J.M. White to investigate the activities of the Special Branch in the State. White pointed out that the South Australia Branch's records and methods were 'influenced by the security forces of the United States of America and the United Kingdom'. The police in South Australia at this time were run by Commissioner Harold Salisbury, previously Chief Constable of York and later of the North and East Ridings of Yorkshire.

White found that the police had prevented Prime Minister Dunstan from 'learning of the existence or nature of substantial sections of Special Branch files on political or trade union matters, in spite of specific enquiries by the Premier in October 1970, July 1975 and October 1977'.[62] The files held by the Branch included 3,000 dossiers and over 40,000 index cards – about 28,500 of which referred to individual persons. As well as communists and terrorists these comprised information on all politicians of the Australian Labour Party at state and federal level, all current and former State Governors, half of the judges of the Supreme Court, magistrates, all university personalities whose views could be classed as 'left' or 'radical', all prominent demonstrators, most prominent trade union officials, most prominent clergymen in peace movements, homosexuals, supporters of the women's movement, divorce law reform campaigners, anti-race discrimination campaigners, all members of the National Council for Civil Liberties, most prominent socialists and over a thousand others who 'came under notice'. There were no files on any heads of government departments and no files on the Liberal Party or Country Party corresponding to the files on the Labour Party.

Judge White concluded that the files were based on 'the unreasoned assumption that any persons who thought or acted less conservatively than suited the security force were likely to be potential dangers to the security of the State.' He condemned the 'width of the interpretation of "domestic subversion".' Most of the files, he said, were on people who 'appear to be genuinely concerned persons who appear to believe in the justice of various causes.' The dossiers were 'scandalously inaccurate, irrelevant to security purposes and outrageously unfair to hundreds, perhaps thousands of loyal and worthy citizens.' Prime Minister Dunstan's response was to disband the Special Branch, burn their files and sack Police Commissioner Salisbury.

Parallels between the South Australia experience and British Special Branches are obviously speculative. But there are points of similarity. There is the breadth of the definitions on which the Branches work. There is the tradition of non-accountable secrecy in which they have worked for years. There are the command structure and close links with the national security services. There are the information gathering and record keeping techniques. And there is the historical link; the South Australian Branch was established on the British model by British police officers.

Yet it is important to appreciate that though Special Branch work is specialized, all police are trained to be able to make highly political judgements in their daily work. Such judgements have nothing to do with spotting criminal acts, or even identifying criminals. These judgements are part of the police's job – as they see it – of preventing 'subversion'. In case this may seem crude and alarmist, consider the evidence offered in a 1977 police 'field manual', written by a very senior officer, Deputy Assistant Commissioner (Crime) David Powis of the Metropolitan Police. His book, *The Signs of Crime*, received the unusual accolade of a foreword by his serving chief officer – Robert Mark – expressing his approval of its contents and commending the author's 'fair-mindedness'.

Here is an example of that fair-mindedness:

Watch for:
Criminals using vehicles who, although not dishonest in the ordinary sense, may, owing to extreme political views, intend to harm the community you have sworn to protect. While there are subtle differences between these types of extremists and thieves, it is difficult to put one's finger on material distinctions. However, they seem to have a motivation or dedication, whatever their appearance (they are usually scruffy and,

occasionally, personally dirty), markedly dissimilar to the cynicism of the greedy or dissatisfied thief ... You see, political immoderates consider themselves soldiers, rather than 'smart operators' who think the world owes them a living. This will show in their ordinary conversation, where almost unconsciously they will use the jargon of their beliefs. This intense and extremist gabble, if spoken with a cultured voice, particularly if the speaker is a woman, should make you pause and think through the likelihood that you have stumbled over an important matter.[63]

Powis's book contains other rich examples in this vein, notably the advice to be suspicious of people carrying ' "These are your rights" cards or pamphlets ... they are carried by male homosexuals, by industrial and other agitators, by "Angry Brigade" inadequates and similar amateur criminals.'[64]

The tendency to use absurd and prejudiced stereotypes is dangerous in any form of work. In political policing it means that people fall under suspicion because of their appearance or lifestyle. A recent history of the Metropolitan Police quotes approvingly this confidential Scotland Yard report of March 1971:

> In addition to the overt revolutionary activity which pervades the far Left of the political spectrum, there is a sizeable 'underground' composed of persons intent upon grasping every opportunity to challenge, denigrate and, if possible, overthrow the form of society which finds acceptance by the majority of the population. These persons are, in the main, in their early twenties, follow no employment, have no settled address, but live fleetingly in various 'communes' ... They will attach themselves to any cause, however hopeless or impractical, which they consider will aggravate or cause embarrassment to authority. They are, in the main, persons of considerable intelligence and cunning and have usually had the doubtful benefit of university or collegiate training.[65]

Political policing is indicative of the trend in police work towards general, speculative evidence and intelligence gathering – a trend which would be greatly advanced by the adoption of Sir David McNee's proposals to the Royal Commission on Criminal Procedure. This trend is not confined to the investigation of known offences, nor even to the red-handed prevention of probable offences. It is signalled by the move from the collection of evidence to the collection of intelligence, into the surveillance of sections of the community whose behaviour or very existence is suspicious to a force dominated by right-wing assumptions. It is the style of policing exemplified by Federation chairman James Jardine's call after Southall to allow the police to investigate the groups which called demonstrations 'to see whether or not those responsible were committing criminal offences.'[66]

Such an approach to policing all too easily becomes the policing of ideas. As far back as January 1971, the political correspondent of *The Times*, David Wood, wrote in the week of the Angry Brigade bombing of Robert Carr's home:

> I, for one, share Michael Foot's liberal horror of a society in which ideas have to be policed as lawless acts. Yet this is hypocrisy, the liberal fallacy. The idea preceeds the act and the best hope of counteraction lies in catching the criminal idea on the wing. We are hypocrites to pretend otherwise.[67]

The police no longer maintain this pretence.

Conclusion

This section of the book has tried to illustrate some of the trends which make a nonsense of the police's traditional claim to be 'non-political'. As the Powis excerpts show, everyday policing policy and training regard certain kinds of people – including the overwhelming majority of those engaged in political activity – as legitimate targets for police suspicion. The modern urban police officer is trained to regard such groups in exactly the same light as criminals – as people from whom 'society' (which by definition does not include these groups) requires protection.

The police view of the world – and this term is used in the full knowledge that there are many shades of police view – is based upon this deep and simple contradiction. The police claim their authority on behalf of the whole of society but they use that authority on behalf of a part of society.

The part on whose behalf they police changes according to circumstances. It will be different in the case of a hit and run motor accident and the case of a racist demonstration, for example. It would be ludicrous to pretend that the part of society served by the police is always merely the capitalist class – though in a capitalist society the police will obviously tend to protect the capitalist system. But it would be just as ludicrous to pretend that at Southall or Grunwick or the Windsor Rock Festival they police on behalf of society in consensus.

Yet this remains the police's claim. In the twentieth century, our political parties, editorial writers and other opinion-makers have failed to challenge it. In spite of the very real disputes which could and should take place over subjects like police powers, operations, organization, training, accountability and – not least – spending, there is no tradition of political disagreement over any aspect of policing.

As a result, the police have been allowed to run their own show, make their own definitions and operate behind a rhetoric of their own choosing. Whatever they decide to do becomes, by definition, in the interests of 'law and order' and therefore of 'society' too. Whoever opposes them is, equally by definition, 'anti-police' and thus hostile to 'law and order' and therefore hostile to 'society'. Some sections of society are already safely consigned to this camp: demonstrators, pickets, squatters, blacks, gays, feminists, immigrants, the Irish. There is no reason why a free society should put up with this. Unless we recognize the importance of continuing real debate about the police (with the participation of the police, of course), freed from taboos about mixing politics and policing, then the list will grow ever longer.

NOTES

1. See 'The Complaints System' by Derek Humphry in *Policing the Police*, Volume 1 (John Calder, 1979).
2. Robert Mark, *Policing a Perplexed Society* (George Allen and Unwin, 1977), p. 12.
3. Ibid, p. 20.
4. Robert Mark, *In the Office of Constable* (Fontana, 1979), p. 161.
5. Ibid, p. 160.
6. *Security Gazette*, April 1979.
7. R. Mark, op.cit. pp. 258-9.
8. R. Mark, op. cit., p. 260.
9. *Report of the Commissioner of Police for the Metropolis for the year 1972*, Cmnd 5331 (HMSO), p. 18.
10. *Report* 1974, Cmnd 6068 (HMSO), p. 10.
11. *State Research Bulletin*, No. 9 (December 1978-January 1979).
12. Foreword to T.A. Critchley, *A History of Police in England and Wales*, 2nd edition, (Constable, 1978) p. xiii.
13. Tony Bunyan, *The Political Police in Britain* (Quartet, 1977), p. 89.
14. R. Mark, op. cit. pp. 144-5.
15. R. Mark, *Policing a Perplexed Society*, Ch. 5.
16. R. Mark, *In the Office of Constable*, p. 156.
17. Ibid, p. 156.
18. See Christopher Price and Jonathan Caplan, *The Confait Confessions* (Marion Boyars, 1977).
19. L.H. Leigh, *Police Powers in England and Wales* (Butterworths, 1975), p. 141.
20. *Police*, June 1979.
21. *The Royal Commission on Criminal Procedure: Part I of the Written Evidence of the Commissioner of Police of the Metropolis* (1978).
22. *Hussein v. Chong Fook Kam* (1970).
23. Leslie Male, *The Challenge of Crime* (Police Federation, 1976).
24. See Robert Reiner, *The Blue-Coated Worker* (Cambridge University Press, 1978). Also the same author's paper 'Fuzzy Thoughts: The Police and Law and Order Politics', delivered to the 1979 Conference of the British Sociological Association.

25. Leslie Male, op. cit.
26. Ibid.
27. *Police*, July 1979.
28. Reiner, 'Fuzzy Thoughts', op. cit.
29. R. Mark, *In the Office of Constable*, pp. 159-60.
30. For a detailed treatment, see Christopher Whelan: 'The law and the use of troops in industrial disputes,' Working Paper No. 2 available from Centre for Socio-Legal Studies, Wolfson College, Oxford. See also *State Research Bulletin*, Nos. 4 and 6.
31. R. Mark, *op. cit.* p. 174. However, the then Prime Minister, Harold Wilson, was not consulted at all. Even in his capacity as head of security, it was a surprise: see Penrose and Courtiour, *The Pencourt File* (Secker & Warburg, 1978), pp. 240-2.
32. R. Mark, *Policing a Perplexed Society*, p. 30.
33. *State Research Bulletin*, No. 10 (February-March 1979).
34. Critchley, *op. cit.*, p. 54.
35. *Report of the Commissioner of Police for the Metropolis for the year 1970*, Cmnd 4680 (HMSO), p. 11.
36. *Report* (1972), Cmnd 5331, p. 11.
37. *Report* (1973) Cmnd 5638, p. 14.
38. *The Red Lion Square Disorders of 15 June 1974: Report of Inquiry by the Rt. Hon. Lord Justice Scarman, OBE*, Cmnd 5919 (HMSO), pp. 35-7.
39. *Report of the Commissioner of Police for the Metropolis for the year 1978*, Cmnd 7580 (HMSO), pp. 25-6.
40. D.W.P. Varwell, *Police and the Public* (Macdonald and Evans, 1978), p. 92.
41. Report (1978), Cmnd 7580, p. 8.
42. Ibid, p. 28.
43. *Daily Telegraph*, 24 August 1979.
44. *Police*, May 1979.
45. 'Law and Order: the problem of Public Processions'. Speech to Manchester Rotary Club, 27 October 1977.
46. 'Crime and the Community', speech to the International Fire, Security and Safety Conference, 24 April 1978.
47. Critchley, op. cit., p. 300.
48. *Police*, May 1979.
49. R.S. Bunyard, *Police: Organization and Command* (Macdonald and Evans, 1978), p. 44.
50. R. Mark, *Policing a Perplexed Society*, p. 19.
51. 'Crime and the Free Society', speech to the International Fire, Security and Safety Conference, 24 April 1979.
52. *Police Review*, 6 April 1979.

53. John Alderson, *Communal Policing* (Devon and Cornwall Constabulary, 1978), and *Policing Freedom* (Macdonald & Evans, 1979).
54. *State Research Bulletin*, No. 2 (November 1977).
55. *Report of Her Majesty's Chief Inspector of Constabulary 1978* (HMSO).
56. *Hansard*, 6 April 1978.
57. *Report of the Chief Constable to the Merseyside Police Committee for the year 1978*, p. 70.
58. *Greater Manchester Police: Chief Constable's Report for 1978*, p. 33.
59. *State Research Bulletin*, No. 13 (August-September 1979).
60. R. Mark, *In the Office of Constable*, p. 311.
61. Quoted in *State Research Bulletin*, No. 10 (February-March 1979).
62. *Special Branch Security Records*: Initial Report to the Honourable Donald Allan Dunstan QC, LLB, MP by the Honourable Mr Acting Justice White (Adelaide, 1977).
63. David Powis, *The Signs of Crime* (McGraw-Hill, 1977), p. 12.
64. Ibid, p. 92.
65. Quoted in David Ascoli, *The Queen's Peace* (Hamish Hamilton, 1979), p. 324.
66. *Police*, May 1979.
67. *The Times*, 18 January 1971.

Section 2

SOCIETY UNDER SURVEILLANCE

I am considerably indebted to a number of friends, colleagues and contacts who have provided important information and advice for this section. It would unfortunately be uncharitable to list their names here to further swell Special Branch files.

In a quite separate category, I am also obliged to the Home Office for courteously and helpfully providing otherwise unpublished factual material.

Comments and conclusions drawn are of course solely those of the author.

Society Under Surveillance
Duncan Campbell

During the last twenty years, police forces in the UK have gone through a remarkable series of reforms. A collection of separate county and borough constabularies, with a loose centre at Scotland Yard, has been reformed into just 52 forces, with a high degree of integration and co-operation. Each force now operates sophisticated communications systems for deploying police resources, and participates in the collection of considerable quantities of information for local and national records. The nature of police operations has changed considerably, diminishing local autonomy and accountability in favour of precise and rapid central control. The emphasis in investigation has changed from evidence gathering after the commission of crime to intelligence gathering in advance of any particular crime being committed. In this 'pre-emptive' view, any citizen, certainly any socially uncharacteristic citizen, is a target for suspicion and observation. This quite explicit development in police planning has virtually put the whole of society under surveillance.

In one sense, this has always been the case. The local constables and detectives who, before the introduction of unit beat policing, were rigidly attached to a particular area would normally make it their business to be as well informed as possible. But they themselves were a part of the community they policed; the forces for which they worked were smaller, and potentially at least, more responsive to local control and accountability through the Watch Committees of local councils.

But the progressive reforms instituted by central government have eroded this accountability, and created police forces which instead place society at arm's length – and under observation. Substantial evidence of this development can be found by examining the role of police information and intelligence gathering. The advent of major new computer systems for storing police information and intelligence has rightly aroused widespread concern. The best known of these systems is the Police National Computer (PNC) in London, which is one of the most advanced systems for disseminating police information in the world. But a variety of other major and minor projects have grown up in the wake of the PNC, including a project to place on computer the records of the Special Branch and other police national intelligence units. This development has received a major boost from the conflict in Northern Ireland, where the army's campaign against the IRA has provided political support for the instigation of extraordinary systems of surveillance and control over the entire population. The Army's records are now on computer too. Traditional military doctrines on the importance of good prior intelligence – but now turned inwards on much of the British population – have encouraged police units like the Special Branch to make advances in the same direction. One local force other than the Metropolitan Police, Thames Valley, has already placed its local intelligence records on a computer.

Prior to 1964, the Central Criminal Records Office at Scotland Yard was the only major national source of information about convicted criminals. There was no national repository of what is now called 'criminal intelligence' although of course even at that stage the Special Branch and the closely related Security Service (MI5) had substantial indexes of and files about persons in whom they had an interest for political reasons. The subsequent creation of Regional Criminal Records Offices, and attendant rationalization of record keeping brought about the first stage of the reforms. Even in the early 1960s, there was official interest in the possibility of harnessing computers to the task of providing police with a national information pool.[1]

The most important reform from the local point of view was the introduction of Unit Beat policing. The domain of a police force would now be divided up into areas under the control of a team of detectives and uniformed officers. A less publicized aspect of the reform was the new arrangements for reporting and record keeping. At the centre of the system was a new post, a collator, who would receive the daily reports of patrol officers and detectives, together with copies of all other communications to and from his police station, and from these build up comprehensive indexes of people, addresses, vehicles, incidents and crimes which had come to the attention of the police. No statutory power existed for this (or indeed many other police information gathering activities); it was merely not prohibited.

The collator is, however, better called a local intelligence officer. He represents at the local level the same type of prior intelligence gathering and surveillance as is carried out by major squads such as the National Drugs Intelligence Unit, the Fraud Squad and the Special Branch. The late sixties reforms of police organization put collators to work in every local divisional and sub-divisional police station. Their resources and methods do vary from place to place, as does the responsibility placed on them or the frequency with which they are consulted. Nevertheless, the collators have now created a co-ordinated nationwide network of basic intelligence records. There is clear evidence that the basic motive behind the collator system was to collect information on as many people as possible who cross police paths. This will include not just persons suspected or convicted of criminal offences as well as their families, friends and 'associates', but also politically active people, and even those who are the victims of crime, or people who have complained to the police.

The British police are yet a long way from possessing or exercising the undisciplined and repressive excesses which are common in totalitarian regimes. But the demands of police spokesmen, at public forums and to official bodies, indicates an underlying intent – witting or not – to go in that direction. Spokesmen like Sir Robert Mark and his successor, Sir David McNee, have repeatedly asked for drastic curtailment of suspects' rights, for the removal of the right to jury trial for many offences, for widespread new powers to stop and search and question, and to detain for questioning without any charge. When the political climate seems right, often in the emotive wake of a terrorist outrage or suchlike, tentative proposals for the carrying of identity papers and compulsory registration with the police are mooted. The police campaigns on such matters go so far as to state quite plainly that the law needs to be reformed because the police themselves regularly break it, often exceeding their powers of arrest, search and so on.

These proposals are steps towards a rigidly controlled society, where there is comprehensive surveillance of many non-criminal aspects of people's lives. Instead of policing from within society, the police are now moving outside – and in so doing they inevitably sacrifice essential trust and goodwill. The new aggregated police forces have become remote from public control – often, indeed, physically remote, setting up operational headquarters away from major towns.

For them, the PNC at present provides a basic and very rapid check on up to 4 million people, and 19 million vehicles and their owners. As well as providing basic factual information, such checks will reveal if the person concerned has a criminal record – however old, however trivial – and will also indicate if some policeman or unit has an interest in the person or vehicle. An explicit part of the development of the PNC was the provision of new communications networks, nationwide, which would enable any beat policeman – on foot or in a vehicle – to communicate immediately with his police station or control room, and obtain information from the PNC via a computer terminal situated there. Again, it has not been widely appreciated that the *raison d'être* of police personal radio – at least at the time it was introduced – was to establish this direct net of communications from the computer to every policeman, rather than to assist in the other tasks, such as summoning urgent assistance in case of need.

This aspect of the PNC project helps to draw what amounts to a net across society. The activity of stop checks, for which no statutory legal power exists unless the police officer suspects a specific crime, now constitutes a basic part of the surveillance system. These checks are not only encouraged by official police doctrine, but in some forces at least are carried out as a minimum duty if no crime is being dealt with. An officer who does not carry out a sufficient number of checks is under-performing.

On each such occasion, radio contact will be made with headquarters and the name or vehicle registration will be checked with the PNC – and quite often also with local collators' files. It is easy to see how well proposals for national identity cards fit in with this sort of scheme. At present, vehicles can be checked on the PNC *en masse* and more or less at whim, and indeed such practices are encouraged – for example, motorway patrols can radio in a series of registrations observed for a 'block' PNC vehicle check. There is no need to stop a car to obtain sufficient identification. Compulsory identity cards would make the same facility available to police to check individuals *en masse*.

Notwithstanding the fact that straightforward police checks can on their own be intimitadory and tantamount to harassment, their exact social effects are subject to two further separate aspects of police behaviour; the nature of information stored and retrieved on demand about an individual being checked; and the behaviour of and powers available to the police. At its simplest, the law may be applied unequally. Someone who is unknown in police files might be cautioned for an offence whilst another with a record – criminal or not – may be charged or at least apprehended and detained further. If new powers to detain for search and questioning are allowed, then the scope of such unequal treatment may be extended to what are in effect non-judicial punishments, whereby the person concerned is detained and thus punished without appearing before a court.

The information passed in response to a police enquiry, whether from the PNC or local intelligence, is intended to assist and help determine the policeman's course of action. If the message is that someone is to be arrested for an offence, then the course of action taken is obvious, and the fact of passing the information is wholly unobjectionable. But where a previous conviction or, say, a record of political or industrial campaigning, is indicated, whilst no offence is currently being committed, it is both offensive and unnecessary that such information should so readily be available.

A very few leaks of information held in police files to the press and so on have more than substantiated the case for concern about the information held. There is no denial from the police that both local and national files will and do already hold records on people who have never been convicted of any offence. Files which have been leaked have shown that, apart from this, it is certainly the practice of local collators to record on an individual's files details of every type of policing activity concerning that person. This will include stop checks, hearsay and gossip, charges resulting in a caution or an acquittal, simple cautions, policemens' and others' suspicions, and even such things as notes about the person standing bail for a third party.

It is offensive to individual privacy that such files should be allowed to be maintained at all in the haphazard way in which they have been created. Equally offensive is the practice of opening files willy nilly on anyone whose name has appeared on a police record of any sort, and then continually cross referencing and up-dating the file with any new information. It is manifestly a threat to the liberty of the subject when police behaviour and attitudes towards an individual are determined by the contents of remote files of unknown reliability and accuracy, rather than by a policeman's own judgment and obedience to his task under the law.

This section of the book examines and documents the major police projects in information and intelligence gathering, and explains the circumstances in which they have developed and how they are likely to continue developing. The description of each system should be viewed in the context of police operations as a whole, for it is only by examining – as far as we are able – the exact effects of such files and computers on individuals that one can credibly portray the immense threat to liberty which is contained in new police developments.

The major computer project to be examined is, inevitably, the PNC. In operation now for five years, the PNC has progressively been modified and extended, and there is no doubt that some of its planners, having succeeded thus far, would now like to move on to a more comprehensive national police intelligence system. Besides the PNC, 'C' (Criminal) Department of the Metropolitan Police has now started using a sophisticated computer which will store the files of five national intelligence squads, including the Special Branch. The third project deserving particular attention is run by Thames Valley Police (TVP). Known as the Collator Project, this computer is used to store all the collators' records for the entire force, with access from all police stations in the area. TVP is so far the only force whose entire collator records have been placed on computer; others have extensive manual filing systems of varying sophistication.

The British Army computer in Northern Ireland is worth some attention because of the interplay between the development of police intelligence in Northern Ireland and similar planning in Britain. The use of the Army computer is not confined to the army alone, but includes the Royal Ulster Constabulary (RUC) amongst its customers. Individual military patrols in Northern Ireland use the computer at the Lisburn HQ in much the same manner as mainland policemen use the PNC.

These computers are only a small fraction of all computers in police use, and it would be erroneous to interpret any police use of computers as being in the same category as, say, the PNC. Other types of computer are widely used in the moment-to-moment allocation of vehicles and patrols to deal with incidents reported to the police. Still others (and sometimes computers shared with local authorities) are used to gather and process administrative information ranging from police pay to gun licences. These applications, known variously as Command and Control, Computer Aided Despatch and Management Information Systems, are discussed later. Their use is relevant to an understanding of the style of contemporary policing; moreover, there is some indication that previously rigid boundaries between the various types of system are now blurring. For example, the normal requirement is now for new command and control computers to have facilities which link them to the PNC, so that one computer terminal can be used for both checking police resources and carrying out PNC checks. At the same time parts of some forces' collators' information files have been placed on the command and control systems. Although any major linkage of separate police computers is clearly some time away, it is certainly a proposal being entertained by Home Office planners.[2] A model for such a development is already available in Germany, where the State Police operate a formidable network of computers with regional and national centres, based on the Federal Criminal Records Office (BKA). Overseas police experience also provides some evidence about police behaviour which is unavailable at present in Britain. For example, Special Branch activities in Australia have received considerable scrutiny, and deserve some attention because of the considerable similarity in operating methods and establishment.[3]

The prospect of legislation on privacy and computers, although not immediately significant, is in the long term quite good. Some kind of regulation of computer based records is widely anticipated within the computer industry, not least because of the many laws on the subject which have now been passed overseas. The first major British examination of police computer records took place in 1976-78, by the Data Protection Committee.[4] They took quite a stern view of police records and in particular the unwillingness of the police to give all the evidence the committee required on the subject. The DPC envisaged the establishment of a Data Protection Authority, and it is likely that such an agency will eventually be established.

The creation of a powerful and independent Data Protection Authority would be a necessary first step in reasserting the eroded right to individual privacy. This is one of a number of areas in which British citizens − who have not the benefit of a written constitution or a Bill of Rights − are becoming increasingly powerless against the state and its agencies. Despite goodwill and concern in parliament and elsewhere, the Home Office and successive governments of recent years have proved wholly unwilling to propose legislation reinforcing human rights. In this void, the police have readily and rapidly moved to occupy the strongest position available; whatever legislation comes, dismantling existing or future systems, or prizing open the secret doors will be hard enough. Yet it is vital that the present drift towards speculative intelligence gathering, in which any citizen, however innocent, is regarded as a fit subject for surveillance because of what he may do in the future, must be stopped. The tide of pre-emptive policing needs to be turned back.

The Police National Computer

Plans for the computerization of police records go back as far as 1959, when a new government department was set up jointly by the Home Office, Metropolitan Police and the Prison Commission.[5] Known as JADPU (Joint Automatic Data Processing Unit), its purpose was to introduce appropriate computer applications into the various sponsor departments. A report prepared during the year outlined the possibility of processing and retrieving police records, on computer, including the particularly arduous task of sorting out fingerprints. Various other police applications of computers were canvassed by JADPU. In 1964, at the same time as Regional Crime Squads and Regional Criminal Records Offices were set up, a feasibility study of centralizing police criminal and other records was carried out.

As a result of this, in 1968 JADPU established a Police National Computer Unit to prepare detailed proposals for such a computer. Their report suggested a number of major projects which could be carried out by the computer. These were: Stolen Vehicles, Vehicle Owners, Fingerprints, Wanted or Missing Persons, Criminal Names (of persons convicted of offences), Disqualified Drivers, Suspended Sentences, *Modus Operandi* (techniques used by criminals), Stolen Cheques, Stolen Property, and Stolen Bicycles. The first five of these were intended as the major tasks of the PNC, with Disqualified Drivers and Suspended sentences to be added later. Most of these facilities are now in operation. The remainder were intended as future 'enhancements' of the system, but, at the time of writing, none have been placed on the PNC in a systematic way.

In 1969, the Labour government gave consent to the project, and work started on a new and highly secure building to house the computer. The PNC building is now contained within the Metropolitan Police training centre at Aerodrome Road, Hendon, in north London, close to the M1 Motorway. In 1970, the PNCU became a separate department within the Home Office, autonomous from JADPU.

The first computers to be installed at Hendon were two large

American central processors of considerable power, Burroughs B6700s. These were installed in January 1972. A further Burroughs B6700 computer used for test and development was installed later. Apart from the computer and associated offices, the building contains an 'uninterruptible' power supply. This arrangement provides power continuously to the computer centre in the event of a failure, and ensures that the computer does not stop operating even during the short time that it takes to start running the PNC's four stand-by diesel generators.

Also contained in the Hendon centre is a Communications Network Control for the PNC.[6] This centre controls and supervises the 800 or so terminals which are connected to the PNC throughout the country. A network of post office private wires – ordinary lines but not connected to the public telephone system – each connect a number of terminals to the PNC. The terminals will normally be visual display units (VDUs) which can rapidly display information sent to and from the computer on a television screen. Alternatively, or sometimes in addition, a police station may have a 'dataprinter', which is a teleprinter modified to work with a computer. This can be used for less urgent enquiries, or those where a paper copy is required.

The VDUs accessing the PNC are now situated, in quantity, in the headquarters buildings of all police forces in England, Scotland and Wales. Additional terminals are often provided at police divisional stations, and in London at all sub-divisional stations as well. Each headquarters, division or sub-division operates a radio network – including UHF or VHF personal radios and VHF links to patrol cars. The PNC terminal is always situated so that enquiries can rapidly be made on the computer in response to a radio call. This network – which in effect connects the PNC to every policeman in the country via the radio networks – provides clear advantages to police efficiency in enabling stolen cars to be rapidly traced. This aspect of the system – which was the first application to go 'live' – is often heavily oversold by police spokesmen. The actual stolen vehicles file – with about 30,000 entries – is a tiny part of the 40 million records which the PNC can store.

From the beginning of 1971, a team of programmers started to develop the computer 'software' which would enable a staggeringly fast response to a very high rate of enquiries. The specification for the PNC required that enquiries from a local terminal would receive an answer within five seconds – even when this could involve selecting one of up to 20 million records. At the same time enquiries were expected to come in at the rate of 21,000 transactions an hour. An independent company called Hoskyns co-ordinated the design of the PNC's heart, a group of programmes called Central System[7] which would provide the basic means of searching for information in response to incoming enquiries. Central Systems 1 and 2 were completed during 1973, and the first two files went 'live' during 1974. These were the Suspect and Stolen Vehicles Index, and the Vehicle Owners Index. Delays, blamed officially on the three day week in 1974, mean that the Vehicle Owners Index did not start operating until late that year, and only held the latest vehicle registrations.

Since then all the major applications of the PNC have started operation. These are listed in *Table 1*, below:

Table 1: PNC Applications

Indexes	Size*	Date of going 'live'
Stolen/Suspect vehicles	100,000	March 1974
" (Chassis/Engine serial numbers)	260,000	—
Vehicle owners	23.25 million	October 1974
Fingerprints	2.5 million	1975
Criminal names	4 million	August 1977
Wanted/Missing persons	100,000	1978
Disqualified drivers	(170,000 est.)	due May 1980
Other major facilities		
Vehicles — search by description		1974
Broadcast system		1975
Cross referencing of local, regional and national records (RX).		1977

* *The size of files is as at September 1979, and is based on information supplied to the author by the Home Office.*

Information in this and the following tables which show the contents of records on particular police computers is based on the various references in the text. In some cases the positioning of information has been rearranged slightly in the interests of clarity; in a few cases, where the name given for the item of information was obscure or specialized jargon, a more meaningful term has been substituted.

Apart from these major files, specialized and *ad hoc* applications have been introduced or are being developed on the PNC. In April

1977, for example, it was announced that stolen building materials and construction vehicles would be recorded on the PNC.

A major additional service provided by the PNC quite apart from information retrieval is the so-called 'Broadcast Facility'. This enables the computer to be used as a rapid communications system, and messages can be passed from one terminal to another, or to all other terminals. The 'Broadcast Facility' has been reported to have been extensively used.[8]

The Stolen Vehicle Index is perhaps the most revealing example of the actual nature of the PNC. The idea of centrally recording stolen vehicles is clearly unobjectionable in principle, and the related attributes of the PNC's fast communications systems are an obvious boon. It therefore comes as a surprise to discover that only one quarter of the PNC's 'stolen vehicles' entries are actually stolen. Information on this comes from a 1976 Home Office Conference,[9] attended by foreign police officers and computer specialists: the Home Office wanted to set up 'firm links between (police) research groups ... and make possible scientific co-operation between them.' A paper at the conference by J.R. Cubberley and D. Blakey of the PNCU reported that an average of 120,000 entries on the Suspect/Stolen Vehicles file were recorded for one of eleven reasons. These ranged from 'having been stolen (about 30,000) to being owned by an active criminal or having been impounded by the police ... for obstruction.'

The other reasons for being listed have not been explicitly published, although some details are available. Stolen and impounded vehicles account for two reasons; additional reasons include vehicles in use for police purposes, vehicles which are, or whose owners are suspected of having committed an offence, and vehicles of 'long term interest' to the police. Two larger sections of this file are therefore concerned with stolen vehicles and vehicles used by the police – these perhaps amount to just over half the file at that time, say 65,000 entries. Most of the rest are either the 'SUS' categories or the 'INT' categories, denoting suspicion or 'long term interest'.[10] One senior police officer has confirmed[11] that in his (provincial) force, about 500 vehicles would have been recorded as of interest. Since there are 52 police forces in Britain, this figure would seem to confirm the estimate that at least one third of the 'Stolen' Vehicles file is in fact concerned with vehicles which are under surveillance; whose whereabouts are to be reported but whose drivers are not necessarily to be made aware that surveillance has taken place.

This category should be carefully distinguished from the category of suspect vehicles, where the person concerned is suspected of an offence and will normally be arrested. At least he or she will not be the subject of *secret* surveillance. Unless details of the exact categories become public, however, it will not be possible to separate the shades

Table 2: Details held on the PNC Stolen/Suspect Vehicles Index

```
REGISTRATION MARK:
MAKE:          MODEL:      TYPE:
YEAR:          COLOUR 1: COLOUR 2:
REPORT TYPE:               TEXT DETAILS:
FORCE/STATION:             FOR FORCE/STATION:
```

'Report type' presumably indicates the category in which the vehicle falls.

of grey between 'suspect' and 'long term interest'. Official spokesmen tend happily and deliberately to blur this and other aspects of police computer systems.

Another unusual, and secret mechanism for surveillance, was described to me by a former PNC programmer. Additional information can be inserted into the record of a vehicle in either the Stolen Vehicle or the Vehicle Owner's index to indicate that the Special Branch have an interest in the vehicle. If an enquiry is made on its record, a message concerning the enquiry is sent to the Special Branch at New Scotland Yard at the same time as the enquiry is answered. The local police force making the enquiry is given no indication that it has been flagged to Special Branch in this way. A bell is rung in the Special Branch duty office to ensure that the message receives attention. This system was justified to programmers as being intended to protect the SB's own vehicles from police interference if they were behaving unusually; but this was clearly not the true reason for the facility. It has been suggested by police sources that similar warning facilities are now available to other major police units such as the Regional Crime Squads and the National Drugs Intelligence Unit.

The use of these PNC files has been highlighted in two cases which received attention in the national and specialist press. In March 1975, a company director named David Morrell was arrested after a stop check on a motorway.[12] He was told by police that a computer check had shown him to be wanted. Although there is some doubt as to the exact file which was consulted, he was nevertheless held for two hours while details of the charge against him were sought. It turned out to relate to non-payment of a parking fine by another member of his firm using the same car.

A more serious and perplexing incident took place in January 1977, when three members of the Hunt Saboteurs Association, or 'Anti-Blood Sports League' were arrested and, later found guilty of desecrating the grave of huntsman John Peel.[13] They had been arrested after their car was checked on the PNC. According to the prosecuting counsel at a preliminary hearing, this PNC check resulted in the officer being told that 'the owner was a prominent member of the Anti-Blood Sports League'. Being aware from TV news of the recent offence some 60 miles away, the police officer then arrested the owner and his passengers.

The case raised considerable concern, because if the membership rolls of minor and comparatively innocuous anti-hunting organizations had found their way onto the PNC, what had not? This line of enquiry elicited an interesting parliamentary answer to an enquiry from Jo Richardson MP to the Home Office:[14] 'Information about political beliefs and activities is not held on the Police National Computer', a remark which appears to be a construction suggesting that the information on beliefs and activities themselves was not an indexed subject as such. For the answer continued contradictorily:

Occasionally information about association with an organization has been held for a limited period in the index of suspected and stolen vehicles when a police officer has judged it relevant when reporting a vehicle as suspected of being used in connection with crimes.

It was possible that the information about anti-hunt membership came from the vehicles being recorded in one or other sections of the Suspect/Stolen Vehicles Index. Alternatively, though less likely, the information may have come from a local collator's records. Certainly, the anti-hunt lobby were in little doubt as to how such information was obtained. A local policeman in Oxfordshire, who patrolled in the area where the car driver, David Hough, lived said in evidence that he had 'frequently observed meetings of the Hunt Saboteurs Association at their address, and had noted registration numbers of vehicles in the driveway'.[15] At other anti-hunt meetings, police noted down car numbers of hunt saboteurs vehicles'.

In the presumptions of pre-emptive policing, the recording of such information reflects a view that *all* people with anti-hunt feelings are likely troublemakers, and qualifies them and their associates as 'suspects'. No doubt the arrest of David Hough and his two passengers will be seen as vindicating this view. But what of the dozens of other quite innocent anti-hunt demonstrators and sympathizers who will be harassed by being stopped and checked as suspects?

There are thus three ways in which the Stolen and Suspect Vehicle Index becomes a means, not of apprehending car thieves and escaping criminals, but of exercising general surveillance on those in whom the police are interested. In fact, this latter aspect of the Index is larger quantitatively than any other, according to the figures above. To pass the (genuinely) Stolen Vehicles Index off as being the major part of the PNC is little short of a deception.

The three ways in which this sort of data may be stored are:

● By recording the vehicles registration in one of the 'long term interest' (INT) categories of the Index.

● By using the free text space (See Table 2 – Text details) of the entry to record such things as 'association with an organization'.

● By the incorporation, secretly, of a 'flag' to alert Special Branch or other squads if the record is accessed.

The Home Office conference paper on the PNC[16] also described the use of partial search facilities on this and other indexes. It is possible to search the entire file on the basis of a partial description, such as 'Blue Hillman, with 5 and 7 in the registration'. Authority of a senior officer is required to carry out such searches, which can be expensive and time-consuming, and need to be justified by the circumstances. The conference paper continued to explain how 'a list of all the owners of yellow Volkswagens in London could quickly be made available to police in a suitably serious case'. It then described:

> a recent case where a girl was raped ... and supplied a description of the car ... a green Ford Cortina with the last registration number being L. A search of the Stolen Vehicles Index (sic) produced a handful of possibles one of them being a car belonging to a man in a neighbouring police area suspected of sexual offences and entered as a suspect. He was subsequently arrested.

The presenters of the paper did not say whether this 'suspect' was actually convicted of the offence, however. Nor does it appear that he had any previous convictions for sexual offences, or no doubt these would have been mentioned. It is also clear that the police had no evidence to prove him guilty of any previous such offence, otherwise, since his identity was known, he could easily have been arrested. What the statement 'entered as a suspect' amounted to, then, is a statement of belief by the police that this was a person who was likely to go and commit a sexual offence, not that he had already been proven to have committed such an offence. The recording of unsubstantiated and almost gossipy information is fraught with danger, not the least of which is that the record will become self-fulfilling, as the police will only generally act towards the person concerned in a way which furthers their own suspicion and beliefs.

It may well be that on this occasion, the 'suspect' was guilty. But spokesmen for the PNC are unlikely to recount the failure stories that go hand in hand with such methods; they could not even furnish statistics as to the number of people 'suspected' of being potential sexual offenders who are thereby wrongfully inconvenienced, or even arrested and then acquitted.

The rapid apprehension of vehicle thieves is also often advanced as a justification for the second major application to become operational on the PNC, the Vehicle Owners Index. This is a fairly straightforward file of every vehicle in the country, with a description, its engine and chassis number, and the name and address of the registered keeper. Prior to 1972, this information was held manually throughout the country in council licensing offices. A search through the records took some time, particularly out of office hours. At the same time as the PNC was planned, the Ministry of Transport planned to centralize all these records on a computer centre at Swansea, known as the Driver and Vehicle Licensing Centre (DVLC). From 1974, this Centre started handling the records of licences of new cars and progressively computerized the records of all existing cars. The development of the DVLC proceeded hand in hand with the Vehicle Owners application on the PNC, and as each new batch of car licences was computerized at Swansea, so the information was added to the PNC's files. The Swansea centre records both vehicle and driving licences, and both owners and drivers are required to report any change of address to the DVLC on penalty of a fine. The information on owner's addresses is then automatically transferred to the PNC. Originally this was done by the despatch of a computer tape of 'updates' every three days; updates are now carried out daily, with the PNC often updated faster than the DVLC.

By December 1977, details of 17.7 million vehicles and owners were recorded on the PNC, and at the time of writing (summer 1979), the total has reached almost 19 million. Each owner, by a neat administrative trick, is now legally obliged to inform the police of any change of address. The merging of the two databases created in effect a new law, without any discussion whatsoever in Parliament, let alone explicit statutory authority. The position of driving licence holders is slightly different. As far as is known, their particulars are not

Table 3: Details held in the PNC Vehicle Owners Index

```
REGISTRATION MARK:

MAKE:          MODEL:        TYPE:

YEAR:          COLOUR 1:     COLOUR 2:

KEEPER NAME:                 KEEPER SINCE:

KEEPER'S ADDRESS & POSTCODE:
```

automatically transferred to the PNC, even if their name appears, say, in the Criminal Names Index. To check new driving licence applications or change of address forms to see if the persons concerned were listed on the PNC would require that such information was either screened at the DVLC, or that updates of new or altered driving licence information was automatically sent to the PNC at the same time as information on vehicle owners. The first suggestion would place an unacceptably high burden on the Swansea computers; both possibilities are denied by the Department of the Environment, which now runs the DVLC.

But police have access to this sort of information on request when they wish to,[17] even if it is not as readily available as it would be on the PNC. The new style of computerized driving licence was specifically tailored to their requirements. It contains a new coded 'Driver Number' composed of five letters of the person's surname, six digits which contain, disguised, the person's date of birth, and five other digits containing initials and information of other kinds. The fact that date of birth is contained in the number is disguised by scrambling the digits round. For example, a person born on the second of December 1944 (02/12/44) will have the code 412024; even sex is distinguished by adding a 5 to the second digit to indicate a woman. Since drivers have to either carry the licence or produce it on demand, this move has created for them a form of national identity card tailor made to the process of PNC spot checks. The policeman can of course readily decode the date of birth, and it is this, together with a person's name, which provides the basic 'keys' for searching the PNC Criminal Names and Wanted/Missing Index – together with any other records, such as local collators files.

The Driving Licence is not an identity card in law, though it is often used as such. There is little doubt that in the joint development of plans for the PNC and the DVLC, its potential as an identity card was stretched as far as was legally possible. Once again, there was no debate in Parliament over the introduction of date of birth information onto the new driving licences. (It had not previously appeared.) A more disturbing idea is that the remaining part of the Driver Number code – which seems to be largely unused at present – could be used to encode secret indications to police officers or others about the holder – such as certain types of criminal record or political activity. Such underhand methods are not unknown to the civil service or police. Immigration Service officers were recently discovered to have applied precisely this sort of marking to the passports of legal immigrants whom they nevertheless suspected were not fully entitled to reside in the UK.[18] The marking could be read by other Immigration Officers and some policemen, although the person concerned would be quite unaware that there was any sort of secret message in his or her passport.

Even without the facility of secretly coded Driver Numbers the rapid availability of owner enquiries on the PNC is in itself a form of identity check on the driver, who is likely also to be the keeper. This of course is a legitimate and useful test where it is genuinely suspected that the vehicle has been stolen. But the vast bulk of the owner enquiries are inspired by little more than curiosity, rather than actual suspicion of a specific crime. This can merely be mischievous; a story, of uncertain reliability and possibly apocryphal, tells of two constables in London being reprimanded for using the PNC facilities to obtain the names of attractive women spotted driving. They would then feign familiarity with the women, whom of course they had never met but who would take the fact of their names being known as evidence of acquaintance. More serious is the practice of more or less random stop checks on the PNC. One ex-policeman from a Home Counties force has stated[19] that patrol cars which were not employed in crime work were expected to fulfil a quota of such checks on each evening patrol. This seems a quite improper, if not unlawful, use of police powers and facilities, involving the random harassment of individuals on suspicion of no offence whatsoever.

A dramatic example of just how easy the use and abuse of the PNC has become was provided when a Nottinghamshire police sergeant was suspended in December 1978 for a 'breach of security' concerning the PNC.[20] It was later stated, during a hearing concerning the reissue of gambling club licences to Ladbroke's Casinos, that a policeman had provided anything up to 10,000 names and addresses of vehicle owners whose cars were observed outside rival casinos in London.[21] Scotland Yard stated that this information had been provided at the rate of 50 pence for each number. The gambling company were refused operating licences on the basis of this and other evidence from Scotland Yard. The police authorities considered a prosecution under Section 2 of the Official Secrets Act.

To anyone unaware of the vast traffic in stop checks which are normally performed on the PNC, it is astonishing that such a high number of improper enquiries could escape unnoticed. The fact that an allegedly corrupt policeman found this work so simple that he only charged 50p for each enquiry is quite damning. Such illicit access to PNC files might have been so simplified by another PNC facility described in the 1976 conference.[22] This is a 'multiple check' which is said to be 'useful in car park, service areas, or road check situations' whereby a number of vehicle registrations can be checked on the PNC during a single enquiry. The whole affair makes complete nonsense of the PNC's supposedly extensive security precautions against abuse of its records.

Besides the vehicle registrations themselves which can be examined on an Owner Enquiry (OE), engine and chassis numbers can also be searched for on a separate enquiry, known as an EE. This is used less frequently, such as when an abandoned car is found, or when there is some reason for believing that a car – although bearing a correct registration – is nevertheless stolen or otherwise false.

Since the rapid access to the vehicle records became available, the Customs and Excise Department have been supplied with their own terminals in order to access the Vehicle Owners Index. This move was announced in a written reply in the House of Commons in January 1975, and raised protests over the further extension of the use of the

PNC by departments outside the police.[23] It was stated that the access by C&E would be to 'a limited amount of information from the motor taxation record of each vehicle registered ... at Swansea'. This information was needed for 'investigation', and would be more conveniently available through the PNC. One former PNC programmer has stated that he understoood this new link to be intended not to facilitate existing Customs investigations, but to enable vehicles entering and departing at certain seaports to be checked.[24] If this is so, then the new link is obviously a further extension of the suspect vehicle index, presumably allowing Customs officers to act against vehicles to which their attention is drawn by a 'suspect' entry. This allegation is however denied by the Customs and Excise Department, who say that the direct PNC access has not been used for any new types of work in checking vehicles.

Other such links may follow. At present, considerable numbers of manual enquiries are made of Swansea DVLC records.[25] Details of vehicle licences are available to the Inland Revenue and other departments 'on reasonable cause' – the Inland Revenue are said to make 200 enquiries a week[26] concerning driving licences of persons whom they are trying to trace. This information is also available to the Home Office, normally in cases of disqualification, where it is linked to the PNC index of disqualified drivers. The entries on the PNC for stolen/suspect vehicles and vehicle owners are shown in *Tables 2* and *3* (p. 76, 80).

Personal Files on the PNC

The remaining major applications of the PNC all concern named individuals and are indexed by the person's name. These are the Criminal Names Index, Wanted/Missing Persons, Fingerprints and Disqualified Drivers. A fifth file, concerning persons with suspended sentences seems to have been delayed. It was mentioned in the original plan for the PNC, and listed in the 1975 White Paper,[27] but was not listed in the Data Protection Committee Report or in a 1977 parliamentary answer.[28]

The major file is of course Criminal Names. This consists of all persons who have at any time been convicted of 'more serious offences'. Such offences are defined in 53 categories which are listed in a Home Office circular to police. These 'serious' offences include criminal libel, offences against the Rent Acts, wasting police time, travelling on a railway without paying and other minor thefts. Also included are offences with frequent political connotations – such as obstruction and offences against the Public Order Act.[29] In 1979, there were 4 million names on this file. It appears, however, that less than this number of actual individuals were involved, since entries were also made for nicknames and known aliases. According to the Home Office paper (Cubberley), 'there are 2.5 million people recorded ... and 4 million names'. Its ultimate capacity is said to be 5.7 million names.[30] *Table 4* (below) shows the form of a basic entry in this Index.

Table 4: Response to an enquiry from the PNC Criminal Names Index

```
SURNAME, FORENAME:

DATE OF BIRTH:      SEX:      COLOUR:      HEIGHT:

CRO NUMBER:

DATE FIRST CAME TO NOTICE:         FORCE/STATION:

WARNINGS:                    DISTINGUISHING MARKS:
```

The Criminal Names files do not contain complete criminal records but are intended as an index to the full files which are held, either nationally at Scotland Yard's Criminal Records Office, or locally at Regional CROs. These files were held, until recently, in paper dockets, occupying almost an entire floor of New Scotland Yard.[31] Many of the records have now been converted to microfilm fiches. A copy of the fiche is made and supplied to a policeman on request. All Metropolitan Police Districts and courts now have microfilm readers. Prior to the introduction of the PNC, the National CRO had to handle any enquiries as to whether a person had a criminal record, a task now taken over entirely by the PNC. One result has been a vast increase in the number of checks on individuals thus made, as the very limited capacity of the Scotland Yard CRO – 36 telephone lines – placed a severe constraint on such enquiries.

The PNC does not however record details of previous convictions, only that there have been some. Each entry in the Criminal Names Index incorporates the basic 'search factors' – name, date of birth, sex, race, and height. To make a search ideally at least name and date of birth are required, although it is quite possible to search on a name alone and an estimated age. The response will include a full physical description, the CRO number and the date at which the person 'first came to notice'. (See *Table 4*). It does not contain a list of previous convictions, or criminal intelligence or other background information. It does contain 'warnings' such as that a person may be violent. Another 'warning' is that the person 'alleges' (i.e. has made) complaints about the police. Most of the background information, can however be obtained at the touch of a button, if the terminal operator at the local police station enters a request for a 'description form' to be supplied by the CRO. The details will then be supplied by post.

The Criminal Names Index does contain details of people who have not been convicted of crime, although according to the Home Office 'suspects should not be placed on this index'. A person who has been charged with an offence will be put on the index; this should be removed on acquittal if the person has committed no previous offences. But the information is not removed if the person already has an entry, or is covered by Section 6 (3) of the Sexual Offences Act 1956 or Section 27 (23) (a) of the 1968 Theft Act.

In order to compile the Criminal Names Index, on computer, the files were taken in conditions of great security from the Yard to a special coding centre in Croydon, between 1972 and 1976. The index finally went 'live' after tests with hypothetical information, early in August 1977. The service was introduced gradually, restricting it at first to checks on people who had just been taken into custody. It is now in full operation.

Provision is also made in each entry for special purpose indications to be made about an individual on file. These include warnings such as 'known to be violent', 'drug addict' and 'escaper'.[32] The Data Protection Committee also discovered that these 'indicators' can include information explicitly tailored to surveillance such as 'an indication that the Special Branch has an interest in the subject'.[33] As well as national CRO numbers, records at a Regional CRO will also be indicated on a Criminal Names enquiry. The DPC also discovered other unusual forms of 'intelligence' data on the PNC which had never previously been mentioned. In particular, the PNC 'has facilities for cross-linking subjects with their known associates'.[34]

Considerably more intelligence data can be stored on persons whose names are recorded in the Wanted/Missing Persons file. This is ostensibly an index concerned with persons who should be arrested on suspicion of having committed a particular crime, or people reported missing. But its name, like the 'Stolen Vehicles Index' is once again rather cosmetic. The Home Office 1976 Conference paper once again put it more bluntly:

> It will include details of persons wanted or suspected of offences, vulnerable persons reported as missing, persons found, and other categories of people such as deserters, escapees, or *people we need to locate for many reasons.* (Author's italics.)[35]

Once again this includes categories of people who are under surveillance as 'suspects' or because of 'long term interest' to the police. The same paper noted that the 60,000 entries in a similar manual index at Scotland Yard were expected to 'increase dramatically' when the index went 'live' and local forces were able to add considerably more information to the index. By September 1979 there were 100,000 entries; the capacity of this index is planned to be about 140,000 names.

Table 5(a) shows the response to an enquiry on the Wanted/Missing Index. *Table 5(b)* shows the 20 categories of persons which may be listed in this Index. (This information is read from a photograph of a chart containing the same information which appeared in a booklet on the PNC, published by the Home Office and the Central Office of Information in 1978. The photograph was not entirely clear, so the entries may be slightly in error. I had previously requested the Home Office to provide this information, and on receipt of the booklet requested that they provide the details of the list seen in the photograph; they replied that the 'reproduction (is) deliberately left unclear'.) *Table 5(c)* lists the 'warning signals' used on the Index, with the same reservations as *5(b)*.

Categories of entry like 'locate' and 'PTA' (Prevention of Terrorism Act; presumably imputes that someone has been or should be detained under PTA powers) certainly confirm a surveillance role. The warning signals appear on police VDU terminals as two letter codes, specifying the appropriate warning(s).

Each entry will indicate whether the person concerned already has a CRO number (he need not have been convicted of any offence), which section of the police is interested in him and why, and whether he should be arrested or approached or 'his location merely reported'.[37] The entry also includes space for recording associates, 'warning signs', and a 'free text' space in which any other comments can be recorded. Since the Wanted/Missing Index has only been in operation a short time, no figures have become available for its overall

Table 5(a): Response to an enquiry from the PNC Wanted/Missing Index

```
SURNAME, FORENAME:

DATE OF BIRTH:      SEX:      COLOUR:      HEIGHT:

CRO NUMBER:

WARNINGS:                     DISTINGUISHING MARKS:

REASON FOR INTEREST: (EG SUSPECTED OF BURGLARY)

FORCE/STATION REPORTING:     REFERENCE:

DATE REPORTED:               DATE RECORDED:

DATE TO BE WEEDED:           TEXT INFORMATION:
```

size, rate of growth, or any breakdown of the separate categories. But its introduction clearly has considerably extended the scope of automatic police surveillance.

Not only is 'intelligence' rather than factual information stored on the PNC, but the suspects or others under surveillance will include quite innocent people. This was admitted by the PNC's Director of Operations, Geoffrey Cole, in a recent interview on the BBC programme *Man Alive*.[38] His remarks are worth reproducing:

> INTERVIEWER. ... suspicions can't be classified as factual. Do you agree?
> COLE. Not entirely, no. It is a factual statement of the suspicion.
> INTERVIEWER. It may be factual that the police have their suspicions, but their suspicions may not be grounded?
> COLE. By the nature of suspicion, it may not always be accurate of course.
> INTERVIEWER. (So) information may be stored on the computer about totally innocent people.
> COLE. That's true.'

In order to accomplish the massive task of searching 4 million names or more for a match to 'trace' a suspect whose particulars are radioed in to his local terminal, the PNC makes use of sophisticated methods of storing and retrieving peoples names. The system, known as SOUNDEX, was developed by the FBI and the Customs Bureau in the United States. It was originally used to provide a fast method of

Table 5(b): Categories on the PNC Wanted/Missing Index

WANTED (FOR A CRIME):	SUSPECT (IN A CRIME):
PTA:	LOCATE:
(IN) CUSTODY:	ABSCONDED FROM CARE:
ABSCONDED FROM HOSPITAL:	ABSCONDED FROM DETENTION:
ABSCONDED FROM: BORSTAL:	ABSCONDED FROM PRISON:
ABSCONDED FROM SCHOOL:	ABSCONDED FROM REMAND (CENTRE):
REMANDED IN DETENTION:	REMANDED IN BORSTAL:
REMANDED IN PRISON:	MISSING:
FOUND:	DESERT(ER):
LIFER (?):	IMPENDING (?):

Table 5(c): Warning signals on the PNC Wanted/Missing Index*

WEAPON (CARRIED):	VIOLENT:
ESCAPER:	MENTAL:
DRUGS (CARRIED OR SUSPECTED:	NEEDS TREATMENT (?)
ALLEGES (COMPLAINTS ABOUT POLICE):	EXPLOSIVES:
DEPORTEE:	REFER TO FILE (?):
FAILS TO APPEAR:	ALIEN:
OFFENCES ON BAIL:	ALCOHOLIC:
GENERAL (?):	

* *For reasons explained in the text, there are four categories missing from this list, and others are uncertain.*

searching for blacklist entries against travellers entering the United States. SOUNDEX is automatically applied to all names which are stored on or input to the PNC. Its main advantage is that names which sound the same, or nearly the same, have identical or similar SOUNDEX codes. This technique neatly gets round the problems of a name being misheard on being told or repeated to a police officer, and problems of different spellings.

Under SOUNDEX, a name is converted to a four letter code consisting of the first letter of the name and three digits. Special rules determine how the remainder of the name is converted into numbers. For example, the name Moran would be SOUNDEXed as M650; the surname or forename Jeffrey would be J360 while the similar sounding Geoffrey becomes G360. This process does not affect the PNC terminal operators, who work with the normal version of the name. But when carrying out a personal check, the PNC may produce up to 50 possible 'traces' on an individual. This is likely to happen if the name is a common one and an exact date of birth or description is not available. In such a case, the terminal operator is told the number of 'possibles' and examines them one by one for the best match. The possibles will incorporate a range of variation in each search factor; a search for Jeffrey Johnson aged about 25 will turn up Geoffrey Johnstones aged 20-30. An age variation of five years either side of the policeman's estimate is included. For women, where age estimation is thought to be harder, the age variation allowed is eight years.

The PNC uses a modified version of SOUNDEX to enable very rapid searches to be made of the Criminal Names Index. Similar techniques of data 'compression' to enable rapid search are used throughout the PNC.[39] The Vehicle Owners file, for example, contains the address of every registered vehicle keeper. A system for computer indexing every address in the country was developed several years ago as part of Post Office plans for postal mechanization. The postcode index now provides a code for thousands of small areas throughout Britain — each one actually a section of a postman's walk — and all addresses in each area are kept up to date on Post Office computers. This arrangement makes it very easy to convert full addresses into short and simple computer codes. For example,

12 Chorley Road, Manchester M16 7BA

is uniquely identified by adding the first three or four letters or numbers from the actual address to the end of the post code, as follows:

M16 7BA 12CH

M16 identifies a part of Manchester, 7BA the subsection of the postman's walk including part of Chorley Road. The inclusion of the street number, 12, at the end of the complete code uniquely identifies the house in question. Such a code can readily be searched by computer, just like the SOUNDEXed names and vehicle registration marks.

The inclusion of these facilities means that indexes like the Vehicle Owners can, if need be, be used to search for a known individual's address, or to discover who is living at a particular address. Although the use of SOUNDEX and the PO postcode index facilitates such searches, the information in the Vehicle Owners Index is arranged in order of car registration and not address or name. Such searches therefore remain time consuming, and would have to be specially authorized; these facilities are not normally available from any local police station terminal. The Home Office acknowledge that the PNC does contain facilities for searching out vehicle files by using the postcodes 'to limit the search to a particular geographical area'; there is no reason why such a search might not be used, if need be, to discover the vehicle owning or using occupants who were living at a particular street or address, by confining the search to just a single postcode.

The Wanted/Missing Index provides facilities for automatically weeding out of date files and removing them from the system. Like the Stolen Vehicles Index, any new information placed on the PNC has normally to be confirmed in writing on a special form, as a form of security check on the origin and accuracy of new information.

The new Disqualified Drivers Index was due to start operation in 1979. The DPC were told that this would contain about 170,000 entries,[40] but exact details of the contents of an entry have not yet been published. It will contain details of the date of imposition and period of the suspension, and a note of the court concerned. A manual index of this kind already exists.

Other applications planned or under consideration for the PNC include suspended sentences and *modus operandi* (criminal's personal techniques) but no firm plans for these have been announced.[41] Also planned are stolen property files and cheque indexes. Earlier plans for a register of stolen bicycles appear to have been dropped through a lack of police interest in this type of crime.

Associated with the Criminal Names files are indexes to Scotland Yard's main collection of fingerprints. These fingerprint records are the backup means of identifying arrestees if 'no trace' is found at the CRO or PNC. About 50 per cent of arrestees are identified from their names, and 5 per cent more are identified by means of fingerprints, the remainder all being potential first offenders.[42] The famous Henry System for classifying fingerprints numerically has been superseded by a new computer code, discriminating between 21 basic patterns and providing a four digit code for the print on each finger. Over two and a half million fingerprints have been encoded this way on the PNC; between 100,000 and 150,000 new sets of fingerprints are added every year.[43] The fingerprint application is quite unlike most other PNC files, since it is only accessible to and used by staff of the B12 Fingerprints Branch of Scotland Yard. It is basically an index to be used for identifying prints of new arrestees just as on the old system. It will however be extended to matching partial prints found at the scenes of crimes when its basic task is operating successfully.

An extensive new fingerprints department was opened in 1977, which utilized the PNC in conjunction with other special purpose computers at Scotland Yard. All fingerprints are now stored on a system called the Ampex Videofile, which stores the entire collection electronically rather than on film, and can present prints on a television screen for comparison and matching. New fingerprints for matching to the files are encoded and sent to the PNC using special terminals in the Fingerprint Branch. The PNC matches the new set as far as possible to existing prints – often doing this work overnight when its ordinary workload is reduced – and potential matches are then fed into the separate computer at Scotland Yard which prepares a display of the original prints and preferred matches for a fingerprint specialist.

The Fingerprint Application of the PNC is one of the simplest in principle, since its scope is limited to the handling and identification of fingerprints and no other information can be handled. It is not clear why the application need be put on the PNC. But it is cross-referenced to the Criminal Names Index, and moreover no other computer of similar power size and reliability has yet been brought into police service.

In January 1978, it was announced in a Home Office White Paper that the present capacity of the PNC had been exhausted and that new computers would replace the present processors. The two existing Burroughs B6700s were therefore traded in for B7700s – a more modern design said to be able to double the number of enquiries.[44] The additional cost was £3.8 million, while a small further sum was to be spent on purchasing more up to date disc storage units, on which all the PNC information is held. This new equipment appears to have been installed during July 1978.[45]

The new computers were claimed to be needed because the 'limit for the amount of information it could hold had been reached'.[46] An alternative explanation was given to the author by the Home Office in September 1979: 'the (existing) processors were incapable of dealing with the sheer weight of numbers of enquiries being received'. They suggested that the PNC had already become overloaded with enquiries by early 1977, claimed that this had been predicted some time before, and said that a new order had been put in hand over a year before it was announced. The newer processors would keep the average response time per enquiry down to 5 seconds.

Whichever version is accurate, the PNC's capacity for storing information does in any case seem to have been underutilized in comparison with early estimates of capacity. The number of records held in 1979 was considerably less than the 40 million anticipated in 1972; the actual level was about 30.2 million. A large part of the shortfall was caused by the reduction in the growth of vehicle ownership in the mid seventies.

The 1978 announcement also revealed that the Wanted/Missing Persons Index and the Disqualified Driver Index could not then go on the PNC because of the alleged under capacity.

Why is the PNC 'full up'? Certainly, the present rate of transactions is staggering. The latest published figure is 160,000 messages a day, or about 58.4 million messages a year.[47] The same scale of use is indicated in a letter from the Assistant Chief Constable of the West Midlands Police to the *Police Review*[48] in which he stated that 'in excess of 100,000 PNC transactions were made by (my) force during April 1979' alone. The number of enquiries made each year in Birmingham alone (1.2 million), or those made in Britain as a whole, is comparable to the total size of the population. These figures dramatically indicate the extent to which the PNC has put much of society under surveillance.

Security and Secrecy

The development of the Police National Computer has never been a secret, and police and Home Office spokesmen have always bowed to a minimal extent to the privacy lobby, with the early provision of information on the general nature of the PNC. But attempts to probe more deeply have often been rebuffed with a distinct lack of candour. In October 1972, Leslie Huckfield MP tabled an extremely detailed series of 37 questions on the PNC to the Home Office. He was answered in two brief paragraphs which alleged – quite wrongly – that all the questions were based on 'a misunderstanding of the purpose' of the PNC. Home Office minister Mark Carlisle then enunciated the standard answer to enquiries about systems like the PNC:

> The information to be stored is broadly the same as that already held.

The same sort of anodyne justification was offered when the new 'C' Department computer at Scotland Yard was unveiled:

> The system (is for) those branches of the force who now use this information in manually held records.

On other occasions the most disingenuous answers have been given. A parliamentary question from Arthur Lewis MP on the 'capacity of each (police) computer' and what 'kind of information was programmed' was answered by saying what the size of the computer's electronic store was. The PNC had '547K words' and information 'relating to the prevention and detection of crime'. Other apologists for the PNC are prepared to be quite reckless in its defence. Chief Constable Philip Knights, president of the Association of Chief Police Officers told the BBC *Man Alive* programme in 1979 that it was '100 per cent inaccurate' to say that information about membership of organizations was stored in the PNC.[50] This was in flat contradiction to the Home Office answer in parliament more than a year before. Knights also denied that the PNC would contain information on 'people who were under surveillance'. Once again, this was in plain contradiction to the DPC report issued two months before he spoke (see page 78).

A similar veil of secrecy and inaccuracy has descended over the question of the PNC storing intelligence rather than information. The DPC took the view that 'it held data which could be classed as intelligence rather than information'. The police witnesses however, seemed to regard criminal intelligence as the separate province of collators and specialist squads, and considered the PNC as broadly 'factual'. The Home Office told the DPC that they had decided to 'postpone' linkage of criminal information and criminal intelligence data while the debate on privacy proceeded. This was a welcome reiteration of an earlier declaration; when in 1972 the *Police Review* published an editorial giving an alarming view of the development of the PNC,[52] a Home Office spokesman told the *Guardian*:[53]

> Criminal intelligence is not going into the national computer. That is categorical. There is at present no plan to put in criminal intelligence as opposed to criminal records.

By 1976, it seems that this view had changed at least inside the PNC itself. In the summer of 1976, the new director of the unit made an introductory speech to PNCU staff about the time they were to receive an official visit from members of the Data Protection Committee. According to staff present at the time, he stressed that their main task was to ensure that the DPC did not recommend a right of access by the subject to police records. Then, cautioning that the rest of his talk was 'off the record' and 'if you repeat this, I shall simply deny it', he explained:

> My main function ... is to set up a national criminal intelligence centre

a task which would create a variety of sophisticated new work for his staff.[54] Programming the PNC was carried out in considerable secrecy, created more by compartmentalization of the work rather than drastic guarding. The PNC's main programmes, written in a scientific programming language called ALGOL, were arranged in 'modules' which could be written according to a specification without any knowledge of the rest of the system. Most of the programming was (and is) done at Home Office premises quite distant from the actual Hendon centre, at Charles House in Kensington High Street, in west London. The programmers work, not on the live computer but on the third 'standby' machine, using test information only. It is thus possible for unusual new features to be added to the PNC of which most of its staff would be unaware.

A new 'cross reference' system was added to the main PNC facilities in 1977. It is designed to cross-reference numbers of criminal records at Scotland Yard with the corresponding dossiers at regional CROs and Force headquarters. At the time of writing (November

.1979), the work of cross-referencing the 'RX' enquiry system had not been completed. The Home Office denies that this will involve linkage or pointers to collator records; the description of the 'RX' system given in a 1978 PNC booklet is, however, more ambiguous:

> This facility permits reference numbers of criminal records held centrally to be cross-referenced to local and regional police records, thus indicating additional sources of detailed information.

The relevant references will be built up in 'several years'.

The PNC is certainly stocked with features which are very far removed from the anodyne descriptions of the system supplied to Parliament, press or public. There is no mention of the warning bells to Special Branch, of the 'cross-linking' of associates, or of the small proportion of stolen cars on the so-called Stolen Vehicles Index. Even since the 1976 figures showing that only 25 per cent of vehicles on the file were stolen, that file has more than doubled in size, to over 250,000 entries.[55] This suggests that a far greater proportion of suspect and other vehicles under surveillance are now on the file.

Besides this, public relations on behalf of the PNC stress that the information now on the computer has always been available to the police, and emphasize the (undoubted) success of the PNC in detecting greater numbers of stolen cars. But no previous police system generated 58 million enquiries every year on more than 20 million people, their vehicles and criminal records. The PNC has created a qualitatively different situation for the individual from that which existed a decade before. The Home Office itself, wearing a different hat, pointed out the precise dangers of this happening in their first white paper on *Computers and Privacy*.[56] Computer personal data systems have the following 'practical implications for privacy' in that they:

(1) facilitate the maintenance of extensive record systems and the retention of data in those systems;
(2) can make data easily and quickly accessible from many distant points;
(3) make it possible for data to be transferred quickly from one information system to another;
(4) make it possible for data to be combined in ways which might not otherwise be practicable;
(5) because the data is stored, processed and often transmitted in a

form which is not directly intelligible, few people may know what is in the records, and what is happening to them.

Parkinson's Law-like, the use of the PNC has now apparently expanded to fill all its available capacity ahead of time, a phenomenon police often refer to rather whimsically as 'suppressed demand'.

They have now developed an almost drug-like addiction to its use, so much so that they cannot now imagine how they succeeded before. During the installation of new equipment in 1978, a quite extraordinary letter was written by Scotland Yard's Director of Information Peter Nievens to Fleet Street editors, asking them not to report a forthcoming shutdown of the PNC over the weekend. He then specified the exact periods it would not operate between 29 and 31 July 1978, and commented:

> There is a slight risk that some *subversive elements or* criminals might attempt to take advantage of the reduction of this facility should this become publicly known. (author's italics.)

Whilst it is easy to see how minor criminals might enjoy two days unapprehended without the PNC, it is very difficult to imagine the more serious threat which it is implied would come from 'subversive elements'. The letter is, in itself, indicative of a mentality now prevalent in some senior levels of the police, which assesses political dissent as a greater threat to society than crime.

The political significance of the PNC in time of civil unrest has not been forgotten by its designers. The Hendon centre is guarded by several types of security alarm, and protected by barriers from crashing vehicles. Full copies of its data tapes are held at several locations, at least one of which is said to be a site elsewhere in north London which is protected against the effects of nuclear weapons.

'C' Department: National Intelligence Computer

The Police National Computer may have been developed and put into operation in conditions of considerable secrecy. But compared with the information available on the 'C' Department computer of the Metropolitan Police, it has positively been bathed in floodlights. Like the PNC, this computer grew out of work initially carried out by JADPU. Using ICL computers at Tintagel House, a Metropolitan Police office building on the south bank of the Thames, JADPU computerized the records of several national intelligence squads during the early and mid 1970s. The first such national intelligence squad – apart from the Special Branch – was the Central Drugs Intelligence Unit, whose formation was announced on 19 October 1972. News of its formation was kept secret until it was actually in operation.[57] In July 1973, it was revealed that the names of 100,000 people were on the index of whom only 35,000 had convictions for using drugs.[58]

The National Council for Civil Liberties and other bodies were in little doubt as to where the other 65,000 names had come from. For some time, the intelligence gathering practices of drugs squad officers and others had been quite apparent. Raids and searches were conducted as much for their value in intelligence gathering, as for collecting evidence of offences. A favourite target was an address book, which would be copied out into files with each person listed therein identified as an 'associate'. The cross referencing method was of course a familiar and time-honoured detective technique, in attempting to locate a suspect for a particular crime. But once again, the whole process was reversed, by gathering intelligence on innocent people who in the Home Office's words might be 'suspected offenders'. Apart from the Central Drugs Intelligence Unit, a National Immigration Intelligence Unit was also being set up at Tintagel House at the same time, and using the same computers. This was the third intelligence unit to be set up by Scotland Yard; the first was the C11 Criminal Intelligence section, whose job was to gather intelligence on thousands of suspected major criminals. The squad would compile information from divisional collators and carry out periodic surveillance to check up on the movements of the person concerned.

In Autumn 1973 the Management Services Department of the Metropolitan Police started to assess the possibility of computerizing all the main records of the units in 'C' Department. This study led directly to the computer now in operation, which will store over 1.3 million names by 1985; the vast majority having been entered on the computer by the Special Branch.

The 'C' or Criminal Department of Scotland Yard is responsible for all the criminal investigation and related work carried out by the Yard. The squads covered whose files are being converted to computer are:

C6: Fraud Squad, responsible for the investigation of Companies Acts and similar offences.

C11: The Criminal Intelligence section which now includes the Central Drugs and Immigration Intelligence Unit.

Special Branch: although ostensibly within 'C' Department the Special Branch's work of political surveillance normally involves close co-ordination with the Home Office and directly with the Security Service, MI5.[59]

With the exception of the Special Branch, which has 410 officers in London and 1,250 nationally, all the squads above are comparatively small in size.

Approval for a complete computer system was given in 1974, and a tender issued to manufacturers. The tender document, which is unclassified, provides full details of the record systems of each section as at January 1974, with projections forward to 1985. This information is reproduced in *Table 6* (p. 101). (It should be noted that the tender document, on which much of this account is based was careful not to identify any of the five sections which were to be computerized. However, this protection was somewhat transparent, since, for example, a section which required the recording of father's names was clearly concerned with nationality and immigration. The Special Branch files ('Section 5') were identified by their special security precautions, and were also the most substantial group of files.)

As can be seen from *Table 6* (p. 101), the project is of considerable size. The growth rate of police records – such as 2,000 new Special Branch files every month – is also noteworthy. The award of a contract for the computer to a British company, Computer Technology Ltd (CTL) of Hemel Hempstead, was announced during 1976, but no details were given about the purpose of the computer. The only official statement on this subject was contained in the disingenuously entitled white paper *Computers: Safeguards for Privacy*[60] issued by the Home Office in December 1975. This stated:

A computer system is being planned to handle information held by the Metropolitan Police about crime, criminals and their associates. The system will be internal to those branches of the force who now use this information, and it will not be connected to any other system.

This remained the absolute official line on the computer for more than three years; no more was said, despite repeated enquiries in Parliament. After it had been pointed out that the vast majority of the potential candidates for inclusion on the computer were people in

Special Branch files who were not 'criminals', the official formula was
suitably modified to:

> information ... about crime, criminals and their associates, and matters
> relating to a national security.[61]

The actual nature of the computer was first explored in *The Times*
in February 1977.[62] The newspaper reported some of the details of the
files, and also a series of questions which had been put to senior
officers at Scotland Yard. The questions included: What percentage of
the records concern convicted criminals and what percentage do not?
Are two thirds of the names on the biggest section of records suspects
and associates rather than criminal records? Scotland Yard officials
replied that 'an answer to all (of *The Times'* questions) would be a
breach of security'.

The existence of the new computer had been mentioned in the
Metropolitan Police's own paper, *The Job*, in December 1976, but
very little information had been given about what it was to store. A
parliamentary answer later in 1977[63] gave the cost of installing and
purchasing the computer during 1976-77 to have been £935,000. In
September 1977, a further *Times* investigation exactly identified the
five units whose files were to go on the computer.[64] About 600,000 of
the 1.4 million personal records that the Special Branch would hold by
1985 would be placed on the computer, occupying half of its total
capacity.[65] Although *The Times* had drawn these figures from the
police specification for the project, Scotland Yard clearly indicated
their displeasure with any publicity:

> The publication of any figures purporting to indicate the total number of
> records in any part of the project would amount to speculation.

Despite these revelations, the Home Secretary, Merlyn Rees,
refused to provide Members of Parliament with any further details of
the project whatsoever.[66] This intransigence left Rees appearing rather
foolish when in February 1979, Scotland Yard's Deputy Assistant
Commissioner Jock Wilson explained in a television programme[67]
what sections of the force would use the computer; two days before,
Rees had refused to make any statement about this. Subsequently, the
official Home Office line included Commissioner Wilson's almost
unnecessary confirmation.[68] Later in March 1979, five Labour
backbenchers questioned Rees as to whether files on them were kept

on the computer. His answers were uniformly uninformative, indeed quite disingenuous:

> There is ... a section for the Special Branch. I feel strongly about it, and say firmly that nobody, whatever his political views, needs to worry about this (being in Special Branch files).

Rees, in an earlier House of Commons interchange, had produced an astonishing explanation of the Special Branch's activities as a political police force:

> The Special Branch collects information on those whom I think cause problems for the State.

Late in 1978, the 'C' Department computer was undergoing final software (programming) tests, according to the suppliers, CTL. It appeared then that the computer might have been installed at large new Metropolitan Police office, at Jubilee House, Putney in south west London.[70] It now appears that, although new police computers have been installed there, they belong to JADPU, the joint Home Office and police organization which began the development work leading to both this computer and the PNC.

Police computers did however come vividly to public attention in December 1978, when the report was issued of the Home Office appointed Data Protection Committee. One section of the report dealt with the Committee's unsuccessful attempts to gain any evidence at all about the Metropolitan Police computer. Forced to rely largely on the two. *Times* articles and parliamentary statements, the Committee reported:

> In relation to the Metropolitan Police, we do not have enough evidence to give a firm assurance ... that the public need (not) be unduly alarmed by the use of computers for police purposes.[71]

The Committee had asked a witness from the Metropolitan Police who gave evidence to the committee to comment on the *Times* articles, but they refused to provide any further information. They did however confirm that the computer would have a 'multi-factor searching capability' – in other words, it could look through all the files stored not just for a file which had *one* characteristic (such as a name, vehicle registration, or political affiliation) but combined several. A widely quoted example was:

> Which red-haired Irishmen on record drive a white Cortina with MR and 6 in the registration?[72]

Table 6: Record on 'C' Department Computer

Squad	Index	Net growth Per month	Estimated number of records		Estimated enquiries per month		Estimated amendments per month	
			JAN 1974	JAN 1985	1974	1985	1974	1985
Fraud Squad	Persons	350	26,500	72,700	1,200	3,000	300	820
	Companies	130	15,500	32,660	—	—	300	630
C11	Major Criminals	—	2,500	3,500	—	—	—	—
	Others	1,000	60,000	190,000	—	—	—	—
Immigration Intelligence	Persons	1,600	76,000	287,000	160	600	600	2,300
Drugs Intelligence	Persons	360	13,000	60,500	80	370	100	470
Special Branch	Persons (White files)	1,000	850,000	982,000	16,000	18,500	1,100	1,270
	Persons (Pink files)	1,000	300,000	432,000	3,000	4,600	1,000	1,440

This would require searching on nationality, hair colour, vehicle type and colour, and on a range of vehicle registrations. This type of information retrieval system is an extremely powerful means of finding information; its inclusion in personal records systems multiplies the dangers to privacy and liberty inherent in police or other computer applications. This, said the DPC, 'introduces new dimensions of unease. Because they provide an easy method of browsing through collections of information, they are well suited to surveillance requirements.' The 'C' Department computer is of course intended for precisely such tasks; and, in the case of the Special Branch, political surveillance.

The specification for the 'C' Department national intelligence computer lists some thirty-five manual data systems then in use by the police, some twelve of which were concerned with people. Of these, only half concerned 'criminals' and contained 17,000 names. The other six, containing over 1.3 million names were simply said to be 'persons'. Besides these main nominal indexes, there are subsidiary indexes of vehicles, boats, aircraft, telephone numbers, addresses and other details.

Apart from a general breakdown of the major files used by each section, (reproduced as *Table 6*), the specification provided a detailed account of each section's records and practices. In January 1974, the Special Branch held 1.15 million files on persons, filed in alphabetical order. Of these, some 300,000 persons had special dockets containing more detailed information filed in a seperate index. The main index consisted of two types of cards – 'white slips' – where all details about the person were recorded on a few white cards only; and 'pink slips' – where basic particulars were entered and a reference was given to a larger personal docket.

One 'feature' of the index was that each name was categorized into twenty-seven 'areas of interest'. It is not known what these areas of interest are, but it was initially planned to computerize the names of only eight of these categories. The Special Branch were to decide the order in which the different areas of interest were to be computerized. Since their work includes security checking of the governments' own staff, it is likely that some of the areas of interest which are not immediately being computerized simply concern relatively straightforward security files on key staff. Another feature of the Special Branch's personal files was an extensive amount of cross referencing to its other main index, the Subject Index. But it was not possible to computerize the Subject Index at this stage as part of the project. It would clearly contain massive amounts of both openly and secretly gathered information about political groups and activities, which would not necessarily be held in a systematic way. By 1985, the SB Nominal Index would hold an estimated 1.414 million records containing some 45 million words (226 million characters) of description. In 1974, the Special Branch were adding new names to their files at the rate of about 500 every week.

The Special Branch also maintained special records concerning 6,100 addresses, 1,300 telephone numbers and 2,500 vehicles. Although there is no further explanation of the exact nature of these records, it seems likely that they relate to the interception of mail and the tapping of telephone lines. The number of telephone numbers so recorded corresponds closely with estimates and published figures on the extent of this practice. It is also noteworthy that each of the other sections using the computer had such files – but the numbers of telephones and addresses involved were very much smaller, and exact figures were not given. This tends to confirm the supposition that these were files on tapped telephones.

There was also to be an index of 7,600 records of 'special interest' which required a 'very rapid response to enquiries based on a name'. This requirement is likely to be for Special Branch officers keeping watch at ports and airports, where the names of large numbers of incoming travellers may have to be checked very quickly against a blacklist. It is difficult to think of any other role that such a file could play. It would be an obvious advantage to have the immigration blacklist on a computer, although it does involve the slight security risk of putting terminals to the computer in outside buildings. But lines between terminals and the computer are likely to be coded to prevent anyone intercepting the information sent.

The Fraud Squad (C6) maintained files in 1974 on 26,500 people and 15,500 companies in which they were interested. They expected the size of their files to triple between 1974 and 1985. During 1974, they were also developing new cross-reference systems on addresses and vehicles of people they suspected of being involved in fraud.

The Criminal Intelligence Section itself (C11) which now also controls the Central Drugs and Immigration Intelligence Units, had about 63,000 people on file in 1974. These files included 130 large dockets on 'criminals of particular interest'. These would be their files on major criminals who were frequently kept under surveillance by the section, and on whom they gathered substantial files. To back up their interest in these principal targets, they also had records on 2,500 other 'criminals of major interest' and 60,000 of 'lesser' interest. The 60,000 'lesser' records were held in an alphabetical index, while the remainder were organized to suit their surveillance operations. C11 also kept four seperate sets of files on 'specialist groups of persons' and areas of organized crime, which they would add in to the basic files. Like the Special Branch, and the Drugs and Immigration Intelligence Units they also had records of vehicles, boats and aircraft.

The files of the Central Drugs Intelligence Unit are described as a 'new and fast growing index' which in 1974 covered 76,000 people – most of them would, of course, be 'suspects'. By 1985, this file would almost have quadrupled in size, the drugs specialists expected. The account of these files in the official specification only mentioned that 1,000 people to go on file were 'criminals'. Like the Special Branch, the Unit also had small files on addresses and telephone numbers and a file on boats and vehicles which was shared with Immigration Intelligence.

The files of the Immigration Intelligence Unit were also described as 'new and fast growing'. By 1985, they expect to have files on 60,500 people. The Unit also has indexes on 'nicknames, addresses, telephone numbers and vehicles'.

The whole specification document is remarkable evidence of the way in which the police see their new intelligence gathering role. In describing the existing manual filing systems which have to be put on computer there is scarcely a mention of the word 'criminal' or 'crimes'. The Immigration, Special Branch and Fraud Squad files do not mention 'criminals' at all; the Drugs Intelligence Unit refers only to a small section of 1,000 out of its 75,000 files – under two per cent of the files held. And, it is clear, the situation will become worse, not better. The total number of files in all five sections would, by 1985, cover an estimated 2.03 million people (1.343 million in 1974). That figure is quite seperate from the 3.8 million *bona fide* criminal records of the CRO, though in some cases there would be a sizeable overlap. These records are quite separate again from those held in London divisional and sub-divisional police stations by collators – the 'local intelligence' records. These must number between 200,000 and 600,000 (see section on collators, page 117). All told, the Metropolitan Police alone must have between 3.5 and 5.5 million people on file.

Table 7: Personal Files on the 'C' Department Computer

```
SURNAME:                    FIRST NAMES:
ASSOCIATED FILE NO (IF ANY):    BRANCH REF NO:
REFS TO SUBSIDIARY INDEXES:     NATIONALITY:
PREVIOUS CONVICTIONS:           CRO NO:
SEX:                    FEMALE PREVIOUS NAME:
ALIAS(ES):                      NICKNAME(S):
DATE OF BIRTH:          PLACE OF BIRTH:
ADDRESS(ES):                    FREQUENTS:
REASON(S) OF INTEREST:          KNOWN TO:
VEHICLE USED:-
                    MAKE:       MODEL:
                    TYPE:       COLOUR:
                    REGN NO:
PASSPORT:-          NUMBER:     DATE ISSUED:
                    WHERE ISSUED:
CROSS REFERENCES TO OTHER RECORDS:
DESCRIPTION:-       HEIGHT:     BUILD:
                    RACE:       VOICE/ACCENT:
                    HAIR COLOUR:    HAIR CUT:
                    FACIAL HAIR:
                    EYES COLOUR:    PECULIARITIES:
                    TATTOOS PLACE:  TYPE:
                    OTHER PECULIARITIES:
```

The personal files of the individual squads will, for ease of computerization, be transferred into a standard single format. *Table 7* (p. 105) shows the standard entry for any squad's files. After the name comes a reference to any 'associated files', which would be large separate dockets still held on paper. The 'Branch Reference Number' might denote one of the Special Branch's twenty-seven 'areas of interest', or some other internal classification. The reference to subsidiary indexes may include specialist or general subject files, investigations in progress, or telephone number and address indexes. Most of the other entries are self explanatory; once again a persistent feature is the cross-linking of people and their friends as 'associates', and 'cross-reference to other records'.

In addition to these basic formats, *Table 8* (opposite) shows a selection of additional information which would be held only by some of the squads for their particular requirements. The Fraud Squad file holds details of driving licences (which can be used by them and the Inland Revenue to trace people via the Driver and Vehicle Licensing Centre at Swansea), details of bankruptcy, and other references whose meaning is not apparent. The C11 files include additional information on vehicle or boat ownership, as well as a note whether the person concerned is on their smaller but more detailed set of manual files as a 'criminal of major interest'. The Immigration Intelligence files also record the person concerned's father's name. The Special Branch will include references to their substantial photograph index, plus the 'folio number' for the 25 per cent of people who have larger dossiers kept on them.

A further feature of the Special Branch files is the provision of 'barred access', which means that security clearance is necessary to see a particular file, even within the Branch. There are a number of other sophisticated security measures affecting the Special Branch records; they are, for example, allowed to see all the files of every other section, whilst no one else may see their files. In many cases, an enquiry by a non-Special Branch officer for a trace on someone on whom the SB have a file will nevertheless be answered 'no trace'; although no doubt the system which has been installed will provide notification to enable the Special Branch to pass on information to the enquirer if that suits their interests. Even within the different sections there will be a grading of security levels, which could mean that someone without a suitable clearance would only be able to see the name on a file, or perhaps not even that.

Table 8: Additional data required:—

(a) by the Fraud Squad

```
DRIVING LICENCE:-
                    NUMBER:          EXPIRY DATE:
BANKRUPTCY:-
                    DAY/MONTH/YEAR:
                    COURT FILE NO:
                    DISCHARGE:
GR CORRES REF(S):   LFF REF:
                    OTHER REF(S):
```

(b) by C11

```
?MAIN INDEX PERSON?:
AIRCRAFT TYPE:
                    REGN NO:         HOME AIRFIELD:
                    PHOTO INDEX REF:
BOATS:
                    TYPE:            NAME:
                    REGN NO:         PORT:
```

(c) by the Immigration Intelligence Unit

```
FATHER'S NAME:
```

(d) by the Special Branch

```
FOLIO NO IN BULK FILES:
BARRED ACCESS TO FILE:
PHOTO INDEX REF:
```

(e) relating to associated vehicles

```
REGN NO:
MAKE:               MODEL:
TYPE:               COLOUR:
OWNER:              OTHER USERS:
PLACE KEPT:         UNUSUAL FEATURES:
```

To protect these files, the computer – which operates twenty-four hours a day – will have many precautions against interference. Access to the computer terminals is controlled by special badge, and passwords and codewords, as well as other checks on the user's identity, are required before access to the data stored is allowed.

The specification for the 'C' Department computer also listed the various types of activity that the police were likely to carry out on the system. Over 90 per cent of enquiries were expected to be of the simple 'trace'/'no trace' type, where a name or vehicle number was entered to see if anything was recorded about the person or vehicle concerned. But it was also to incorporate the sophisticated 'multi-factor search' enquiries that the DPC found so alarming. Whereas a 'trace'/'no trace' enquiry should be carried out in a 'few seconds', a search using several factors other than names in the records should take a 'few minutes'. A list of people who satisfied the search factors would be output. A more sophisticated procedure which might take a 'few hours' was also to be available; this would allow what the DPC called 'full text retrieval' by searching the entire content of a record for a particular factor. For example, a general search against 'Queen Street, Manchester' might produce a list of people who had addresses there, who had friends who lived there, who drank in pubs there, or who had been involved in criminal offences there. Such a search would involve a time consuming check of all the records in the computer.

To do all this data handling the computer is programmed using a sophisticated software system developed by the UK Atomic Energy Research Establishment at Harwell, Oxfordshire. The system, called STATUS, controls large files of records efficiently, which is presumably why it was selected for the Metropolitan Police requirements. The actual computer is in fact a set of small interconnected computers, known as the CTL Series 8000.

Eventually, the police hope to develop the computer to handle other applications which have from time to time been set up using the JADPU computers. These include an index of particulars of stolen works of Fine Art, a Stolen Currency Index, and a 'Special Enquiry Information Collation System'. This would be a temporary file system which could be set up during a major police investigation – a big murder case, a search for bombers, etc – where a large police team gathers a vast amount of evidence quickly, with corresponding difficulties in sorting out relevant information. Although in this case, it would be normal to wipe out the information after the enquiry was over, such a new system would obviously facilitate the transfer of suitable information to Special Branch or C11/CDIIU files.

Eventually, the Metropolitan Police proposal states, they would like to have a system like SOUNDEX with 'name coding and matching routines', as well as comprehensive statistics on the use of the new system. But the most startling suggestion is a requirement for 'behavioural pattern recognition'. In other words, the computer would periodically examine new entries on files and determine the way in which someone was behaving, and whether this was likely to be of interest. This development would seem principally to concern the Special Branch and C11 files, where there is considerable interest in following people's friendships and inter-relations, and where a new grouping could be spotted more quickly by the computer itself.

It is small wonder that the drafters of the document, in projecting police file holdings forward from January 1974 chose an unusual 11 year period on which to base their predictions. It is tempting to believe that they themselves were privately aware of how closely a ten year plan to January 1984 would have paralleled George Orwell's fears.

The system was brought into service in 1979, under the joint supervision of the Metropolitan Police Management Services Department, JADPU, and the government's Central Computer Agency. In order to meet the project timing, provincial Special Branch officers who regularly spend three months tours of duty in Scotland Yard at the SB's 'National Joint Unit', were employed during much of 1978 solely in coding personal dossiers ready for the computer. Although development and the loading of files continues, there is little doubt that the 'C' Department computer will indeed be working well and on time by January 1984.

Northern Ireland: Society under control

Since 1978, British army intelligence units working in Northern Ireland have maintained what is probably the most extensive computer based surveillance system anywhere in the world. By now, details of at least half of the entire population are recorded, together with extensive and closely cross-referenced indexes of vehicles, addresses, and activities. Although this system is primarily run by the army, it is run for a policing and not a military purpose *per se*; and army operations are run in more or less close co-operation with the Royal Ulster Constabulary, in support of whom they notionally work.

It therefore falls well within the scope of this study. And it is well worth examining how this system works, as far as is known.

The parallels between the Northern Ireland army computer and other police systems, particularly the PNC, are close. Both, for example, are closely coupled to communications networks for the rapid dissemination of information on a 'stop check' basis – in the army's case, a network of links to personal radios carried by military patrols, known as 'Ulsternet'. Both systems are justified and legitimated by reference to the more fearsome types of crime, so that their everyday effect on personal liberty may be ignored, or written off. And both, perhaps necessarily, embody the same principles for bringing society under surveillance and control – although it is perhaps only by comparing and contrasting the two systems that these principles begin to stand out clearly.

Military intelligence moved into Northern Ireland with the arrival of the first soldiers in 1969, but acted then in a quite haphazard way. By 1971, however, a Special Military Intelligence Unit (Northern Ireland) had been set up under the command of an intelligence Colonel, and at the end of that year a new central intelligence group, the 12th Intelligence and Security Company of the Intelligence Corps, was set up in the Lisburn headquarters. This, and another company formed later, the 14th, are part of the Intelligence and Security Group (UK). By 1972, over 100 army specialists were involved in this work; three years later this figure had trebled.[74] The introduction of internment, earlier in 1971, had pointed up various problems of police (primarily RUC Special Branch) intelligence, and a wholesale overhaul of methods now took place. Although the potential use of computers was canvassed at that stage, no one then knew how long the army would remain in Northern Ireland, or what the likely political future would be. Various manual indexes were however becoming progressively more extensive. Some time in 1974, it seems, the first computer was installed at the Lisburn HQ, to handle checks on vehicles passing through army checkpoints. Full scale computerization of army intelligence records was announced in 1976[75] – although by that stage there had already been several reports that at least some of the 500,000 or more personal records had already been computerized.[76]

The vast intelligence gathering operation in Northern Ireland did not come to public notice at all in the rest of Britain until December 1974, when the *Times* correspondent Robert Fisk reported that the 'Army's computer has data on half the population of Ulster'.[77]

Residents of the province – particularly Catholics – had by this time long been familiar with regular and intrusive questioning and searches by troops, both in the streets and in their homes. Fisk was shown the computer vehicle check in operation, and given a practical demonstration of the speed of information retrieval concerning houses and people. On asking an army sergeant for the colour of the sofa suite in his own Belfast house the correct answer was radioed back, he reported, within 30 seconds.

The major part of the system shown to Fisk involved links to army run blockhouses on major roads intended to monitor vehicles, particularly those travelling in and out of the Irish Republic. The blockhouse checkpoints were connected by landline to the Lisburn HQ. Fisk's story raised a storm in the House of Commons the same day, and the then Northern Ireland secretary Merlyn Rees claimed that 'there is no computer for intelligence' in Ireland. Since he had already conceded that there was 'a computer for vehicle checking and for vehicles crossing the border' the reply was a little disingenuous, for the vehicle checks were themselves an intelligence operation. Rees then less than disarmingly suggested that what was being used in Northern Ireland 'was the same sort that was in police use here' (ie. the PNC).[78] Leslie Huckfield, a backbench Labour MP, told the House that he had investigated the *Times* report from his own sources, and that although the computer had not yet started operating as far as personal data was concerned it was 'already set up and raring to go'. Rees reasserted that such a system would not be introduced without Parliament being informed.

When, finally, the use of a computer as described by Fisk was officially confirmed, it was done at a time of maximum emotion when criticism of the move could most easily be curtailed. The official announcement, on 12 January 1976, immediately followed the murder of ten Protestant workers at Bessbrook. In the same statement, Prime Minister Harold Wilson announced that the Special Air Services (SAS) would henceforth be operating undercover in Northern Ireland. It was a convenient moment for the authorities to legitimate activities that had indeed gone on for many years previously.

The same weary excuses for the intrusion on liberty were trotted out again; Wilson explained that the computer would 'handle *existing* records so that information can be processed and acted upon more quickly'. The MoD added that

Army records, *at present held in manual files* and covering details of suspects, weapons, incidents and vehicles, will henceforward be held on a computer. (Author's italics.)[79]

Parliament cannot now deny that it was informed of the decision to introduce such a system, albeit at a time, of course, when criticism could be stifled and the impact of the news manipulated. Parliament had not at any previous stage been informed of the decisions to set up files on the bulk of the Northern Ireland population, or of the decisions to computerize first vehicle and vehicle checkpoint records, and then the remainder – until it proved opportune to announce that a decision had already been taken. Even Wilson's statement to Parliament revealing the system was deplored by some army sources. In April 1977, the new computer had yet to come into full operation.[80] It was operating by 1978.

The official rubric on the Northern Ireland computer states that it concerns 'information on suspects, incidents, vehicles and weapons'.[81] Rather more detailed and exact information has however appeared in the press describing the four major indexes which are now held on computer. (Incidents and weapons are smaller indexes.) Further information on the contents of these files has come from a 'restricted' army manual on 'Search for Munitions', details of which were revealed during 1979.[82] The four major indexes concern People ('P'), Street Records ('House'), Vehicles ('V') and Vehicle Checkpoints ('VCP').[83]

There are between half and three quarters of a million personal records on the 'P' index. All records are indexed, as with the PNC, by name and date of birth, and the records include particulars of addresses used, associates, a physical description, occupation, details of associated vehicles or associations with political organizations. Information held – and passed out – concerning vehicles includes a security interest rating from 1 to 5. Each car is given a grade which depends on where the owner or user lives, their religion, politics and friends. Grade 1 – detain immediately and bring to army HQ – and Grade 5 – clear, no action – are the extremes. A grade 4 means that the person concerned lives in a suspicious area but has no political connections or friends under surveillance; grade 3 means that the army regards the owner/user as 'subversive'; a grade 2 implies sufficiently subversive tendencies to be detained immediately.

This information is available to foot and vehicle patrols, who can radio in for a check through Ulsternet. The treatment given to an individual strongly depends on his or her religion and 'security interest'. The army have a wide range of special legal powers of detention for questioning which can be exercised at whim, quite apart from their ability to intimidate and harass. In more involved cases, street records giving details of particular houses may be called up for use in interrogation. This is, for example, the major reason for recording such recondite information as the colour of someone's sofa, or the type of television owned. Such particulars provide simple-minded identity checks for Army and police interrogators.

The Street Records cover most of Northern Ireland dwellings, and the bulk of the data on these files comes from the regular army searches. The basic index for the file, as far as the computer is concerned, is likely to be the Post Office postcode index, which provides a record of all dwellings coded in an easily accessible way. The data input to this file includes details of television and furniture, the number and type of outbuildings, the number of rooms, even the type of fire in use in the main room. A full list of such details is contained in *Table 9* (p. 114), which draws on the army manual 'Search for Munitions'.

The vehicle records detail the colour, make, type, registration number and licence details of a vehicle, as well as the names and addresses of the owner and of other users. The files also record the 'usual locale'[84] of the vehicle, noting also if it has been stolen or involved in crimes or other incidents.

The VCP index is an index of vehicle movements, apparently arranged according to the time a vehicle was seen and the checkpoint or other position where it was seen. All information from passive checks on vehicles as well as stops and searches is recorded on this index, which can by now presumably be cross-referred onto the main vehicle index, to generate a list of the whereabouts of any given vehicles.

The weapons index details the type and serial numbers of both legally held weapons and those found by the army and police, together with firearms certificate numbers, when applicable. Not much information has become available about the sixth, 'incidents' index, although it may be presumed to record basic details of any crime or terrorist incident and other events of interest to army or police, such as a particular set of individuals meeting in, say, a pub or a park. An 'occurrences' index is in operation on the Thames Valley Police

Table 9: Information routinely recorded during army search in Northern Ireland

ADDRESS: HOUSE TYPE:

OCCUPANT'S RELIGION:

DETAILS OF PREVIOUS SEARCHES: DATE:

UNIT: RESULT:

OCCUPANT'S NAME: OCCUPANT'S DATE OF BIRTH:

LENGTH OF TIME IN RESIDENCE:

OWNER'S NAME: OWNER'S DATE OF BIRTH:

KEYHOLDER'S NAME: KEYHOLDER'S DATE OF BIRTH:

OCCUPANT'S PROFESSION: OCCUPANT'S HOBBIES &
                                 INTERESTS:

OCCUPANT'S WIFE/HUSBAND/FAMILY DETAILS:-

   NAME: DATE OF BIRTH:

   RELATIONSHIP:

RELEVANT DETAILS ABOUT OCCUPANTS OF ADJACENT
   BUILDINGS:

ASSOCIATED VEHICLE:-

   MAKE: MODEL:

   COLOUR: FEATURES:

ASSOCIATION: MOTOR TAX DETAILS:

ASSOCIATED PROPERTY:-

LEGALLY HELD WEAPON:-

   TYPE: SERIAL NO:

   FIREARMS CERTIFICATE NO:

TELEVISION TYPE: COLOUR/BLACK & WHITE:

TELEVISION LICENCE NO:

TELEPHONE NO AT ADDRESS:

NUMBER OF TELEPHONE EXTENSIONS:

NUMBER & TYPE OF OUTBUILDINGS:

COLOUR OF FRONT DOOR:

NUMBER OF ROOMS: COLOUR OF SUITE:

TYPE OF FIRE IN MAIN ROOM:

TYPE OF DOMESTIC POWER SUPPLY:

HOUSE TYPE: DISPOSITION:

computer (see next section) which indicates the likely scope of such a category. The incidents index will involve links to each of the other basic indexes (P, House, and V).

Besides the extensive personal detail recorded on the P index there is reported to be[85] a system of 'flagging' people of interest indicating, say, that the encounter should be reported to a particular intelligence agency, or that the person should be left unimpeded for the time being. Until the main computer was in operation, the P indexes were reportedly held in duplicate at local level and at one of the three brigade headquarters in Northern Ireland. The new project has now centralized all records at the Thiepval Barracks HQ at Lisburn.

The Northern Ireland army computer is thus the most extensive surveillance operation known in any country. It has of course been set up and operates against a background of ten years of turmoil, terrorism and brutality on all sides. It operates in circumstances where extraordinary legal powers are available to the police and the army, and where the 'war' against the Provisional IRA and other armed groups is presumed to legitimate almost any removal of liberty for the population as a whole. It is worth noting in passing that, despite this massive surveillance, military intelligence commanders do not now think that there is any hope of a victory against the IRA for the foreseeable future. A secret intelligence report by Brigadier J.M. Glover, who shortly afterwards became the commander of land forces in Northern Ireland, was leaked early in 1979. It revealed that the considered view of the army leadership was that the IRA had the 'sinews of war' to continue to fight indefinitely, despite what the army and its intelligence activities could do to 'attrite' terrorist activities.[86]

The links between army intelligence operations in Northern Ireland and various police files and computer systems are considerable. The RUC and the army work closely together on most levels and data is exchanged. There are representatives of the internal and external intelligence agencies, MI5 and MI6, at the army HQ, while military intelligence officers are detached to liaise with local and national Special Branch units. Major co-ordination of this kind takes place at Scotland Yard, where the Special Branch National Joint Unit has representatives of provincial SB units, including the RUC. It co-ordinates the exchange of information and has supervised the pooling of information in SB files on the 'C' Department computer, described above. Through the NJU, information can be exchanged between the two computer centres.[87]

The RUC have yet to get a computer of their own, although like every other police force they have had and operated PNC terminals for several years. Early in 1979, however, it was stated[88] that the RUC would receive a new computer for command and control purposes. The new computer will contain interfaces to the army system, the PNC, and the local Criminal Intelligence Retrieval System (CIRS) which may also be installed in Belfast. It will also interface to the 'PSS' – Packet Switched System of data transmission, presumably that now being developed for public service by the Post Office, so that more links may be developed in future. These interfaces will enable RUC operators to obtain information directly from any of the other computers and supply it to patrol policemen.

The Data Protection Committee, once again, attempted to discover what was taking place on the army intelligence computer, but were rebuffed: 'We were unsuccessful in obtaining any detailed information',[89] they reported. The Northern Ireland Civil Rights Association had told the DPC that 40 per cent of the population were on file and that the files held a wide range of personal information, including 'any form of suspected ... political activity'. NICRA claimed that the army deliberately used its powers of arrest and interrogation under the Emergency Provisions Act to gather information to update the files. But the DPC took this matter no further.

Whilst some aspects of the Northern Ireland army computer are clearly related only to the exigencies of the present campaign, it will be apparent that the general philosophy of the computer is identical with that of the PNC. It has even been alleged that these links go further; that PNC software techniques and programmes have been adapted for use by the army. In fact, it would be surprising if this were *not* the case, as many of the applications and tasks are very similar. The police in Britain lack the legal powers, and indeed the manpower, political justification or public support necessary to carry out continual and extensive surveillance by means of checks and searches as happens in Northern Ireland. But as the previous sections make clear, they would like to have these powers at least latent, as well as the technological means to use them effectively. Contingency plans and contingency legislation undoubtedly await a suitable moment – like the Bessbrook incident – when, if needed, such powers may be legitimized and authorized. The only factor lacking in the Ulster situation, paradoxically, is identity cards. This, presumably, is one reason for the elaborate interrogatory identity check facilities available. The implications of the Northern Ireland computer are clear – nothing apparently exists in constitution or law to prevent a similar project going ahead in Britain, secretly, until it was too late to stop.

Collators: Local Intelligence Gathering

Collators are local intelligence officers employed by each British police force. The explicit title of 'local intelligence officer' may sound repugnant to many and difficult to accept or comprehend. But local intelligence gathering is the quite explicit task of these specialists, who (with variations from force to force) maintain card indexes on people, events, vehicles, addresses, crimes and so on. The collator is now an established, and indeed central part of any British police force, yet the scope of his work has very infrequently come to public attention.

The job was institutionalized from 1966 on as part of the unit beat system of policing. One of the few official references to this innovation is, unusually, in a careers booklet for schoolchildren[90] which describes the collator's office as 'the information centre of the unit beat system' (see *Fig. 1*, p. 118). The collator will update files from every possible information source within a police station – officers' daily reports, crime investigations, cases before the courts, information from police files elsewhere, hearsay from any kind of source, stop checks and vehicle checks, and so on. All of these are entered on a person's record and are available to local police officers on demand, and to all others

Figure 1: Unit Beat Policing: The Collator's Role

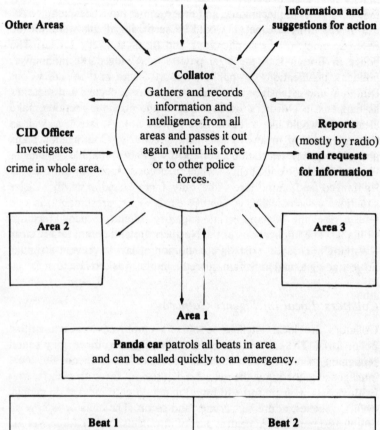

UNIT BEAT POLICING

Adopted from HMSO Careers Booklet 80, The Police.

either directly or via their own local collators. Detectives now rely heavily on obtaining information from collators during the early stages of an investigation.

A number of leaks of police information have shown that almost any sort of information is regularly finding its way onto this kind of file, and that they are potentially capable of immense harm. They regularly record gossip, hearsay and unsubstantiated information, and permanently file details of any kind of police activity against an individual, irrespective of any charge or conviction. They open and update files on people who have never been convicted or even suspected of a criminal offence, on the hypothesis that anyone at all may someday attract police attention – and therefore (in the absence of any legislation forbidding such activity) should be recorded if encountered.

Except for one police force, Thames Valley, these files are still largely kept on manual card index filing systems, and will remain so for some time. Information from them does of course find its way into the computerized systems described elsewhere in this section of the book. Information is also circulated in the form of local or force-wide intelligence bulletins, often with folksy titles to ensure officers attention (such as the London 'Bush Telegraph' issued by Shepherd's Bush police, and the 'Lima Lantern' issued by L (Lima) division in south London). Collators' status and importance can vary widely and be as idiosyncratic as their files; some may have civilian or uniformed assistants and extensive areas for file storage and photographic display, others only minimal facilities.

In 1972, the Home Office set up an experiment in the computerization of collator's files, using terminals in Uxbridge police station, on-line to the Home Office's JADPU computers in central London. This trial was, presumably, sufficiently encouraging for the Police Scientific Development Branch of the Home Office to start planning for a full scale version. The decision to computerize the records of Thames Valley was taken early in 1974. The National Council for Civil Liberties learned of the plan in March 1974, but any enquiries about the propriety of proceeding with the project were stalled until the order had actually been announced by the computer manufacturer, the US Honeywell corporation.[91] The computer, a Honeywell 6025, was handed over to the Home Office at Thames Valley's Kidlington HQ near Oxford during September 1975. It was operational by the end of 1976.

An early note of caution about collators was sounded by the *Police Review* which argued in 1972:

> Since 1966 the Service has collators in most Police divisions and they have amassed information which in both quantity and quality would surprise most people on their books. Police intelligence is now forward-looking, anticipating who is going to commit what, when, and where – and because it is so purposeful it is also frequently libellous ... Much of the information stored in collator's files is tinged with the calculated guesswork of the officer who has provided it. Much of the information is personal detail (and) it may seem a trespass on the freedom of the individual ... There is a serious danger that once a person is in the system he may remain there – there is no way of opting out until the Police consider he has reached the age of criminal ineffectiveness.[92]

In 1978, their editorial fears about the 'automated detective' were borne out by the cutting remarks of two FBI visitors to the system, whom the Home Office invited to inspect its operations. During the demonstration, the visitors were shown the record of one man about whom it had been noted that he 'fancies little boys'. This report was based on a conversation overheard by a policeman's wife in a local village shop, after which it had been entered by the policeman in an 'occurrence book'. The *Police Review* commented that the allegation was untrue, and that although much information going on to such a computer was 'valid intelligence', 'a substantial proportion is unchecked bunkum'. Such a system would, the visitors believed, have been 'wholly unacceptable' in the USA where the constitution and other legal safeguards protected personal privacy to a greater extent than in Britain.

Thames Valley Police and, until recently, the Home Office have refused to provide details to the press or public about the system known as the Collator Project. However, a very comprehensive description was given by a member of the Police Scientific Development Branch in November 1976, which enables the characteristics of the computer system to be more precisely described.[94] By then, the computer capacity had already been increased with the installation of a more powerful model (Honeywell 6040) and extra facilities.

The computer links the Kidlington HQ with 30 terminals at collator's offices in 21 police stations throughout Oxfordshire, Buckinghamshire and Berkshire. The maximum capacity of the files on the Collator Project computer, and the present current numbers of records stored, are given in Table 10.

Table 10: Thames Valley Police Collator Project – Current and Maximum Size of Files Stored on the Computer

Index	Actual Size*	Maximum Size	Percentage of design capacity
Persons	99,825	150,000	66.6
Vehicles	17,156	300,000	5.7
Place (Addresses)	77,834	300,000	25.9
Occurences	66,998	250,000	26.8
Crimes	5,943	120,000	5.0

* Figures, current at September 1979 were supplied to the author by the Home Office who stated that the number of persons with criminal records amongst the 99,825 recorded was 'unknown'.

With a population of 1.5 million in the entire Thames Valley area, this ambitious planning means that 10 per cent of the entire population may eventually be on file; given that most police records, criminal or otherwise, tend to concern adult males, this suggests that between a quarter and a third of all adult males in the area would be likely to become the subject of computer dossiers.

The actual utilization of the files shows quite a remarkable divergence between planned and actual number of files recorded. Although virtually 100,000 people are on file – two thirds of the planned capacity – only a tiny and disproportionate number of vehicles are recorded. The PNC has probably proved a tempting alternative means of retrieving vehicle information; for the rest, the figures seem to indicate that the Thames Valley Police are enormously more interested in recording personal details and non criminal events (occurences) than in recording crimes.

The designers of the system aimed to create a sophisticated database, where, for example, each person of interest could be electronically linked to up to 100 'associates' and the same number of vehicles, addresses, crimes or occurrences. The astonishingly exact and disturbingly detailed data formats for the Collator Project are contained in *Tables 11* to *15* (pp. 123-128). They are largely self-explanatory, but do merit further comment. Because of the extensive cross-linking of records, much of the material entered can appear repetitious; although the details of a particular person's house will appear when his personal record is examined, the particulars are actually stored under the house in the address index, with a link to the person as a 'frequenter' or 'occupant'.

The personal record starts with the normal police identifiers, name and date of birth, followed by criminal record numbers if any, in Thames Valley and nationally. The security level which is applied to the record determines who can see the record. A number of security levels are in operation with, presumably, Special Branch at the top, followed by senior detectives, and with uniformed constables at the bottom. Each user's password also determines his maximum security level. If a record is graded higher than that, he is unable even to discover that it exists. The same principle applies for other records, including crimes and occurrences. Security levels can also be assigned to sections of records, such as the reasons for police interest, or to links between records, such as the details of associates or premises frequented. There appears to be no provision for coping with a situation when a police officer needs details of someone whose records are too highly classified; at the moment he has no way of finding out whether police really do not have any information, or whether the information exists but is classified out of his reach.

The format of the personal record indicates the numerous ways in which people may become the subject of police files. Most startling is the third of three major categories at the bottom of the file – 'aggrieved in crime'. In other words, even the victims of crime are put on file. This may on occasion be a convenience in investigating their complaints but it is more likely to be the product of an intention to get everyone on file, without differentiation. Thames Valley Police (TVP) do not deny keeping records on victims; indeed it is not denied by other forces, such as the Metropolitan Police who have acknowledged that collator's files may include people who make 'frequent complaints' to the police.[95]

Besides victims, suspects, or committers of crimes, files may also be opened on someone because they have associated with someone else on file, or frequented or occupied a house on file, or been involved in a non-criminal 'occurrence', or been a user of a car on file. One effect of the use of a computer is to make the recording of such information, which might often be irrelevant or of questionable value, so simple that little discretion is exercised about what is put onto the system. The provision of extensive standard storage spaces for information on everything from 'habits' and 'gait' to 'driving disqualification' and

Table 11: Thames Valley Collator Project — Information Stored in Personal Records

```
SURNAME:                        FORENAME:
THAMES VALLEY CRO NO:     NATIONAL CRO NO:
DATE OF BIRTH:      PLACE OF BIRTH:     SEX:
SECURITY LEVEL:
ALIASES/NICKNAMES:-   SURNAME:     FORENAME:
REASON(S) FOR INTEREST:    (SECURITY LEVEL:  )
KNOWN TO:                        JOB:
ADDRESS:                        PREMISES:
COLLATOR AREA:                  HOUSE NO:
STREET NAME:                    STREET TYPE:
LOCALITY:                       TOWN:
ABOVE ADDRESS VERIFIED ON (DATE    ):    NOTE:
ASSOCIATE(S):-  SURNAME:        FORENAME:
                          (SECURITY LEVEL:  )
VEHICLE(S):-      REGISTRATION MARK:
HEIGHT:                         PHOTO NUMBER:
EYE COLOUR:                     BUILD:
EYE PECULIARITIES:        RACE/APPEARANCE:
VOICE/ACCENT:                   HAIR COLOUR:
FACIAL HAIR:                    FACE TYPE:
TATTOO PLACE:                   TATTOO TYPE:
ABNORMALITIES-TYPE:      ABNORMALITIES-PLACE:
MANNER:                         HABITS:
GAIT:
FREQUENTS:-(DETAILS OF PREMISES FREQUENTED,
          WITH SECURITY LEVEL:  )
```

```
LAST CONVICTION DATE:              COURT:
DRIVING DISQUALIFICATION-DATE:     PERIOD:
MODUS OPERANDI-OFFENCE:            TEXT:
              ENTRY:               TEXT:
              PROPS:               TEXT:
      CHARACTERISTICS:             TEXT:
OFFENDER IN CRIME(S)-REFERENCE NOS:
SUSPECTED IN CRIME(S)-REFERENCE NOS:
AGGRIEVED IN CRIME(S)-REFERENCE NOS:
LINKED OCCURRENCE(S)-DATE:         INPUT DATE:
AREA:                      OCCURRENCE NOS:
REMARKS:
```

'linked occurrences' tends to encourage the maximum amount of input.

Records for vehicles include links to users, locations, occurrences, and crimes as well as the usual descriptive details. The TVP computer, like the PNC, can retrieve any vehicle registrations matching to an incomplete registration, or even just to a particular description. Address records include details of locality and collator area as well as the basic address. As seems usual, the postcode is also kept as part of the computer record. As well as links to other records, each address record can contain up to 100 lines of explanation of 'reason-for-interest' or 'comment'.

Both crime and occurrence records include space for extensive details of *modus operandi* (MO), a criminal's working methods in a particular crime. The form for entering a crime shows how, if possible, the police will enter the name and date of birth of the 'aggrieved' as well as the offender. The remainder of the entry includes links to other files and other fairly standard detail.

Occurrences can of course include a wide range of events which are merely of interest to the police, without, any criminal involvement. It

Table 12: Thames Valley Collator Project – Information Stored in House/Place Records

PREMISES:	COLLATOR AREA:
HOUSE NUMBER:	STREET NAME:
STREET TYPE:	DISTRICT:
LOCALITY:	TOWN:
COUNTY:	POSTCODE:
REASON(S) FOR INTEREST:	SECURITY LEVEL:
COMMENT:	

OCCUPANT(S):	SURNAME:	FORENAME:
	DATE OF BIRTH:	
FREQUENTER(S):	SURNAME:	FORENAME:
	DATE OF BIRTH:	

CRIME LINK(S):	REFERENCE NOS:
DATE:	AREA:
LINKED OCCURRENCE(S):	
OCCURENCE DATE:	INPUT DATE:
AREA:	OCCURRENCE NO:
VEHICLE(S) ASSOCIATED:	REGISTRATION MARK:

is therefore open to Special Branch or other sections to record (and if need be, classify to prevent others seeing) details of attendees of political meetings, demonstrations, strike pickets and so on, or any other kind of information obtained by surveillance. There is no requirement that this information should be directly or indirectly related to crime.

The TVP system is, as its designers intended it to be, a very comprehensive local intelligence system, capable of recording, linking and retrieving information about almost any aspect of peoples lives. Although such systems may be disastrous for personal privacy, they

Table 13: Thames Valley Collator Project – Information Stored in Vehicle Records

REGISTRATION MARK: MAKE:

SECURITY LEVEL:

COLOUR 1:   COLOUR 2:   TYPE:

DETAILS:

USER(S):   SURNAME: FORENAME:

           DATE OF BIRTH:

PLACE LINK(S): (DETAILS AS IN HOUSE/

               PLACE RECORD):

OCCURENCE LINK(S):   (DETAILS OF OCCURRENCE):

STOLEN IN CRIME: REFERENCE NO:

DATE: AREA:

SUSPECTED IN CRIME: REFERENCE NO:

DATE: AREA:

REMARKS:

have equally not been an untarnished success for the police. Many police officers have been critical of the TVP system and the way it operates, seeing it more as an over-engineered product of the sweeping ideas of the Home Office's Police Scientific Development Branch rather than as an aid to practical policing. According to one chief constable who has reviewed the TVP project, the experiment will not be repeated in any other force in the same or a similar form. One member of the Home Office/police committee reviewing progress on the system reportedly remarked that the TVP system operated on the well established computing principle of 'Rubbish in ... rubbish out'.[96] A technical assessment of the system by the staff of *Computing* magazine described the type of database system used as 'primitive', and prone to serious difficulties if the size of files stored were significantly expanded.[97] This may have contributed to the 'operational' difficulties experienced.

Table 14: Thames Valley Collator Project – Information Stored in Occurrence Records

```
OCCURRENCE DATE:        TIME:     SECURITY LEVEL:
OCCURRENCE TYPE:                  SOURCE:
PLACE LINK(S):   (DETAILS AS IN HOUSE/PLACE
                  RECORD):
PERSONS INVOLVED:   SURNAME:      FORENAME:
                    DATE OF BIRTH:
VEHICLES INVOLVED:       REGISTRATION MARK:
CRIME(S) LINKED:   REFERENCE NOS:
DATE:                           AREA:
OTHER LINKED OCCURRENCES:   (DETAILS OF
                             OTHER OCCURRENCES):
MODUS OPERANDI:             (DETAILS AS IN
                             CRIME RECORD):
COMMENT:
```

The official evaluation of the results of the Collator Project has only recently begun, and no future developments are yet envisaged by the Home Office. Local forces have however pressed ahead with less sophisticated plans for Criminal Intelligence Retrieval Systems (CIRS). Some twelve forces were, by late 1979, either planning or had implemented some computerization of collator or intelligence records. Apart from Thames Valley, Suffolk and Cheshire Constabulary already had systems in operation. Greater Manchester, Merseyside, Humberside, Kent, Lincolnshire, Staffordshire, Devon and Cornwall, West Yorkshire, and Lothians and Borders (in Scotland) were all planning computerization. It was reported in 1978 that Humberside Constabulary had set aside up to £250,000 for this purpose because 'it would be near impossible to do a full check on an individual (now) ... because everything known isn't contained on the PNC'.[98] In Dorset, the collator's offices at force headquarters are strategically located

Table 15: Thames Valley Collator Project – Information Stored in Crime Records

REFERENCE NUMBER: COMPLAINT DATE: COMPLAINT TIME:

DETECTED?:   CRIME DATE: CRIME TIME:

SCENE OF CRIME: SECURITY LEVEL:

PREMISES: (DETAILS AS IN HOUSE/PLACE RECORD):

OFFENDER: SURNAME: FORENAME: DATE OF BIRTH:

SUSPECTED PERSON(S):   SURNAME: FORENAME: DATE OF BIRTH:

AGGRIEVED PERSON(S):   SURNAME: FORENAME: DATE OF BIRTH:

SUSPECTED VEHICLE(S):   REGISTRATION MARK:

MODUS OPERANDI:-   OFFENCE: TEXT:

                   WHERE: TEXT:

         MODE OF ENTRY: TEXT:

                   PROPS:.   TEXT:

           CHARACTERISTICS: TEXT:

VALUE OF GOODS(£):   EXACT FIGURE(£):   VALUE OF GOODS RECOVERED(£):

COMPLAINANT'S NAME: COMPLAINANT'S ADDRESS:

COMPLAIN RECEIVED BY: BEING DEALT WITH BY:

HOME OFFICE CLASSIFICATION: REMARKS:

beside the control room itself, with access to PNC terminals and with some of the collator records – in particular with address or street index files available almost as rapidly on an automated card index as if they were on computer.

Apart from the 'little boys' story and other general comments, no other information on the quality or type of information stored by the TVP computer has been available. At least one academic study has been made of collator files. During 1979, a set of Metropolitan Police 'Section Intelligence' files were lost or stolen, and copies later passed to the press.[99] The academic study observed that some unusual descriptions had found their way into collator records, such as remarks that a man was 'grossly obese' or had an 'effeminate appearance'. Most of the information stored concerned men; the proportion of women rose when organized checks such as on vehicles were being carried out. In one collator's office, they reported that there was a file marked 'cows, queers and flashers'.

The Metropolitan Police collator files referred to above provide a useful insight into the operation of the police collators. Most of the cards concerned members of a single family, the 'Wilsons' (they asked for their real names to be suppressed). A file on a middle aged mother of three, Mrs Carol Wilson, who had no criminal convictions of any kind, was opened in 1975 when her car was 'seen parked outside' the address of a man with convictions for rape, burglary and grievious bodily harm. But it does not note whether she was the driver or, indeed, whether the car had anything to do with the house. (In fact she had, on the day concerned, lent the car to a friend, and has never heard of the person concerned.) Nevertheless a file was thereafter maintained on her, and updated when she moved address. A note of her purchase of a new car in 1979 was made following a message from Scotland Yard. But the entry does not explain why this should be relevant, if at all, to preventing or detecting crime. Curiously, the address of her husband who had lived elsewhere for thirteen years was still shown as being the same as hers; when she moved, his address was erroneously 'updated' at the same time.

Files on her sons provided examples of the recording of hearsay, and gossip, and details of offences of which they were acquitted. One entry on Ted Wilson noted that 'a private person ... overheard ... a conversation' between Ted and a friend 'about a load of nicked stereo gear that they had'. The report was never investigated and remains unsubstantiated. Ted's file had been started in 1972 when he was fined

£1 after being convicted of the trivial offence of being carried in an uninsured car. Several years later he was convicted of a number of more serious offences, which may have been the reason he was singled out for special attention by the Special Patrol Group. A plainclothes SPG group walked along the street one afternoon, pushed him up against a wall and searched him, without explanation. This too was recorded in his collator file – 'stopped by SPG ... whilst washing car belonging to Dad'. He had not, of course, been committing any offence.

Other files in the same group showed how files were readily opened on anyone with whom the police came into contact. The file on Ted's brother, Joe, contained details of five other people, only two of whom had criminal records, not all of whom were listed as 'associates'. Three are marked down for the simple reason that they were stopped in the street one day whilst walking with Joe, and asked for their names. All are now listed as associates of a convicted person. Joe's file also contained details of charges of which he was acquitted and overheard gossip.

A file on another man, who had a long criminal record, listed a woman as his 'associate', and claimed that he had had a child by her. The claim is untrue, but the police never bothered to verify it or otherwise, and it remains on both people's files.

All these files contained details of description, criminal record number, and so forth. They also contain a racial 'Identity Code' ranging from RC1 (RC for Racial Classification) meaning white caucasian to RC7 (half-caste or unidentified). The range takes in Asian and Arabic variations, and use of this classification system is standard in many police documents and communications.

Collators may also keep individuals' political activities or political associations on file. Quite recently, Scotland Yard prepared a standard form for reporting on the organizers of and speakers at political meetings, which information no doubt finds its way onto collators' and Special Branch files. Collators vary widely in their selection of relevant material, and also in the way they select items of interest for attention by the station staff. A few local intelligence bulletins, such as those mentioned above, have been passed to NCCL. An extract from one such bulletin entitled 'Local Intelligence Bulletin – D Division – 1/78' which circulated in Buckinghamshire, illustrates the gossipy flavour of these circulars (real names have been altered):

John Smith, a well known local druggy, has moved into 15 New Road together with Ann Brown and child. As we know, Brown is also on the stuff and this new combination should prove interesting. As far as we know Mr Brown is still at home in King Street. It will be interesting to see who visits the new couple.

The bulletin finished with an exhortation not 'to let up on information coming in' despite the temporary absence of the normal collator.

The TVP computer has not been linked to the PNC, nor would it be obviously useful to do so at present (but information from both can be accessed from the same offices and the results passed out together to beat officers.) There have been official discussions on the linking of collator records into regional or national pools, presumably as a national criminal intelligence databank. Regional databanks might be related to the regional crime squad structure. A committee under the Chief Inspector of Constabulary has reportedly been reviewing such proposals.[100] (See also pp. 74, 94-95).

No figures are available for the extent of collator file holdings, even in London. If Thames Valley's allocation of 150,000 records is typical of the country as a whole (it is in fact likely to be a lower proportion than for metropolitan districts) then there may be 5-6 million such records, which will inevitably cover a wide range of people who are innocent of any crime – indeed, as with Carol Wilson, innocent of any suspicion. Collator records are more likely to affect an individual directly than other kinds of record keeping, since the attitude of local police officers is intended to be directly influenced by anything contained in the files. It is unfortunate, therefore, that the Data Protection Committee did not examine the TVP scheme, although it is clear that it and any other collator computerization projects should in the DPC's view come under the scrutiny of the independent Data Protection Authority.

Command and Control/Management Information

Although the storage of personal information is the purpose of the largest and most sophisticated computers in police service, these are by no means the most numerous. Many more computers and new projects concern two further types of police computer – used for management information, and the operational control of police resources. Command and Control ('C2' or some times 'Computer Aided Despatch' (CAD)) is the general title for computer systems employed in police control rooms, which keep track of the location and activity of individual police units. Management Information Systems (MIS) contain administrative police information, and may also include 'intelligence' usually of a non personal nature, such as the whereabouts of keyholders to large buildings, and so on. Because of their different character, these systems do not generally contain personal data, and their use is less controversial. Nevertheless, the boundaries between different sorts of work are merging, and command and control computers are already usually 'interfaced' to the PNC so that PNC data may be obtained at the same time as information about police resources. Although no data is transfered out to the PNC or elsewhere from this sort of link, this may change as more experience is gained in the linking of police computers.

The development of command and control systems has been one facet of the rapid increase in mobility and in the provision of extensive communications systems. The first computer to be used in this way was planned in the late 1960s, and became operational in Birmingham in 1972. The objective of such computers is to provide force controllers with rapid access to details of police resources – who is doing what, where – and other helpful information, with which to despatch forces to deal with incidents. Most forces do not try to direct all units from a central control room, but operate with a split of units between 'force' – controlled centrally on VHF radio networks – and 'divisional' – controlled from divisional or sub-divisional stations, usually using UHF radio. In order to provide the best possible '999' service, emergency calls are normally handled centrally. When police forces amalgamated both before and during 1974 local government reorganization, many problems arose in reorganizing their operational control systems, and a wide range of command and control systems have now come into use.

The term 'command and control' is itself of course military jargon, and the technology and practice of these systems very much reflects the military mode of organization. The predominant command and control system for large British cities, for example, is to be the Ferranti Argus computer. This machine and its associated programmes and other hardware are the product of Ferranti's military systems division, and are primarily designed for military use.

The military emphasis was very much apparent in plans for

Computer Aided Policing (CAP) which were presented to the Greater Manchester Police in May 1979.[117] The plans set out details of a computer for command and control and other purposes. The computer centre, it appeared, would be defended as though it were a key military target. It required to have a high level of 'survivability' under attack; the report noted that:

> the time when the full power of the Force's CAP may most be required could be under the conditions of the severest threat

which extraordinary belief in the importance and power of computers is rather akin to Scotland Yard's feelings about the temporary shutdown of the PNC (see p. 96).

The GMP computer was planned to be in operation by 1984. The computer and operations room will be housed in an annexe to the GMP's existing headquarters at Chester House, Manchester and will be 'hardened'. It was recommended that personnel working there should be positively vetted for security.

The second stage in command and control developments was the provision of a larger and more sophisticated system for the (then) City of Glasgow police. This used two Argus 500 computers, one of which was available to the Home Office for experiments and development while the other was in operation. Whereas the Birmingham system included only information on incidents reported and resources available, the Glasgow version includes crime reports, facilities for handling major incidents, and the automatic sending of messages to and between police teleprinters.[101] The Glasgow system could produce a range of statistical information, such as daily and weekly analyses of crime reports. The next stage in development was the extension of the Glasgow system to cover the whole area of the new Strathclyde police, and the replacement of the Birmingham system with a new one for the West Midlands. Besides these, similar Argus based command and control systems have been installed in West Yorkshire and Staffordshire police HQs, while Dorset and Suffolk police have obtained computer systems made by the US Digital Equipment Corporation and Marconi respectively. The newer Argus systems contain additional facilities:[102] integrated data communications; automated incident handling; management information; and crime information. The rural forces tend to spend less time dealing with incidents, therefore have different requirements. With this in mind different forces have developed varying facilities; in Staffordshire and

Dorset, one 'module' shows the 'duty state' of all officers. The Dorset system includes terminals in the CIU, the Intelligence Unit inside the force's headquarters.

A 'module' linking each computer to the PNC was developed for the Birmingham system and has become virtually standard. This module allows any video display unit (VDU) terminal on the command and control computer to be used also as a terminal to the PNC, thus making the PNC and its files much more accessible at divisional level and below. Suffolk police, according to the Home Office in one report,[103] have developed a 'local information retrieval' module on their computer which could provide information on, say, a car which 'has been seen in the docks area after midnight ... in suspicious circumstances.' Collator information on people and vehicles is stored and accessed on the Suffolk computer. Patrol officers can get such details from their 'area controller' at the same time as a PNC check. A major facility in the standard computer software now provided by the Police Scientific Development Branch to any potential user is a 'Local names and vehicle index' which may hold the same sort of information.

Alongside these developments for central control rooms have come several types of equipment for automatically transmitting data from individual police vehicles, or even patrol officers, to their headquarters. The systems work by sending a series of tones over the normal radio link, which can be decoded and interpreted by electronic or computer equipment at the control room. The earliest of these devices simply sends a short code signal each time a vehicle moves into a new area. Later developments included codes indicating what a unit was doing – patrolling, dealing with a road accident, carrying prisoners, and so on.

One system of this type is in use in conjunction with the Glasgow command and control computer.[105] Each vehicle carries a console with a set of push buttons, which can indicate the vehicle's position to within a one mile square, anywhere in the Strathclyde Region. Up to 88 different codes can indicate the 'state', or activity in which the unit is engaged. The console also includes two special facilities: an 'emergency' button which will put out a 20 second warning message when pressed; and a 'PNC' button, which will alert an 'Enquiry Unit' at the headquarters to handle a PNC check or other enquiry. The Enquiry Unit is said to have 'comprehensive information files'[106] which may include collator information and other criminal intelligence information, as well as having access to the PNC.

Four other British police forces are now trying out a dramatically more sophisticated type of data communication system, known as MADE (Mobile Automatic Data Experiment). In this system, vehicles carry a somewhat unwieldly array of communications equipment: typewriter-style keyboard, a miniature teleprinter for incoming messages, electronic message displays, and an automated map positioning system. The map merely needs to be touched in the right place for a signal indicating the vehicle's exact location to be sent to headquarters. The two way printer-keyboard system means that written messages can be sent to and from the cars, an advantage in circumstances where communication is difficult or noisy, or where additional security is wanted. A casual listener would be unable to decode the messages transmitted. MADE has been tested on the command and control systems of the West Midlands, West Mercia, Staffordshire and Warwickshire police. A related development, also manufactured by the Marconi company, is a computerized system called LANDFALL which uses a micro-computer on board each vehicle to automatically track its movement around a local road network. This obviates the need for the vehicle's personnel to radio in their position, since it can be sent automatically by their computer, after an 'interrogation' signal is sent from the central computer. The system first became available in 1976; in 1977, the Metropolitan Police ordered LANDFALL to equip Y Division, in North London. It will only cater for some 50 vehicles, at a cost of over £500,000. At the time, the police hoped eventually to extend the system to cover the entire area within a radius of 16 miles from the centre of London. But such sophisticated vehicle tracking systems have not, as yet, found extensive use as part of police command and control systems.

The first eight command and control systems, and some of the facilities they provide, are shown in *Table 16* (p. 136). By March 1979,[108] there were 24 police force command and control systems either operational or on order. The standard facilities now provided on new systems are:

Computer aided despatch, comprising:
— Incident Handling
— Police Resource Availability
— Automatic reminders (to take particular action, institute checks, etc.)

Table 16: Command and control projects implemented in UK, with some facilities

All the systems incorporate incident handling and police resource availability facilities. Computerized command and control systems are also now on order for Cleveland, Derbyshire, Essex, Greater Manchester, Gwent, Hertfordshire, Lincolnshire, Merseyside, South Yorks and the Metropolitan Police (London) forces. The Manchester, Merseyside, and Metropolitan Police systems incorporate 'management information' application.

Force	Birmingham	West Midlands	Glasgow	Strathclyde	Staffs	Suffolk	Dorset	West Yorks
Operational	Feb 72	April 78	May 75	March 78	June 77	March 77	May 77	April 78
Facilities:–								
PNC link	yes							
Crime reporting			yes	yes	yes	yes		yes
Local index retrieval			yes	yes	yes	yes	yes	
Local authority link					yes		yes	
Street index		yes		yes	yes		yes	yes
Automatic map displays			yes	yes				

— Street Indexes
Message switching (between teleprinters at each police station)
Major incident handling
Duty states of all police units
Interface to the Police National Computer

In the autumn of 1979 the Metropolitan Police placed an order for the largest command and control system in Britain. This multi-million pound scheme will involve a complex of six new control rooms taking up an entire floor at New Scotland Yard, and an extra 70 new control centres at major police stations throughout London. Although the Met already have an elaborate control centre at New Scotland Yard, its major activities have not been computerized. One computer installed in 1977 handles '999' calls in the North London and South Hertfordshire areas.

As mentioned above, the Suffolk command and control computer at Martlesham Heath, near Ipswich, was the first to incorporate local intelligence information retrieval. This is said to include 'nominal (i.e. concerning people), property and firearms indices'. South Yorkshire police have ordered a similar special record keeping system.[109] And the possibility of computerizing local intelligence at the same time as other computer applications is now being explored by many local forces (opposite and p. 145). The Humberside police committee have been told that the plans for their new computer will include details of:

> people with criminal records, the vehicles they are likely to use ... the
> places they frequent, ... and the crimes they have committed.

A more limited experiment in management information computerization is now being undertaken in Devon & Cornwall, where a microcomputer is in use at divisional, rather than force, level in order to discover its value to smaller police units. The Devon & Cornwall force have been particularly innovative in computer experiments; amongst other projects, in 1977 they carried out a 'Delphic poll' in which higher ranking officers gave their opinion on the likely date of introduction of various technological innovations. On the question of 'full criminal and collator records (being) available anywhere within the country within one minute ... from a computer', these policemen's expectation was that this would happen before 1985 and probably in 1983. More commendably, however, they did not see it as likely that identity cards would become mandatory in the UK between now and the year 2000.

Management information systems are seen by Home Office planners essentially as a set of programmes which can be grafted onto an existing computer which has basically been provided for command and control. These programmes are generally concerned with providing analytical information – such as how policemen spend their time – or simple forecasting – such as the likely number of 'incidents' in a given future month. Further programs can enable police administrators to carry out simple experiments in examining the effects of different deployment policies in response to hypothetical incidents. These systems are respectively known as MIS-1 and MIS-2. MIS-3 develops the principle further, and examines ways of obtaining maximum police 'productivity' in dealing with incidents. No detailed information has been published about the social assumptions on the role of the police involved in such sophisticated computer studies. But one Home Office researcher has summarized the following reasons for developing MIS to deal with 'growing problems ... facing the police':[110]

> range of crime expanding ... more 'political' incidents require a more sensitive approach ... growing racial problems; ... growing hooliganism ... fast road network.

It is clear that, while the implementation of management information systems and similar projects does not involve dangers to privacy or civil liberty on the same scale as the massive databanks discussed earlier, it does involve political questions about the role of the police. As such, the subject ought to be more open to public debate. The statistical analyses which are produced by MIS and similar systems are intended, naturally, to guide the deployment of police resources. The profiling of a particular area as, say, a 'high crime rate district' will eventually lead to more police resources being deployed in the area. The greater police attention is likely to lead to more crime being reported and investigated, and so on. If the area is one in which police/community relations are poor, then conflicts are likely to be exacerbated, and policing inevitably worsened if the conflict in fact increases crime rates and decreases local co-operation with investigations. In a number of studies, this sort of effect – a vicious circle of stigmatization of a particular area – is shown to be parallel to the effects of stigmatizing an individual in a personal file.

Included as a facility in many command and control projects, and elsewhere, are programmes for 'Major incident investigation'. Every year, a number of major cases of considerable complexity are taken on by the police. The information generated in a major enquiry can often be so overwhelming as to be counter-productive; recent cases have involved as many as 28,000 statements from witnesses, and cross-referencing of information by hand involved 400,000 index cards. Such a case only occurs twice a decade, but less extreme examples are rather more frequent.

After a number of trials on the Home Office JADPU computers, a major incident investigation package was included as part of the specification for the highly secret 'C' Department computer. A 'pilot experimental indexing system' was being developed in 1976,[111] to be evaluated on a number of real investigations. The major incident investigation system, like the rest of the 'C' Department computer, uses the STATUS software system to obtain 'full text retrieval'; this allows the entire information store to be searched rapidly for any word or phrase of interest. The computer and its STATUS software are 'located permanently at a secure site', but computer terminals will be transported rapidly to the location of the major incident, and the Post Office will provide emergency direct telephone lines.

Major incident investigations by the police do not ostensibly appear to pose different questions of principle from ordinary investigations. But the programming of such work on computers which are likely to be handling collator type information – and especially the major work of this kind on the 'C' Department national intelligence computer – puts it beyond doubt that information gathered in the investigation is unlikely to be deleted in its entirety once the case is over. Above, I have set out several examples of the police practice of attempting to index everyone whom they come across, in whatever context. Given the powerful capabilities of the 'C' Department computer, it would strain credulity for the police to suggest that details of members of the public coming forward to help in an investigation – or others whose names may be innocently mentioned – will not be added to the swelling database. Whereas in the past the sheer effort of indexing or filing information from manual records made it unlikely that confidence would be abused in this way, the computerization of major incident investigations will remove this safeguard – and, in the long run, may lessen public co-operation.

Society and Privacy

Throughout this study, it is clear how poorly Parliamentary democracy has served to protect our liberties. This is not entirely the fault of Parliament, and certainly not that of some, at least, of its practitioners. There exists no constitution, Bill of Rights, or more exact instrument than the Magna Carta, which requires the executive to explain and justify itself before placing society under further surveillance. Police surveillance of society by means of computerized records has boomed in the last decade, and the next few years' development is also clear: more intelligence data and files on 'persons of interest' will be sneaked onto the PNC; some local forces will have computerized local intelligence records, and arrangements will have been made for the standard interchange of such data; the police and security agencies will have a formidable new weapon for political surveillance and control in the shape of the 'C' Department national intelligence computer. The security service (MI5), moreover, has its own comput r centre, comprising several ICI 2900 computers at a classified central London location. We may only surmise how much further MI5, which has many times more staff than the Special Branch, a vastly larger budget, and no policing duties, has taken political surveillance.

All of these developments show a common pattern. Low level officials begin the systematic recording of information which they wish to keep. This system is turned into a manual record index, and eventually a decision is taken to place the whole on a computer. Some time after the decision to computerize records has been taken, a public announcement will note that the public need not be alarmed as the information has 'always been available on manual records'. In no case has public discussion of police computers been full and frank; the official responses range from the stonewalling of a government committee by the Metropolitan Police, to dishonest and misleading answers given in Parliament. In most cases, minimization of public discussion has rested on the simple proposition that the public and its representatives are best kept in ignorance. This view is generally supported by arguments about security, or the difficulties arising from explaining complicated technology. Such views are elitist, arrogant, and dishonest.

The most seditious argument is that of security. The concept of 'national security' is a well established bureaucratic mechanism for skating over differing group and class interests in society and substituting the state's desired prerogatives.

The police do have good arguments for some of their computer applications; moreover, it would be luddist to suppose that they will be willing to stay on paper while every other sector has the benefit of cheap computing. But while the police are ready to proclaim the acceptable arguments – the PNC is scarcely mentioned in a Chief Constable's report without a reference to its efficacy in dealing with stolen cars – they employ 'security' as a cover-up for the inconvenient and distasteful parts of their exercise, such as the 'flagging' of political dissidents' car numbers. Our liberties are most often threatened not by the bulk of the entries but by the footnotes – such as the 'warning' that someone may make a complaint about the police, or that they belong to the civil liberties lobby, which emerges on a PNC check.

A major remedy is disclosure. There is no reason why someone should not see, for example, their entry on the PNC Criminal Names file, if it contains no more than the police say it does. This alone would not be enough; the provision of the Rehabilitation of Offenders Act ought to apply at the very least to the PNC files, so that policing action toward a person is not affected by a 'spent' conviction. To do otherwise is wholly out of keeping with the spirit of the Act.

The same should be true of almost all collator information. Any information stored on such a system should be open to inspection and challenge by the individual (subject to some deletions), say six months after its entry. This would allow the retention of information relevant to current investigations whilst encouraging the purging of out-of-date data or gossip. Again, this would not be enough, and independent scrutiny, of all files at any time by an agency like the Data Protection Authority would be needed.

Attacks on civil liberty always start with minorities, and always the minorities whose public acceptability is lowest. Thus Irish people, Blacks, active trade unionists, left-wing socialists, communists and anarchists, bear the brunt of direct police surveillance, harassment and disruption. Their liberties therefore require the strongest defence of all. They may also require the strongest defence at the most difficult time; the unprecedented police powers in the Prevention of Terrorism Act, for example, (reviewed in Volume 1 of *Policing the Police*) were legitimized and enacted at the moment of maximum outrage – as was the first official announcement of the army's new Northern Ireland computer. Such manipulative official public relations are not the mark of integrity in democratic government.

The Data Protection Committee has of course already set forth quite a strong view on the subject of police records. Some of their comments are worth setting out again:

> We have not been able to satisfy ourselves that ... the information (we were given) is adequate,[112]

concerning the Metropolitan Police computer. They added, in relation to the general question of connecting 'factual' files (name, address, vehicles owned, convictions) to 'intelligence' data that:

> the linking of factual personal information about an identifiable individual with speculative data about criminal activity could pose a grave threat to that individual's interests ... (this) should only be done ... in special circumstances ... with caution and subject to the most stringent safeguards.[113]

The DPC recommended that all police computer systems, including applications for criminal intelligence, should come under the control and supervision of the proposed Authority. A Code (or Codes) of Practice specific to police files would be drawn up, and published. The Authority would be independent of the government, and its inspectors would be empowered to make checks of computer installations, their data and operations. There is one major deficiency in the DPA proposals, in that their scope is confined to computer and not manual records systems. Nevertheless, the DPC took a strong view in opposition to the Home Office's determination that no outside scrutiny of so-called criminal intelligence data should be allowed.

The next move is of course back in the hands of the Home Office itself, who have shown little enthusiasm for early legislation. Like the first report on privacy (the Younger Committee on Privacy, 1972) the DPC report and its important recommendations for safeguarding privacy and liberty seem to have been quietly filed in Home Office recesses. Labour governments have not acted and no proposals have been advanced in the Conservative government's legislative programme.

Sections of the police have, however, treated the subject with some seriousness, and have developed plans for dealing with potential privacy legislation. The head of the Police Scientific Development Branch outlined proposals in 1979 for separating information and records into three computer systems – one for criminal records, one for crime reports, and a third for force and collator intelligence. This might facilitate implementation of the varying Codes of Practice affecting each application.[114] It might also, of course, facilitate avoiding the irksome effects of the DPA altogether, by having a separate computer handling 'sensitive' information exempted from scrutiny.

One of the major problems in dealing with the impact of police computers on privacy and liberty is the difficulty in knowing what role a computer may have played in a particular police action. There are some examples of this above, but they are very few – and investigations, for example by NCCL and the BBC *Man Alive* programme failed to find very many more. But the argument that the police computers have caused no harm because no certain victims can be found is, of course, specious. Who is to know whether a computer or a file clerk was responsible for, say, creating and extracting a dozen files on supposed anarchists who are then the target of 6 am raids?

We have a rather better idea of who is likely to suffer and how from the increasingly wide-ranging police information on file when we see in detail the type of information recorded. For this reason, this study includes comprehensive details of all types of information stored in the major police computers. Examples of actual files do, sometimes, come to light. There could be few more dramatic demonstrations of this than when, in the course of the police 'vetting' of the jury for the 1979 trial of six anarchists,[115] details of the police files on the prospective panel of 93 jurors were published in the *Guardian*.[116] Although Special Branch and sensitive collator information had obviously been 'sanitized' from the files, it still contained intelligence on 20 people out of 93. Less than half of the 20 had criminal records. Five were the victims of crime, four were claimed to be friends or relatives of 'criminals', one was filed for having made a complaint about the police. One was believed to live in a squat. Of the ten who had criminal convictions, at least four of those were 'spent'.

All of this omitted the more sensitive information which the police did not wish to reveal. But even the amount of information recorded was evidence enough of the scope and scale of police information and intelligence gathering; of a random selection of adults in London, the police already had files on over 20 per cent. Society is, indeed, increasingly under surveillance.

Afterword

During the summer of 1979, I sought to arrange interviews with senior Home Office personnel responsible for police computer policy and related matters, in order to discuss the material in this chapter. In the course of some two months, this was apparently impossible to arrange. The Home Office nevertheless offered to supply answers to a series of written questions, and did so. Substantial parts of some of the answers are incorporated in the text, and indicated as such in the absence of a reference to a published source.

Some of the questions which I put to the Home Office were intended to establish the areas which were now officially permissible for discussion in the light of recent and growing concern over computer files, and which areas were not. Others requested details of policy. Below are set out most of these answers, on which no particular comment is needed:

Please state whether the concept of 'pre-emptive' policing is a part of official policy, and if so please describe the policy, if not please describe/explain official attitudes towards this description of policing.

The methods of policing within a force area is an operational matter and it is for the Chief Constable to decide in the light of prevailing circumstances how best this could be done.

Please describe the sub-categories of the Stolen Vehicles Index and the Wanted/Missing Persons Index, and state how many entries are in each sub-section. Please state the regulations concerning the placing of entries in each sub-category, and provisions for their deletion.

Please state the data elements stored in each record in each PNC application (in other words, what types of information can be stored in each file).

Will the Home Office permit me to see a copy of the Operators Handbook for the PNC, which I understand to be unclassified?

This information although not classified in a formal sense is restricted to police use only. To make it available publicly could jeopardize the security and effectiveness of the PNC and could put at risk the privacy of individuals recorded thereon.

Are there provisions for weeding information from the Criminal

Names Index after a fixed period of time, or according to any other provisions?

— Provisions are made for weeding information from the Criminal Names Index after a fixed period of time and depending upon the nature of the crime for which the person has been convicted.

Please describe any future plans or studies concerning general criminal intelligence retrieval systems, their facilities and likely implementation.

— There are no central plans or studies relating to criminal intelligence retrieval systems as such but ... research in the general area of information retrieval (is available to local forces).

Please describe policy and any plans concerning the computerization or centralization of criminal intelligence records at local, regional or national level.

— Apart from local systems ... there are no plans to computerize criminal intelligence records.

Concerning the Metropolitan Police 'C' Department computer, please state the number of entries in each file on the computer. Please state what percentage of persons in each section have criminal records. Please describe the 27 categories of interest for inclusion in the computerized or manual files of the Special Branch.

— As stated in the Home Secretary's reply to a Parliamentary Question on 25 January 1979, it would not be in the public interest to give detailed information about the Metropolitan Police 'C' Department Computer.

NOTES

1. J.F. MacLeod, *The fingerprint application of the Police National Computer, Conference of the Science of Fingerprints*, September 1974, p. 1. (hereinafter, 'MacLeod').
2. *Report of the Committee on Data Protection* (Chairman Sir Norman Lindop), Command 7341, HMSO, 1978, 8.16, p. 82, (hereinafter 'DPC Report').
3. See, for example, *State Research Bulletin 4*, Feb-March 1978, pp. 58-60. (hereinafter 'State Research'; the Bulletins are also republished annually by Julian Friedmann, as *The Review of Security and the State*.)
4. See DPC Report for report and recommendations.
5. MacLeod, p. 1.
6. See for example: J.E. Barrett, 'A long arm of the law', *Post Office Telecommunications Journal*, Spring 1975.
   Communications for the Police National Computer, Intercom (Home Office Directorate of Telecommunications), *8*, June 1976, supplement on Communications 76 exhibition.
   International Aeradio Ltd, publicity brochure on communications systems, 1976.
   P.P.H. Smith, *Communications Control Centre for a Central Computer*, Home Office Conference on Communications for Police and Fire Services (Directorate of Telecommunications), Leicester, September 1971.
7. C. Hipwell, 'The hard labour of building a secure police system', *Computer Weekly*, 10 May 1973.
8. J.R. Cubberley and D. Blakey, *The Police National Computer System in the United Kingdom*, Home Office Conference on the Use of Computers in Police Operations', London, November 1976, p. 56. (hereinafter 'Cubberley').
9. Ibid.
10. Tony Bunyan, *The Political Police in Britain*, Quartet, 1977, p. 81 (hereinafter 'Bunyan').

11. Private communication, January 1979.
12. *Computer Weekly*, 10 April 1975, editorial.
13. *Datalink*, 24 October 1977, and 13 December 1977.
14. *Hansard*, 2 December 1977.
15. Private communication from Hunt Saboteurs Association to *Datalink*, 20 November 1977.
16. Cubberley, pp. 5 & 6.
17. *Computers: Safeguards for Privacy*, Command 6354, HMSO, 1975. See application EN05, p. 19 (hereinafter 'Cmnd 6354').
18. *Guardian*, 5 July 1979.
19. Private communication, July 1979.
20. *Observer*, 13 December 1978.
21. *Datalink*, 19 July 1979.
22. Cubberley, p. 54.
23. *Computing*, 23 January 1975.
24. Private Communication, June 1979.
25. DPC Report, p. 399.
26. *Guardian*, 11 April 1977.
27. DPC Report, p. 359.
28. *Hansard*, 2 December 1977.
29. *State Research 1978*, p. 45.
30. Address by the Director of the PNCU to a meeting of the British Computer Society, 31 March 1973.
31. *The Job*, 5 August 1977, pp. 4-5.
32. DPC Report, 8.08, p. 81.
33. Ibid.
34. DPC Report, 8.16, p. 82.
35. Cubberley, p. 56.
36. As for note 30.
37. DPC Report, 8.12, p. 81.
38. *Listener*, 8 March 1979.
39. Private communication, June 1979.
40. DPC Report, 8.15, p. 82.
41. Ibid.
42. Macleod, p. 3.
43. *Hansard*, 2 December 1977; see also *Table 1* (p. 74).
44. *The Times*, 3 January 1978.
45. Letter from Scotland Yard to Fleet Street editors, 27 July 1978. (see page 96).
46. *The Times*, 3 January 1978.
47. *Listener*, 8 March 1979.
48. *Police Review*, 27 July 1979.
49. Cmnd 6354, *45*, p. 31.
50. *Listener*, 8 March 1979.

51. *Hansard*, 2 December 1977.
52. *Police Review*, 8 May 1972.
53. *Guardian*, 9 May 1972.
54. Private Communication, June 1979.
55. DPC Report, p. 359.
56. *Computers and Privacy*, Command 6353, HMSO 1975. *6*, p. 4. (hereinafter ('Cmnd 6353').
57. *Guardian*, 4 October 1972.
58. *Sunday Times*, 1 July 1973 and 15 July 1973.
59. See, for example, Bunyan.
60. Cmnd 6354.
61. *Hansard*, 2 December 1977, 15,25 and 29 January 1979, and 16 February 1979.
62. *The Times*, 14 February 1977.
63. *Hansard*, 7 July 1977.
64. *The Times*, 9 September 1977.
65. See *Table 6*.
66. *Hansard*, 2 December 1977 (and see 61 above).
67. 'Your life in their files', *Man Alive*, (BBC2), 18 February 1979; see *Listener*, 8 March 1979.
68. *Hansard*, 2 March 1979.
69. *Hansard*, 27 and 29 March 1979.
70. Duncan Campbell, 'New computer for the Special Branch', *New Statesman*, 25 August 1979.
71. DPC Report, 8.23, p. 84.
72. DPC Report, 8.20, p. 83.
73. Duncan Campbell, 'Facts and figures on phone tapping', *New Statesman*, 9 February 1979.
74. Information about military intelligence in Northern Ireland comes from the journal of the Intelligence Corps, the *Rose and Laurel*, for the relevant years (1969-74).
75. *Hansard* 12 January 1976. See also *Computing* and *Computer Weekly*, 15 January 1976 and the *Sunday Times*, 18 January 1976.
76. *The Times*, 5 December 1974 and *Sunday Times*, 7 September 1975.
77. *The Times*, 5 December 1974.
78. *Hansard*, 5 December 1974 and *Times*, 6 December 1974.
79. *Computer Weekly*, 15 January 1976.
80. *Computing*, 21 April 1977.
81. *Computer Weekly*, 28 April 1977.
82. *Time Out*, 13 and 20 April 1979, and *Computing*, 13 April 1979.
83. Most information in this section (but not all) comes from the *Sunday Times*, 18 January 1976.
84. Ibid.

85. *Time Out*, 13 April 1979.
86. Duncan Campbell, 'The army's secret opinion', *New Statesman*, 13 July 1979.
87. *Time Out*, 13 April 1979.
88. *Computing*, 12 April 1979.
89. DPC Report, 8.36, p. 87.
90. HMSO Careers Booklet No. 80, *The Police*.
91. Ed Harriman, 'Computerizing the Police Notebook', *New Scientist*, 1 August 1974.
92. *Police Review*, 12 May 1972.
93. *Police Review*, 21 April 1978; see also State Research 1978, pp. 108-109.
94. T.R. Mann, 'The United Kingdom Thames Valley Project', in Home Office Conference on the Use of Computers in Police Operations, November 1976, p. 97.
95. Stated by Scotland Yard on enquiry to the Press Office, July 1978.
96. *Guardian*, 20 February 1979.
97. Private Communication, November 1978.
98. *Datalink*, 23 January 1978.
99. Duncan Campbell, 'Keeping tabs on everyone', *New Statesman*, 10 August 1979.
100. State Research 1978, pp. 108-109.
101. A detailed description of the development of command and control systems is given by G. Turnbull, L.P. Coates and A. McNair: 'Command and control in the United Kingdom', Home Office Conference on the Use of Computers in Police Operations, London, November 1976, p. 7. (Hereinafter 'Turnbull'.) See also, A.T. Burrows, 'A new command and control system for the Birmingham City Police', International Electronic Countermeasures Conference Proceedings, Edinburgh, July 1973.
102. Turnbull, p. 6.
103. Turnbull, p. 7.
104. Turnbull, p. 12.
105. Strathclyde Police Command and Control, Ferranti Ltd. leaflet No. MSD 77/9, 1977.
106. Ibid.
107. *Computer Weekly*, 30 November 1977.
108. A.T. Burrows, 'Technological developments in policing and the liberty of the subject', Joint Summer Conference of the Association of Chief Police Officers and Local Authority Associations, Harrogate, May 1979 (hereinafter 'Burrows, 1979').
109. Ibid, p. 9.
110. G.G. Duckney, 'Management Information Systems in the UK', Home

Office Conference on the Use of Computers in Police Operations, London, November 1976, p. 196.

111. D. Wyeth, 'Major Incident Investigation in the UK', Home Office Conference on the Use of Computers in Police Operations, London, November 1976.

112. DPC Report, p. 79.

113. DPC Report, 8.16, p. 82.

114. Burrows, 1979, p. 10.

115. The case of R v. Stewart Carr and others (1979); better known as the 'Persons Unknown' case.

116. *Guardian*, 20 September 1979.

117. Duncan Campbell, 'Computer-run policing', *New Statesman*, 26 October 1979.

Section 3

THE SPECIAL PATROL GROUP

... if industrial policy follows this course the next instrument of the Cabinet will be the Special Patrol Group as the problems created by deindustrialisation come to be presented to the public in terms of law and order ... I warn the right hon. Gentleman [Sir Keith Joseph, Secretary of State for Industry] that if the industrial policy he follows leads to ... social tension the Special Patrol Group will not be a substitute for the National Enterprise Board as a way of dealing with it. This policy will lead to an inevitable attack on our democratic freedoms.

Tony Benn, M.P., speaking during the Second Reading of the Conservative Government's Industry Bill, House of Commons, 6th November 1979.

The Special Patrol Group   Joanna Rollo

Prologue

> *If you kill me that's murder. If I kill you, it's simply a matter
> of preserving law and order.*

> (Special Constable to demonstrator at the Chartist rally on
> Kensington Common in 1848.)[1]

On 18 July 1975 a policeman was stabbed to death in Birmingham,
outside a West Indian club called the Rainbow Rooms. PC Green had
been in the Force for 18 months, had been cited three times for
bravery during that period, and was a regular patroller of the Rainbow
Rooms, a man with something of a mission.

> His reputation amongst the youth was that of a consistent
> troublemaker who launched a campaign of real terror against black
> people, young and old, male and female. On that night he went as
> usual with his dog to the club ... Outside the club he set his dog on
> a young black girl, which provoked the incident leading to the
> stabbing. Within an hour of the stabbing the police force counter-
> attacked by launching what can only be described as a military
> operation. It was aimed specifically at the black community. Road
> blocks leading out of the city were set up: hundreds of black people
> were rounded up in the streets, taken to the police stations
> photographed and finger-printed. Any protest was met with
> beatings up and young women were forced to submit to having
> their knickers searched for the weapon by male policemen. Black
> people were taken out of restaurants and cinemas and buses were
> halted and black passengers removed. In all that night
> approximately 600 West Indians were rounded up. Only one was
> charged.[2]

On Monday 23 April 1979 a young man was killed in a back street in Southall, West London. He died as the result of one deadly blow, and although the weapon which killed him vanished in mysterious circumstances, a post mortem suggested that his skull had been fractured by a leadlined rubber cosh. Several witnesses saw him coshed and immediately made statements to both the police and press. No roadblocks were set up, there were no searches of houses and clubs, restaurants and cinemas, no 'rounding up' of suspects, no spot searches, no photographing, no finger printing.

The murderer was not found. Why? Because the dead man, Blair Peach, was not a policeman. He was a member of the Socialist Workers Party and he was in Southall to demonstrate against the National Front. He was murdered by a member of the Special Patrol Group.

The National Front was meeting in Southall Town Hall that Monday, with the permission of the Conservative-controlled council, to publicize its platform for the General Election to be held the following week. It was an act of outright provocation. First, because 70 per cent of Southall's population are Asian-people, the National Front's election manifesto stated, who would be deported immediately, should the NF ever come to power. Second, because the first victim of the racist onslaught on the black communities back in 1976 was a Southall boy. Gurdip Singh Chaggar was stabbed to death in a Southall street by a white youth. The outrage in the community which followed the murder, particularly amongst the youth, meant that any National Front activity in Southall would meet a determined response.

Almost as soon as the National Front announced their intention to meet, it became clear that the police were equally determined that the meeting would take place, supporting this stand with references to the Representation of the People Act, and invocation of the right to 'freedom of speech'. Other 'principles' such as the feeling amongst the majority of the population in Southall, or laws such as the Race Relations Act, or even the Public Order Act, which could have been used to support a ban on the meeting and were rather more applicable to the situation, were not considered to be as important by the police.

So the Asian community planned to protest against the National Front, with a demonstration the day before the meeting, a half day strike and a mass-sit down outside the Town Hall where the meeting was to be held, organized chiefly by the Indian Workers Association, the Southall Youth Movement and the Anti Nazi League. Two months later William Whitelaw, Home Secretary gave this interpretation of subsequent events to the House of Commons:

> Regrettably the preparations for opposition to the National Front meeting revealed a growing difference of view between young Asians and their elders which was easily exploited by extremist elements.[3]

This was not true. It was true that in 1976, after the murder of Gurdip Singh Chaggar, the Asian youth responded much more radically than their elders both to the growth of racism and to police attempts to contain their opposition. But, in 1979 the community was united in its determination to oppose the 'right' of the National Front to meet in its midst: and the determination of the police to uphold that 'right' met with growing local anger.

It was clear, early on in the day, that the police were preparing for a confrontation. Thousands were drafted into the area; some stationed there overnight in a local school requisitioned to accommodate and feed them. From mid-day they lined the streets surrounding the town hall, streets that were rapidly emptying as shops shut down for the afternoon. Groups of Asians were consistently 'moved on' from the area round the Town Hall, a nearby pub was closed early and people doing their shopping in the vicinity found themselves in the midst of a police cordon. Asian youth were spot-searched on the streets, some were verbally abused. 'Move on you black bastard' was one remark overheard by journalists, and those who didn't immediately 'move on' were being pushed and shoved. A spontaneous demonstration formed under the banner of the Southall Youth Movement. The police grabbed the banner and it was trampled underfoot. Some youths were arrested. The temperature rose, scuffles between police and young Asians broke out and by mid-afternoon there had been a series of violent clashes up and down the length of the High Street. The police, with riot shields, mounted officers and spearheaded by the Special Patrol Group, 'cleared' the street.

Part of the reason these clashes erupted was the police policy of arresting anyone who had a loud hailer and thus removing at an early stage leaders of the Asian youth who were trying to keep control of the situation and stop the then three hundred or so youths retaliating. But the youth were provoked. First because the police had made it clear that they were going to get the National Front into Southall whatever the community felt, and second because they adopted tactics of harassment and intimidation from an early stage. The Legal Action Group, in its demand for an inquiry into Southall, noted:

> Police tactics in Southall seem to have made disorder inevitable. Streets were sealed off and residents prevented from going about their normal business. People were allowed to enter streets and not to leave. The local council had allowed the Town Hall to be used for a public meeting under the Representation of the People Act 1949. Before there was any reason to suppose that members of the public would cause disruptions, the police sealed off the hall.[4]

After the events of the afternoon Southall was put under a virtual state of siege. Every approach to the Town Hall was closed down with road blocks and massed ranks of police, with SPG units and mounted contingents in reserve behind the cordons. A local legal advice centre was closed down. It had all the trappings of a carefully planned para-military operation with the aim of preventing any protest whatsoever against the National Front meeting. Vishnu Sharma, President of the Southall Indian Workers Association, described Southall that day as an example of the 'total police state in operation'.

An hour before the National Front were due to arrive for their meeting the police began to 'clear' the streets round the Town Hall. Charge after charge was launched against the demonstrators, mounted police with drawn sticks singled out and 'rode down' those who became separated from the crowd. The Special Patrol Group smashed through the crowds in flying wedges and its snatch squads grabbed and arrested at random. Resistance met with even greater violence. Demonstrators who had fled down alleyways were trapped and forced to 'run the gauntlet' – dodging blows from police with drawn truncheons as they went. It was a terrifying experience – the police were striking people at random with what looked like a determination to hurt as many as possible. Asians and West Indians were singled out for 'special attention'.

The Peoples Unit House, being used as a medical centre for the, by now, dozens of injured, was raided. Those inside were forced to run a gauntlet of truncheon-wielding police as they left. One of the doctors inside the house described the scene:

> There was myself, a lawyer and a bloke who was an ambulanceman for six years. The Police came in beating down the door. They herded us downstairs and in the hall they systematically hit each of us on the head with a truncheon, including myself. We were all bleeding from this. The

ex-ambulance driver I saw in a corner whimpering – by the time the ambulance arrived he was shivering, unconscious and his pulse rate was over 120. Another bloke, black, was shoved into the room. He also had been hit badly by the police. By the time the ambulance came he was an unconscious heap on the floor. The police refused to put him into the ambulance, they said that he was shamming. The rest of us were taken to hospital – I had six stitches.[5]

From six to ten o'clock that night the streets of Southall were 'controlled' with equally violent tactics. The Special Patrol Group were brought into the frontline of police operations, charging and chasing groups of demonstrators. The National Front meeting went ahead – a coach load of them were brought into Southall with a guard of police outriders. Police helped National Front stewards to vet those going into the meeting, a reporter from the *Daily Mirror* being refused entry because he represented a 'nigger loving rag'.

By the end of the night, the community had paid a high price for opposing the National Front. Three hundred and forty-two people were arrested – more arrests than had been made in any single day since 1961 – and dozens were injured, many severely. Gareth Peers, one of the defence solicitors for the 342 arrested, was appalled by the injuries:

Usually after a demonstration which results in confrontation with the police there are a fair number of bumps, bruises and grazes. But it was the number of serious injuries that really startled me. One man had a fractured pelvis and an Asian boy had to undergo an operation for the removal of his testicles as a result of his injuries. I personally saw 13 serious head injuries in one day – one man lay in a coma for days with a blood clot on his brain. Young girls were coming into the legal advice centre with half their hair shaved off so that wounds could be stitched. *I found it personally sickening. At times it was more like being in a casualty ward than a legal advice centre. But I was struck over the recurrence of head injuries – even after Grosvenor Square, or Red Lion Square, there weren't injuries as serious as those sustained by so many people at Southall.* (Author's italics.)

Blair Peach died from the head injury he received in Southall. He was on his way home when he was trapped by a Special Patrol Group charge down Orchard Road. Parminder Atwal, one of the residents, witnessed the events that followed. This is the statement he made to the press:

Demonstrators were at the top of Beechcroft Road. I decided to move my car in case there was trouble. I was in my garden when two police vans came and about twenty policemen got out. The police were carrying shields and black truncheons. They tried to break up the line of people and came running down the road, pulling people, pulling them by the hair and hitting them with their sticks.

This boy was standing on the corner next to the wall when everybody came running past. He got tangled up in it and was knocked over. Then, when he was lying on the ground, the police came rushing past him as they chased these other blokes down the road. As the police chased past him, one of them hit him on the head with the stick. I was in my garden and I saw this quite clearly.

When they all rushed past he was left sitting against the wall. He tried to get up but he was shivering and looked very strange. He couldn't stand. Then the police came back and told him like this: 'Move! Come on – move!' They were very rough with him and I was shocked because it was clear he was seriously hurt. He managed to get up and try to cross the road. He saw me standing in the garden of my home and he came towards me. He dropped into my garden. I held him and asked my sister to get a glass of water. I gave him the glass but he couldn't hold it.

He couldn't move his hands. His tongue was stuck to his upper jaw and the upper part of his head was all red as if he was bleeding inside. I cradled him in my arms, but I got pretty scared. I could see it was serious. He could not speak. I picked him up and carried him inside by the heater. I put some water in his mouth and he couldn't take it. Somebody else called for an ambulance and I cradled him in my arms until it came.[6]

By the time the ambulance arrived Blair Peach was unconscious. Three hours later he was dead. There were three other witnesses to the scene Parminder Atwal describes – Mr Bhatti, also a resident of Orchard Road and two teachers, both friends of Blair Peach. They made statements to the police and the press that they had seen Blair Peach struck by a member of the Special Patrol Group.

Celia Stubbs, who lived with Blair Peach, was called to Ealing General Hospital to identify his body. As she was about to leave at 3 am, she was approached by two police officers. They asked her to go with them to Southall police station to make a statement. She wanted to go home, she was distressed, but they insisted. They only wanted a short statement, they said, they would not detain her for more than a few minutes.

At Southall police station Celia Stubbs was 'interviewed' for more than an hour by David Powis, Deputy Assistant Commissioner at

Scotland Yard. He cross-questioned her about her relationship to Blair, about her children, about her job, about her movements on that day. Friends who had accompanied her attempted to persuade Powis to stop what was becoming an 'interrogation'. They were bluntly warned to shut up. At 4 am Powis was joined by Commander Cass – Head of the Yard's Complaints Investigation Bureau, who continued the questioning. When Celia asked if she could leave Powis insisted that this 'interview' was essential. *'I must remind you', he said, 'that this is a very serious matter. A man has died. The police are treating this as a murder inquiry.'* (Author's italics.)

The first hearing of the inquest into the death of Blair Peach took place a month later. The police asked the coroner for *a further three months* to complete their investigations. In the week before, the *Daily Mirror* had carried a report by its crime correspondent stating that police had narrowed down their investigations to six officers – all members of the Special Patrol Group. Yet no charges had been brought by the police, no officers had been suspended from duty, not one identity parade had been held. It appeared that the police were not investigating the murder at all but constructing a cover-up operation. That belief was strengthened by the Home Secretary's refusal to hold a public and independent inquiry. A police investigation was, as Paul Holborow, the Anti Nazi League's Secretary put it: 'like Tweedledum investigating Tweedledee.'

The Anti Nazi League launched a campaign against this cover-up and called for the SPG to be disbanded:

> With the Tories in power and the subsequent mounting attacks on trade union organizations and the increase in racist legislation, such as the tightening up of the immigration laws it is clear that the SPG will be required more and more to control opposition to such developments ... Blair Peach's murderer is still at work in the ranks of the SPG. Will you be the next victim of their violence when you go to the picket line at your workplace to defend your job, or your pay or your working conditions? Or if you, like Blair did, go to protest the activities of the National Front or any other fascist or racist organization?

At Blair Peach's funeral, Ken Gill of the General Council of the TUC, called for the disbanding of the Special Patrol Group: 'Everyone of us must take up this call,' he said. Six weeks after Southall the Anti Nazi League broke the news which immeasurably strengthened that call when they published the results of the independent post mortem on Blair Peach, carried out by Professor Keith Mant, Head of Guy's Hospital Department of Forensic Medicine. His conclusions were startling.

Mant found that

> death has resulted from a single heavy blow to the left side of the head ... the instrument used must have been very weighty and yet at the same time was malleable and without a hard edge as there were no lacerations to the scalp ... a police truncheon is relatively light and when used usually lacerates the scalp ... *the instrument used could have been a lead weighted rubber 'cosh', or hosepipe filled with lead shot, or some like weapon.* (Author's italics.)

It could mean only one thing – the SPG officer who murdered Blair Peach had gone to Southall with a weapon specifically designed to inflict serious injury. The police emphatically denied that such weapons were 'authorized'. Yet after the pathologist's report was published, the crime reporters on several national newspapers uncovered the following sequence of events from 'inside sources'.

The evening before the Anti Nazi League released the report on Wednesday 6 June, a member of an SPG unit was secretly detained for questioning at Rochester Row police station. Further, 'SPG offices and locker rooms at Leystonstone and Barnes police stations had been searched as part of the inquiry'.[7] The following day the *Daily Telegraph* reported that police forensic scientists 'were examining items from policemen's lockers. Some items could be described as coshes.'[8] It was confirmed by the *Daily Mirror*: 'A cosh has been found by detectives investigating the death of Anti-Nazi League demonstrator Blair Peach'.[9] The *Daily Express*, which described the coshes as 'Riot Souvenirs' revealed that 'A deputation of colleagues from the SPG went to Scotland Yard yesterday to enquire about the two-day detention of their colleague. They were told it was a matter of routine investigations.'[10]

The following day the SPG officer was released, and suspended from duty, but Scotland Yard stated that this was not in connection with the death of Blair Peach. The officer, according to the *Sunday Express*[11] was PC 'Chalkie' White, and 'officers who raided his locker found a collection of "souvenirs" from previous duties and from America which he had visited as a member of the International Policeman's Association.' Coshes such as described by Professor Mant are issued to American Policemen and are easy to obtain.

Apart from one final news item the press revelations came to an abrupt end at this point. On Sunday the *Mirror*'s Chief Crime Reporter, Norman Lucas,* told his readers:

> I now learn that in addition to a driver of the Yard's Special Patrol Group being questioned and suspended, two police constables and an inspector have been interrogated. The inspector insisted he had a solicitor with him at Rochester Row police station when he was questioned. The suspended PC was a driver of a Special Patrol Group vehicle on the day of a riot.[12]

Before Southall, the Special Patrol Group had already acquired a reputation for violence. It now appeared that members of the group deliberately equipped themselves with lethal weapons for use against demonstrators. The Special Patrol Group went to Southall prepared for a riot – which is one of the principal reasons that there was a riot in Southall on 23 April.

The police 'cover-up' was officially completed in the 'independent' police investigation conducted by Commander Cass which reported to the Director of Public Prosecutions in the late summer of 1979. The DPP announced in early October that the police report did not contain sufficient evidence to enable a prosecution to be brought against any police officer. However, unusually, the DPP did leave the way open to further consideration of this decision if sufficient evidence arose from other, non-police sources. It is, moreover, known that officials at the DPP were most dissatisfied about the police report submitted to them: they felt that there was abundant evidence that Blair Peach had been killed by an SPG officer but the unwillingness of the police to identify that officer within the half-dozen suspects made it impossible to pinpoint the man responsible and to bring charges.†

Long before Southall and the murder of Blair Peach there was a

---

* Some months later Norman Lucas carried out a small public relations exercise on behalf of the Special Patrol Group, when he told his readers: 'Professional agitators are conducting a campaign to brand members of the SPG as a Nazi type unit that uses unnecessary violence and makes indiscriminate arrests. To further the campaign for the disbanding of the SPG agitators at demos have been known to plaster tomato ketchup 'blood' on their faces, then move as close to SPG officers as possible, just for the benefit of the TV cameras. Yet Susan (female SPG member) and her colleagues will tell you that the SPG always ends up with a longer list of injured than do the demonstrators.' (*Sunday Mirror*, 16 September 1979.)

† Whether or not the delayed Coroner's hearing and any subsequent hearings or proceedings lead to a prosecution is not known at the time of going to print in December 1979. However, the substance of the argument in this section on Southall is not altered either way: the facts stand as presented and their serious lesson remains the determination of the police *themselves* to cover up the crime committed by an SPG officer. So far as the police, at least, are concerned, they were above the law in Southall on 23 April 1979.

volume of evidence that the police are capable of using brutal and sometimes fatal methods of getting evidence, in the form of 'confessions'; to intimidate and humiliate, and sometimes simply for revenge. It has been known for police officers to equip themselves with 'unauthorized' weapons, in the knowledge that they can expect a fair degree of immunity when they do so.

In Sheffield in 1963 a newly formed special crime squad, alarmed at a fall in the crime detection rate, snatched six 'suspects' from a pub and used a rhinoceros whip on two of them as a 'lie detector'. One of the constables involved later claimed he carried the whip 'in case of conflicts between coloured informants'. The men were beaten in relays, with the whip and the truncheon, one of them suffering a total of 70 blows. The subsequent inquiry, some months afterwards, was only brought about because of the determined efforts of a local lawyer and a campaign by the local paper. The incident was common knowledge in the local force, yet not one officer felt it necessary to report it and an inspector told the inquiry that 'these things go on fairly frequently don't they'. The inquiry disclosed a wholesale cover-up operation and even fabrication of evidence by several officers.[13]

In 1969, £2,280 damages were awarded against the Cheshire police for physical injury they had caused to workers on strike at the Roberts Arundel factory at Stockport. Three men had been beaten at Stockport police headquarters until they obeyed demands to shout 'Mercy, mercy'. Yet no policeman was prosecuted, suspended or even brought before a disciplinary hearing. During the Fine Tubes strike in Plymouth in 1972 a police assault on pickets injured several workers, who then brought complaints against the police. The police were asked to attend an identification parade for the resulting inquiry. They refused pointblank to do so and their senior officers refused to compel them to participate.[14]

In Leeds in 1971 a detective sergeant and a former detective inspector were jailed for assaulting David Oluwale, a Nigerian immigrant, who was later found dead. The cause of his death was sustained harassment by the Leeds police who had singled him out for 'special treatment'. He had been beaten, kicked and urinated on, and on one occasion driven miles into the countryside and abandoned. It took eighteen months before the offences for which the two policemen were convicted came to light. In the cover-up, police notebooks and other station records had been doctored, which would only be possible with the connivance of several officers. During the trial, several officers said they had seen Oluwale assaulted, but none had seen fit to report this. All sixteen policemen accused of offences in connection with the case remained in the Leeds force.[15]

In 1976, Liddle Towers, a thirty-nine year old electrician died from injuries received when the police set on him outside a Gateshead Club. His doctor, Alan Towney, said, 'I've never seen injuries like them. He had been pulped. He had about forty bruises and seven large abrasions.'[16] Although three eye-witnesses saw police officers kicking Towers as he lay handcuffed on the ground, the police claimed that he received his injuries when one officer accidentally fell on him! The first inquest returned a verdict of 'justifiable homicide', and a second inquest resulted in an equally unsatisfactory verdict of 'misadventure'. The verdict was challenged but the Home Secretary refused to set up an inquiry.

In November 1978, twenty-two year old James McGeown died in Strathclyde 'A' division police station. He had been arrested in Glasgow city centre by two police officers who became suspicious because he was carrying a partially opened suitcase. One of them punched McGeown in the throat and then smashed his head against a wall. McGeown struggled to defend himself and the Strathclyde Support Unit were called to the scene. He was taken to the police station where, with his hands held behind his back in handcuffs, he was actually kicked to death. The blow that killed him split his liver in two. One of the officers involved in the incident, Sergeant Alexander Meechan, was subsequently tried for culpable homicide and found not guilty on the grounds of insufficient evidence. It was an astonishing verdict, because the chief witness for the prosecution was PC Alan Johnson, one of the two officers who had first arrested McGeown. After the trial Johnson said: 'I was so sickened by my experience that I left the police force. Despite the fact that Sergeant Meechan was found not guilty, I could never go back to the police force.' Johnson testified to seeing Meechan deliver two massive kicks to McGeown's body: 'I think you finished him that time,' said Johnson. 'Yes, it's ages since I've been in a good fight. It's a long while since I had a kick at someone,' Meechan replied. Finally, Johnson told the court, another SSU constable, Hugh Dewar, lashed into McGeown shouting 'That's nothing but a bastard!' Dewar said Johnson was wearing steel toecapped boots. Although Johnson's evidence implicated several members of the SSU in kicking a helpless man to death, only one was actually charged.[17]

The police were forced to re-open the case after the trial only because McGeown's family and friends openly challenged the verdict, and organized a campaign in the community, collecting 4,000 signatures for a petition demanding a public inquiry.

It was similar action in Huyton, Liverpool, that first brought the case of Jimmy Kelly to public attention in 1979. Several witnesses saw Kelly set on and beaten by police from the Huyton station, as he walked home from the pub, late on the night of 20 June 1979. Kelly died in police custody and the hastily commissioned report conducted by the police pathologist suggested that the cause of death was a heart attack. Finding no serious injuries, Kelly's family instructed an independent pathologist to conduct a post mortem on their behalf (several they approached refused to take on the case) which established that he had been savagely beaten, that the injuries could have been caused with an iron, bar-like, instrument and that they certainly caused his death. The police were forced to conduct a third post mortem as a result, but Kelly would have been buried without the full facts ever coming to light were it not for, first, a campaign organized in Huyton by his family and friends to demand a public inquiry into the case, and second, the tireless investigations of a local journalist, Rob Rohrer, who was the first to publish details of the Kelly case in the *New Statesman* and who subsequently uncovered a long trail of beatings and brutality suffered by Huyton and Knowsley residents at the hands of the local force.

In only one of these cases was an SPG-style unit involved. Yet all bear the hallmark of behaviour that is associated with the SPG, particularly after the events of Southall: brutality; 'tooling-up' with unauthorized equipment that is designed to cause infinitely more pain and injury than the standard police truncheon; and that sense of 'solidarity' amongst the police which leads to incidents like these being covered in a conspiracy of silence (in only one case, that of James McGeown, was an officer so appalled by what he had seen that he came forward to testify). The victims are always poor or black working class people who live in what the police describe as 'high crime areas' but which are those communities that have borne the most savage effects of crisis and decline.

There are, however, crucial differences between these cases and the case of Southall. First, the Special Patrol Group use violence openly and publicly on the streets and have done so for some considerable time. Second, they use violence not in order to 'fight crime', but for political ends – as a deterrent to protest.

The campaign against the Special Patrol Group gathered widespread support after Blair Peach was murdered. But it was not the first occasion on which people had felt sufficiently concerned about the actions of the SPG to call for it to be disbanded.

Had the police *themselves* taken the step of prosecuting an SPG member for the murder of Blair Peach that campaign would have been immeasurably strengthened. But the Special Patrol Group is central to the role the police play in our society, and it was crucial that the SPG be maintained intact. That is why they are 'beyond the reach of the law', and why the police tried so hard to avoid being forced to account for the murder of Blair Peach.

Solving the 'Worst of all Crimes'*

> ... *the worst of all crimes is the furtherance of political or industrial aims by violence* ...[18]
> Sir Robert Mark

> *I say the government must have a strong body of police* ... *to uphold the law without calling for troops on every occasion: the soldier forms the reserve and should not be the advanced guard.*
> Sir Charles Napier, Commander of the Northern District, at the height of the Chartist Movement between 1839 and 1841.[19]

A month after Blair Peach was killed, TUC General Secretary Len Murray gave a talk to police cadets at the Metropolitan Police training centre at Hendon. He called for the Special Patrol Group to be disbanded and campared its activities to those of the CRS in France. 'There are dangers of using a mobile reserve of this kind,' he added, 'and I hope they are recognized by the police.'[20]

Fortunately the Special Patrol Group is a pale shadow of the 15,000 strong Compagnie Republicaine de Sécurité, a rigorously drilled, highly efficient and ruthless force. When ordered onto the streets of Paris in May 1968, they killed five demonstrators in six weeks and injured 1,500 in a single night. The CRS are a 'third force', brought into action in situations beyond the control of the police and an intermediate step to calling in the army.

There is no 'third force' between the police and the army in Britain.

* I am grateful for the assistance of the *State Research* group whilst researching this section.

Instead the Special Patrol Group is being developed to fulfil the functions of such a force and is now an experienced paramilitary unit within the police force.

Over a hundred years ago, Britain's Liberal Prime Minister William Gladstone wrote: 'We have got to govern millions of hard hands and it must be done by force, fraud or goodwill.'[21] In Britain the state has relied on goodwill (albeit liberally seasoned with fraud) with force kept in reserve for exceptional situations, such as the dockers strike in 1912, Tonypandy, or the 1919 police strike. Alongside that concept of governing, British policing has always been based on the idea that the police act with the consent of the community to enforce the law. T.A. Critchley, a police historian, writes that 'the British idea of the police' has always depended on public approval. 'So long as the police are unarmed and have few powers not available to the ordinary citizen, they are compelled to rely not on the exercise of oppressive authority, but on public support.'[22]

Government through goodwill, or policing through consent, was a viable policy during a period of calm and economic stability, such as Britain saw in the fifties and early sixties. Thus the Royal Commission on the Police in 1962 found 'that there is a peculiar quality in the relationship between the police and the public of this country ... It is attested by the foreign visitors whose favourable comments on our police are well known, and it is demonstrated in the common everyday instances in which people instinctively consult a policeman when in difficulty or perplexity even of a minor kind ... It is not generally disputed that there is a kind of relationship between the policeman and the man in the street in this country which is of the greatest value.'[23]

The same conclusions could not be drawn today; the popular image of the 'friendly bobby on the beat' has collapsed under growing evidence of the violent and sometimes fatal methods now used by the police, most acutely apparent in Britain's major cities. The last decade has seen radical changes in the police.* Not only are their specialist functions far more highly developed, there is also a growing militarization of the force – between 1970 and 1972 the police were

---

* A startling example of how attitudes in the police are changing can be found in a police training manual written by Kenneth Sloan, Training Officer for the Greater Manchester Police Force. He concludes his discussion on riot control with the following paragraphs: 'The last word is given to the officer, who must remain anonymous, who offered an alternative solution for the control of rioting mobs. He said simply: "All you have to do is spray them with machine gun bullets".'[25] William Whitelaw, now Home Secretary, wrote the introduction to this pamphlet, which he described as an 'admirable booklet'.

issued with guns on 5,244 occasions; between 1975 and 1978 they were issued with guns on 14,574 occasions. One in every three policemen in London is trained to kill. And the priorities of policing are changing. In the words of Sir Robert Mark, ex-Chief Commissioner of the Metropolitan Police, the highest police post in the land:

> ... crime is never likely to be more than the conventional costly nuisance it is today and terrorism as today, is in reality a comparatively insignificant issue. Freedom (to operate) and public order, in the widest sense, must be the priorities for the police of tomorrow.[24]

Changes like these do not come about in isolation. They developed in response to the acute crisis of the early seventies when dissent reached new heights and 'goodwill' broke down. The ruling class faced a serious challenge to its authority and new means of controlling society were sought.

Economic Crisis and Industrial Struggle

At the beginning of the seventies Britain was swept by a wave of industrial struggle more bitter and prolonged than any since the war. It followed on the radical student and anti-Vietnam War movement which had brought thousands onto the streets in Britain, and it was provoked by the onset of a severe recession in the economy. Unemployment soared, so did the cost of living and thousands of workers took action to defend their living standards and their jobs. They came into head-on conflict with a government that was determined to curb, if not crush the power of the trade unions. During its four years in office, the last Conservative Government under Edward Heath, was forced to declare a State of Emergency on five occasions, each time in response to a national strike: the dockers' strikes of July 1970 and 1972; the electricity workers' strike in December 1970, and the miners' strikes in February 1972 and 1973-74.

1972 saw the highest total of working days lost through stoppages since the war – almost 24 million and twice the 1970 figure. Only once in British history was the number of strike days greater – in 1919. The first national miners' strike since 1926 was victorious. Building workers staged their biggest ever strike – 300,000 were out for over twelve weeks. Nor were the strikes solely concerned with wage claims;

there were strikes against redundancies, against victimizations, and there was a purely political strike to free the 'Pentonville Five'. There was a strike of 50,000 engineers in Birmingham in support of the miners in 1972 and the previous year over 200,000 workers joined a solidarity strike for the Upper Clyde Shipbuilders work-in. There were strikes in support of old-age pensioners for the first time ever – 6,000 construction workers came out at the Anchor site near Scunthorpe.[26] Dozens of factory occupations took place, the most famous being the UCS work-in, in support of which the trade union movement collected over half a million pounds.

Workers successfully challenged and defied the power of the law and the courts by taking on the 1971 Industrial Relations Act, which the Tories rushed through Parliament in a desperate attempt to control the unions, but which even the employers considered an ineffective if not an inflammatory means of coping with the situation. The big ones – Leyland, ICI, Ford would not touch it. The reasons were obvious even before the Industrial Relations Act became law and were pointed out by the representative of the Shipbuilding Employers Federation in evidence to the Donovan Commission:

> I do not see how you are going to make a sanction work. You cannot just put 5,000 strikers in jail and if you fine them and they do not pay the fine, what are you going to do? I do not see how this would work out in practice, unless everyone observed the law voluntarily. If people kick over the traces in large numbers the law is helpless ...[27]

It was not only the militancy and the strength of the movement that concerned the authorities – new tactics were being developed in pursuit of wage claims, but with much wider implications. The flying pickets were the best example of this. Delegations of workers travelled the country to close down sites, factories and depots in order to win their strikes, the most famous example, being the miners and the building workers. This led to a decision in 1973 that the police would be used to try and stop the flying pickets *en route*. As Robert Carr, then the Home Secretary, put it, 'We want to stop the masses forming to start with.'[28] It was the miners' victory in closing down the Saltley depot in their 1972 strike that prompted that and several other decisions on the role the police should play. It is worth remembering the experience of Saltley, for that very reason. Arthur Scargill, the Yorkshire miners' leader, who played a central role in organizing the

Saltley Gate picket, later recalled the experience in an interview:*

They (the senior police officers) said to us that we could only have twelve people on the picket line, and we said 'no we're having all the pickets that we've got and more besides.' So it was obvious there was a confrontation in the air. ...

... If I tell you we had 180 arrested, it gives you some idea. I was black and blue. They were punching with their heels into the crowd, they were hitting with elbows. They were in the crowds with plain clothes on – a copy of the *Morning Star* in one pocket and The *Workers Press* in the other shouting: 'Shove the bastards!' and as soon as you did you were arrested. They had telescopic lenses on top of the buildings, filming the incidents all the time, they had police officers changing their uniforms each day with different numbers on them so you couldn't identify them. No question about this, its quite true ... In spite of assurances from the police that there would be no violence they were really putting the boot in. The lads who were embarrassed on that picket line were in two parts: the ones who were local Birmingham police didn't like what was happening at all. That's a fact. *But we had an even more embarrassed set of police officers – the ones who had originated from Yorkshire, and who had previously been miners. They were really upset. They said: 'Look we don't mind fighting troublemakers in football crowds or hooligans on the streets; but we're not happy about dishing it out to boys we've worked alongside with in the most appalling conditions underground.' There were a handful of them. They certainly didn't do a lot to implement their own police instructions; but the boys who were brought in, the heavy brigade, they really did. These blokes in white steel helmets who came were supposedly motorcyclists, but without actual motorcycles, and with heavy jackboots on.* (Author's italics.) They were marching them down, seventy at a time, and they were changing them every hour. Seventy marching down like stormtroopers, you could see them on both sides. Then they started to bring them down every half hour to intimidate. I yelled through my megaphone: 'We've got them on the run, lads, they can only last half an hour now instead of an hour' ...

... And then over the hill came a banner and I've never in my life seen as many people following a banner. As far as the eye could see it was just a mass of people marching towards Saltley ... They were coming from five directions ... I heard the police talking – Sir Derek Capper was one – the tactic was simple: get the pickets coming from the east to go through to the west and get the pickets from the west – the striking engineers – to

* We acknowledge with gratitude permission to quote extensively from this interview in *New Left Review* (July-August 1975).

go through to the east. I got this megaphone and I'm yelling like hell: 'When you get to the picket line, Stop! Stop!', they were trying to tell me to shut up and I said 'You try today, no bloody shutting up today. These boys are coming to our picket line.' And they were piling up like sandwich cake, as far as the eye could see they were just pouring in, Saltley was now just a mass of human beings arriving from all over, with banners: The only time this crowd opened was when a delegation of girls from a women's factory came along all dressed in bright white dresses. They plunged through and one of the lads shouts: 'Go on officer, tell them they can't come. Try and hold them.' And no police officer moved. Who'd have dared to try and stop those girls coming into that square? Nobody. The crowd was absolutely dense by this time ... Everybody was chanting something different. Some were chanting 'Heath Out', 'Tories Out', 'Support the Miners', 'General Strike', a hundred slogans were being chanted. I got hold of the megaphone and I started to chant through it: 'Close the gates! Close the gates!' and it was taken up just like a football crowd. It was booming through Saltley. 'Close the gates'. And Capper, the Chief Constable of Birmingham, took a swift decision. He said 'Close the gates' and they swung them to. Hats were in the air, you've never seen anything like it in your life. Absolute delirium on the part of the people who were there ... I gave a political speech to that mass of people and told them that it was the greatest victory of the working class in my lifetime ... *Here was the living proof that the working class had only to flex its muscles and it could bring government, employers and society to a total standstil!. I know the fear of Birmingham on the part of the ruling class. The fear was that what happened in Birmingham could happen in every city in Britain.* (Author's italics). Had that occurred in every city in Britain that would have produced a whole new concept in what was after all a wage battle as far as the miners were concerned.[29]

Precisely. For the Conservative Government, the police chiefs, and the heads of the armed forces, Saltley was the stuff of which nightmares are made. Saltley forced the ruling class to re-examine its means of control and both the army and the police were found wanting. An illustration of the atmosphere during these years is provided by recalling the discussion of private armies that followed the defeat of the Tories in 1974. There was 'GB75', a secret volunteer organization trained to take over factories, power stations and essential services in the event of a strike, set up by Colonel David Stirling, founder of the Special Air Service (SAS) units. A similar body, 'Unison', was formed by General Sir Walter Walker. After the fall of the Conservative Government, one of its Ministers, Geoffrey Rippon, called for a Citizens Voluntary reserve to be formed because

... at a time when the foundations of our society are being shaken by violence and extremism we must take steps to ensure the maintenance of order. A Conservative Government must provide for an adequate level of reserves and for the strengthening of the Territorials, and strengthen the police and create a Citizens' Voluntary Reserve for home defence and duties in aid of the civil power.[30]

In the same spirit a group of Conservative MPs, including Jill Knight, Angus Maude and Airey Neave wrote to Mr Heath and Sir Keith Joseph, then Shadow Home Secretary, advocating a force of volunteers to aid the police.[31]

But private armies were far from the solution the authorities had sought. One of the leading experts in counter-insurgency, Major General Sir Richard Clutterbuck, gave an insight into mainstream thinking when he argued that such forces would not only be useless because they would not have the expertise to run essential services in the event of a general strike, but that using them would only serve to increase the confrontation:

> Pouring 100,000 of General Sir Walter Walker's and Colonel David Stirling's volunteers into the power stations, pumping stations, transport depots and docks in a time of national crisis would achieve less than nothing if it drove another million (or conceivably ten million) out of the gate ... Neither military nor volunteer labour can ever break a general strike, though they could easily provoke one. General Walker is God's gift to all militants.[32]

The 'Third Force'

Overriding even these considerations was the fact that a private army even if it was on the 'right' side, was an unacceptable means of maintaining control simply because it falls outside the direct control of the state, and also unnecessary since the state was already equipped with contingency plans for dealing with widespread disorder, even to the point of insurrection. In *The Political Police in Britain* Tony Bunyan describes the

> National Security plan ... formulated over a number of years to tackle anything from a temporary outbreak of disorder in one city or region to a more prolonged confrontation. Contingency plans cover a strike limited to one or two essential services; a general strike; insurrection in one or more regions; and finally a general insurrection over a large area of the country

(e.g. Scotland and the North of England) under a unified command of the military, the police and the administration at regional and national level.[33]

During the winter of 1973-74 contingency plans existed, according to Brigadier W.F.K. Thompson, then Military Correspondent for the *Daily Telegraph* and a member of the Institute for the Study of Conflict, for

> use of troops in the event of a national emergency arising from strikes in key industries such as coal, the docks and transport ... (which) include the use of armed forces in an internal security role and as a substitute for civilian labour. The former could include helping the police deal with illegal picketing and providing escort for transport drivers and others engaged in carrying out essential services.[34]

Yet all these are extreme solutions – last resorts which also have the potential of escalating the conflict, as Clutterbuck predicted. His conclusions may have been based on the experience of the 1945-50 Labour Government, which called in the troops to break strikes on ten occasions. In all but two, their use provoked such outrage amongst trade unionists that the strikes spread.

Using the troops to break strikes by running essential services is one thing; sending troops into street battles with mass pickets altogether another. The problem after Saltley was not how to keep the economy running in the event of widespread strikes, but how to stop mass pickets achieving their objectives without actually opening fire on them.

Saltley showed that the police were not prepared for that task. Shortly afterwards Brigadier Brian Watkins of the Army General Staff wrote:

> The whole period of the miners' strike has made us realize that the present size of the police force is too small. It is based on the fundamental philosophy that we are in a law-abiding country. But things have now got to the state where there are not enough resources to deal with the increasing numbers who are not prepared to respect the law.[35]

But police inability to stop the mass picket was not merely a question of numbers. They were beaten at Saltley because they were not trained or equipped to break up a massive crowd of determined and angry engineers, miners and other workers. A paramilitary unit, like the French CRS, might have been able to do so but at that time the only other force in Britain that could have been used was the army. Troops were being held in reserve at Saltley, equipped with riot shields and truncheons but they were never used and it is not difficult to see why.

After Saltley the creation of a 'third force' – a paramilitary unit to back-up the police – was discussed anew. The formation of such a body had previously been discussed and rejected. As early as 1961 a Home Office Working Party was formed to investigate the need for a 'third separate policing force'. It recommended, ten years later 'that the British public would not support the creation of a paramilitary force and that the existing police forces should be re-trained and re-equipped to fill the gaps that existed'.[36] 'The strongest argument in favour of a third force,' say the authors of *State Research*, 'was that it would relieve the conventional police of their aggressive role and enable them to maintain friendly relations with the public. Against this the continental experience demonstrated that riot police generated more hatred and counter violence than ordinary police.'[37]

In the wake of the miners' strike and the confrontation at Saltley the National Security Committee (NSC) was created.[38] It drew together representatives of the military, the intelligence services, the police, the Home Office and the Department of Trade and Industry. Its task was to prepare for emergency situations and 'a possible internal threat to the security of the state'. According to *State Research*, the NSC also discussed the creation of a paramilitary unit and

> reached the same conclusions as the Home Office Working Party, largely because the police argued vociferously against the creation of a new force ... The National Security recommendations went beyond those of the working party; the police should revamp training in riot control and firearms, and clear lines should be laid down about when the army was to be called in; joint police-military exercises should be held regularly and plainclothes units of the Special Air Service should be on permanent standby for any situation the police could not handle.[39]

The SPG Comes of Age

Those recommendations were put into practice with the re-organization of the Special Patrol Group, which effectively became a third force within the police force. The SPG had been formed seven years earlier, under a Labour Government, allegedly as a squad that could better control rising crime and vandalism on London's decaying housing estates than the local police, although, in the words of a senior police officer, 'The Special Patrol Group was set up as an elite force.

But after a short time the people at the top got cold feet and brought them back under control'.[40] It was a highly mobile unit that could be rushed into an area to 'saturate' trouble spots within minutes; that and the special training and discipline such a unit receives made the SPG a suitable candidate for adaption into an anti-riot, paramilitary unit. It was already experienced in 'public order', the field in which it was to develop a specialization, having been used during the Grosvenor Square demonstration in 1968, and again in 1969 when it was part of a police-military contingent sent into Anguilla in the West Indies to put down a movement for independence.

Today the SPG consists of 204 officers, divided into six units, with each unit having 3 sergeants, 28 male PCs and 2 female PCs under the command of an Inspector. A Chief Superintendent is in overall charge of the SPG. The SPG thus has its own independent command structure – the A.9 Branch at Scotland Yard – and for this reason they wear the letters CO (Commissioners Office) on their shoulders.

Since its formation, SPG recruits have been drawn from volunteers from the London police divisions. Last year there were three volunteers for each place. Their average age is 31 and many have ten years service or more. The turnover rate is however high – currently around 25 per cent a year. This is partly due to the unsocial hours the work entails (they are always on call 24 hours a day for an emergency) and partly because service in the group is limited to two years.

Each of the six units has three blue Ford Transit vans and a number of unmarked cars for surveillance. The Transits carry 12 officers, one of these being the driver and another the radio operator. The vans have two radio channels, one the general Metropolitan police wavelength, the other specifically for the SPG. The driver and the radio operator are responsible for issuing arms or other equipment. As *State Research*, put it:

> To deny that they are a para-military force ... also flies in the face of the evidence. A Southern Television hour-long documentary put out in 1976, called 'The Man in the Middle', showed SPG training exercises and equipment. At their main training centre, near the River Lea in East London, they were shown practising the 'wedge' (to break up demonstrations) unarmed combat and the use of riot shields and CS gas. The programme also showed the equipment carried by a fully-equipped SPG Transit van. These included riot shields, pistols, rifles, sub-machine guns, smoke grenades, truncheons and visors.[41]

One of the key men behind the revamping of the Special Patrol Group was the Deputy Assistant Commissioner responsible for Public Order, John Gerrard, who had been appointed superintendent of the Group when it was formed. In 1971 Gerrard had attended the US Police National Academy in Atlanta, Georgia, where, together with other police chiefs he examined riot control techniques and the use of paramilitary forces.* The other key man was Robert Mark, appointed Chief Commissioner of the Metropolitan Police in April 1972. Mark joined the Metropolitan Police in 1967 and had been involved in preparations for the Vietnam demonstration the following year, remembering it for having exposed 'critical weaknesses in our resources for surveillance and communication.'[43] In 1969 he was sent to Northern Ireland by the then Home Secretary James Callaghan, on the night that troops went in. His brief was to study the Royal Ulster Constabulary and the B Specials, as a member of the Advisory Committee set up under Lord Hunt to investigate policing in Northern Ireland. His experience led him to observe that 'Policing in a free society depends on a real measure of public approval and consent. This has never been obtained by military or paramilitary means.'[44]

The following year he was appointed to the Ministry of Defence Working Party set up to review the army's policies in respect of aid to the civil power. In the company of former SAS 22 Division Commander, Major General Anthony Deans Drummond (author of *Riot Control*), and Lt. Colonel Bastick, Mark, in his own words 'travelled the world first class at the expense of the Ministry of Defence' visiting Lancashire, Ulster, Berlin, Paris, the USA, Canada, Rome, Singapore, Hong Kong, Tokyo, Cyprus and Holland. The working party report recommended no changes in existing relationships between the army and the police in Britain, but Mark found the exercise 'valuable in affording an insight into police methods elsewhere'.[45]

In February 1971 Mark joined Home Office and Ministry of Defence representatives on a 'Special committee to co-ordinate the use of police and troops in the event of civil disorder in Britain (which) has started meeting in London.'[46] By the time he was appointed he must

* ' ... In view of the growing subversion, mounting terrorism and violence against citizens, and the rapidly expanding population, it is essential that the training programme which brings military and police personnel from other hemisphere nations to the United States be continued and strengthened ... The United States should respond to requests for assistance of the police by providing them with the essential tools to do their job.' (Nelson Rockefeller, 8 December 1969.)[42]

have had considerable first hand knowledge both of the operation of paramilitary units and of the ongoing discussion of police-army co-operation. Between 1971 and 1975 there was a series of joint exercises, seminars and conferences with the consistent theme of preparation for a serious confrontation or widespread disorder. Mark saw the police as 'very much on their own in attempting to preserve order in an increasingly turbulent society'.[47] But at the same time they were developing much closer links with the military and in a position to utilize much of its experience in that field.*

It was during Mark's first years as Commissioner that the Special Patrol Group were prepared for their new role, with Gerrard taking responsibility for their reorganization, training and equipment. Mark later wrote in a significant passage:

> Some of the tactics adopted by the London police, and later by other forces were those developed and used by the army and the RUC SPG in Northern Ireland. The introduction of 'snatch squads' and 'wedges' in demonstrations, and random stop and searches and roadblocks on the streets were based on the Army's experience in Ulster.[49]

In April 1972 a sixth and final unit was added to the Special Patrol Group. Robert Mark's first annual report as Commissioner made explicit their new role. Two units had been sent to carry out 'protection duty at London airport' for two months. One unit was permanently assigned, from October 1972 to guarding embassies in the centre of London; special attention was given to drugs; and units of the group 'also acted as a reserve at demonstrations at which militant elements were thought to cause disorder, and in particular assisted police in the protracted industrial disputes involving dockers and building workers.'[50]

But neither the re-organization of the Special Patrol Group, nor the

---

* Mark's autobiography provides an insight into how smoothly these links operate with his account of the decision to send the Special Patrol Group and the army into operation at Heathrow in 1974: 'Late in the afternoon of Friday 4 January John Gerrard ... called on me with the Head of Special Branch. ... It appeared that there was a possibility that terrorists had undertaken a reconnaissance of Heathrow and that they might be in possession of one or two ground-to-air missiles.' Mark decided the army must be called in, then 'I tried to reach the Home Secretary and Permanent Under Secretary, but without success. I had no better luck with the Minister of Defence. There was nothing else for it but to cross the Rubicon. I asked the GSOI of London District to get the GOC's agreement to move troops into Heathrow by the first light on the following morning and he readily agreed. During the night we managed to find the Home Secretary who gave us his blessing.'[48]

consequences of its operations as an armed and highly mobile squad became public knowledge until the India House shootings in 1973. On 15 February 1973, two Pakistani workers from Bradford, Basharat Hussain and Mohammed Hanif Hussain, both aged 19, 'invaded' the Indian High Commission with toy pistols as part of a religious protest. Within minutes they were dead, shot by PC Stanley Conley and PC George Burrows of the SPG. They were not asked to throw down their 'guns' and they were not warned that they would be shot if they did not do so. Conley later told an interviewer 'I could tell by the look in his eyes that he was going to fire. We are trained to watch their eyes'.[51] The two police constables became heroes overnight with the press largely sympathetic to their actions and Home Secretary Robert Carr was joined by his Shadow Cabinet opposite number James Callaghan in praising the SPG's immediate action. Parliament, which must have been taken as much by surprise as anyone else by the existence of this crack squad, its new role never having been reported to, or discussed in, the House of Commons, chose to attack the sale of toy pistols as the most dangerous practice to emerge from the incident.[52] In the *Political Police in Britain*, Tony Bunyan puts the one 'crucial question' that was not asked at the time:

> ... what would have happened if armed policemen had not been instantly available as would have been the case a few years ago? Presumably the streets would have been cleared and entreaties made to the 'gunmen' to give themselves up. Given that these 'dangerous gunmen' were in fact two young and frightened men, who can doubt they might have emerged unhurt? But no attempt was made to talk to them, to discover they were not 'guerrilla terrorists' − there was no time. In just four minutes they were dead.[53]

The Special Patrol Group continued to be responsible for guarding embassies and high commissions in central London up until November 1974 when this task was taken over by the newly-formed Diplomatic Protection Group. They were also used to back up the Bomb Squad (now the Anti-Terrorist Squad) during the IRA bombings in London in 1973 and in other 'anti-terrorist' activities, such as the joint police-army exercises at Heathrow the following year. According to Scotland Yard the Special Patrol Group were first armed for 'the protection of foreign embassies',[54] but they remained armed after that duty was transferred to the DPG. And after the Balcombe Street siege in 1975, in which the crack marksmen unit, D-

11, was used for the first time, it was clear that the SPG were but one amongst a growing number of armed police squads. They still act as back up to these specialized units, but have developed their own specialization in the field of 'public order', and in policing the black communities (or 'high crime' areas in the police phrase), and it is here that they have made their mark in the years following their re-organization.

They have been either in front line or held in reserve at every major strike and political demonstration during the last six years. In the summer of 1972 they were called in to South London to break up an occupation by Briants Colour Printing workers. In July they were used against picket lines at Robert Horne's warehouse, where London dockers and print workers were protesting against the use of scab labour: 'In mid afternoon the SPG moved in, using truncheons against the picket of printers and dockers and throwing middle-aged women against a wall and beating up anyone who fell into their hands. Even the local police officers who normally patrol the pickets were astonished at the behaviour of the "heavy mob".'[55] In August they joined a force gathered from other counties to stop a mass picket of dockers from Hull, Grimsby and Goole at the Neap House Wharves in Scunthorpe. There they used 'road blocks and searches, snatch squads, Special Branch photographers to identify militants and random arrests.'[56] In 1973, barely a month after India House, they attacked a May Day March. Micky Fenn, a Royal Docks Shop Steward, recalled the incident: 'Without warning or reason they grabbed two London dockers, Charles Alexander and George Scott from the middle of that march and charged them with assault and threatening behaviour. Each got three months and £60 fines. Just by chance, these men had been amongst the active pickets at Pentonville prison the previous year.'[57]

The Death of Kevin Gately

It was in 1974 however, that the Special Patrol Group again hit the headlines, once again in connection with a killing. In July 1974 Warwick University student Kevin Gately died during a Special Patrol Group charge into an anti-National Front demonstration at Red Lion Square. One of the demonstrators, Alex Callinicos, shortly afterwards described the events leading up to the entry of the SPG:

We approached the Square peacefully and orderly chanting slogans against the Front and its racialist policies. We entered it to find 500 police – at least 25 mounted – drawn up in front of the (Conway) Hall. The march turned right to await the Front. Then a scuffle broke out between the police and a group immediately in front of our contingent. Batons drawn, the police kicked and punched their way through the march, trying to cut it in half. Demonstrators still entering the square found themselves attacked as they did so. In self-defence we were forced to link arms and fight back. The police, in danger of being overwhelmed, rushed in reinforcements from Special Patrol Group vans parked nearby.[58]

There were no witnesses to the blow which had killed Kevin Gately, established by the pathologist to have been inflicted by a 'round-tipped instrument, travelling at considerable velocity and clipping the six foot seven demonstrator behind the ear.'[59] The inquest into his death returned a verdict of misadventure, despite the fact that the police evidence, presented by Commander John Gerrard, was contradictory on one crucial point – whether Gately's body had been found before or after the SPG charge. One witness, Margaret Forely told the court that she had seen two policemen kneeling on the unconscious man's chest and heard one of them shout 'have you calmed down now'.[60] The resultant public inquiry, headed by Lord Scarman came no closer to establishing how Gately had died, but the Special Patrol Group were widely held to be responsible. *Socialist Worker*, one of the few newspapers which blamed the SPG for the death, was visited by Commander Habershorn and told to 'shut up'.[61]

Robert Mark viewed the inquiry as expedient, but expressed nothing but contempt for most of the participants. 'It is at times like this that a commissioner really earns his pay,' he later wrote:

His men are smarting both from physical injury and from unscrupulous, politically motivated liars. A weak minority government is hanging onto office by its eyelashes unable to run the risk of offending its extreme left in case it should bring it down. Nothing is more certain than that an inquiry will be held if only to placate criticism and defuse the situation. The inquest will clearly not be sufficient because it will be confined to inquiring into the death. *From a police point of view nothing could be worse than to appear to have an inquiry imposed upon the force.* There remains only one sensible course of action, to get in first and to demand an inquiry, though well aware that it will almost certainly be a waste of time, money and manpower. This is in fact what we did and precisely what happened. Lord Justice Scarman sat for a total of twenty-seven days to establish with infinite patience and courtesy, notwithstanding the ill manners of some of the participants, that Kevin Gately had met his death by misadventure and that the International Marxist Group were primarily to blame for it because they had deliberately attacked the police. It is a great pity that the proceedings could not have been televised. It was a field day for the lawyers. Those representing the Warwick University Students' Union and the National Union of Students were paid £9,582, the Liberation lawyers were paid £9,563. Even the representatives of the International Marxist Group received £8,277 with the National Front coming last with a modest £6,270. All these sums were paid from the Metropolitan Police Fund, or, in other words, by the ratepayer and taxpayer. The judge approved them as reasonable, but happily in this country it is open to every citizen to disagree. One quarter of these sums would in my view, have been gross over-payment. The only tangible effect of the inquiry was to relieve an embarrassed government of harassment by its own extremists. It had no effect for the police at all, other than to waste a great deal of time and money.[62]

On the contrary. The police almost certainly agreed to an inquiry because they were confident, following the inquest, that there was insufficient evidence to implicate them directly with the death of Kevin Gately. And whatever Mark claimed the facts of Red Lion Square were simply that Gately died because the police launched an onslaught against the demonstrators. Yet they emerged from the inquiry exonerated from all blame. The Special Patrol Group had gained a 'licence' to use extreme violence to maintain 'law and order', and could expect immunity from the consequences.

After the Scarman inquiry Mark felt sufficiently confident of public opinion of the police to declare that the fines imposed by the courts 'for violence at disputes and demonstrations' were 'derisory and a positive encouragement to the unruly' to the extent that it was scarcely worth prosecuting. The statement had the desired effect — 'the penalties for violence and hooliganism in central London rose dramatically.'[63]

It is worth remembering that this sequence of events was set in motion because the police were determined to protect the activities of a tiny and viciously racist organization whose policies lead to violent attacks and even the murder of black people. Yet it was those who opposed the National Front who were labelled 'extremist', and it was their right to express that opposition which was attacked, and not only through the imposition of much harsher sentences for demonstrators. After Kevin Gately died at Red Lion Square it was clear that anyone who joined an anti-NF demonstration risked rather more than a heavy fine, should the Special Patrol Group be in attendance. However, if it was intended as a deterrent it was ineffective. In the years after Red Lion Square, opposition to the National Front swelled. Increasing numbers took to the streets in protest at their marches and their meetings. Ever larger numbers of police were mobilized to protect the National Front with force more often than not, especially if the Special Patrol Group was in attendance.

Grunwick

1977 saw the police develop their proficiency in riot-control a stage further when riot shields modelled on those used by the army in Northern Ireland, appeared on the streets of Britain for the first time – in Lewisham that August. The year had begun with a large anti-fascist demonstration. In spite of a massive police mobilization, plus units of the SPG, counter-demonstrators attacked a National Front march in Wood Green, North London, and at one point almost stopped it. And that summer the Grunwick strike became a major political issue.

The strike had begun in August 1976 when 150 Asian workers, mainly women, went on strike at the Grunwick film processing laboratory in West London for the right to join a trade union and to improve what were virtually nineteenth century working conditions laced with a strong dose of racialism.

They found they were not only up against their own dedicatedly anti-union employer, George Ward, but that their strike was seen as a test case for those sections of the establishment who shared his views. The National Association for Freedom, a vociferously right wing organization whose members then included Keith Joseph, Robert Moss and Brian Crozier (both the latter were connected with the CIA and both have advocated the creation of a paramilitary force in Britain), threw itself into a vigorous campaign on behalf of George Ward in particular, and 'law and order' in general. Even the 'liberal' press sided with Ward – *The Times* declared in its editorial columns that businesses like Grunwicks 'could not have come into existence ... if they did not have a competitive edge, and the only edge they could have is low labour costs and a willing labour force not restricted by trades union attitudes.'[64]

For trade unionists the issue at stake at Grunwick went beyond the right of workers to join a trade union – the right to picket in defence of that aim was also being denied. From the start of the strike the police displayed a determination to prevent successful picketing that defies any claim to impartiality on their part. Robert Mark retired as Commissioner during the Grunwick strike, although he made it abundantly clear where his sympathies lay when he referred in his autobiography to George Ward, as 'an Anglo-Indian running a small business (who) has courageously and successfully stood firm against politically motivated violence in the streets.'[65] Successfully, yes, but scarcely single-handedly. Robert Mark saw to that. He does not call into question, as he did over the Red Lion Square inquiry, the amount of taxpayers money that must have been spent to ensure that one employer could refuse recognition to a trade union, even though an official inquiry, also under Lord Scarman, recommended he cease to do so. Mark recalls with 'particular pleasure' receiving an invitation to join the Board of the Phoenix Assurance Company, as soon as his retirement was announced. Coincidentally Lord de L'Isle, Chairman of the Phoenix Board, was also Chairman of the National Association for Freedom at that time.[66]

Robert Mark was succeeded by Sir David McNee, whose activities as Chief Constable of the Strathclyde force, the second largest in the country, had earned him the nickname of 'The Hammer'. McNee had already gained considerable experience in the field that was to demand much of his attention. He had developed the role played by Strathclyde's version of the Special Patrol Group, the Strathclyde Support Unit, and had also masterminded the joint police-army operations to break strikes in Glasgow by firemen and dustmen.

When the first mass picket was held at Grunwick on 13 June 1977 McNee sent in the SPG. They remained on duty at Grunwick for the next month, up until the largest of the mass pickets on 11 July. The first mass picket was repeatedly charged by the police, to clear a path for the bus carrying the strikebreakers. Dozens were injured and over a hundred arrested, including Labour MP Audrey Wise and Arthur Scargill. The SPG grabbed people out of the crowd at random and singled out members of the strike committee for special treatment. Len Gristey, a London Regional officer of APEX, the trade union involved in the recognition disputes saw them snatch hold of Mahmood Ahmed, secretary of the Strike Committee: 'They grabbed Mahmood and kicked and punched him hard. They'd obviously wanted him especially. They took him round the side of the police coaches to boot him in.'[67]

Jo Richardson MP told the press that in years of supporting such disputes she had never seen such open intimidation and brutality from the police as at Grunwick.[68] After that mass picket the strike committee held a press conference. On the platform was Maria Duggan, a 25 year-old case worker for the Pregnancy Advisory Service, who arrived on crutches with her foot and leg bandaged. She had been at the back of the factory when the strike breakers' bus went through. She told the Press Conference: 'I linked arms with my friends and tried to move forward to talk to the workers on the bus. Suddenly the SPG men got out of their vans and hurled themselves on us. One of them kicked me on the shin and then dragged me to the ground. The pain was so excruciating that I was vomiting.'[69] Mary Davis, a lecturer in history at Tottenham College of Technology was in a wheelchair with both feet and one leg bandaged. 'The SPG rushed at us like animals,' she said. 'It looked as if they were picking on women and smaller men. I was dragged out by one of them and my shoes came off. They stamped on my feet several times.' The bones in her feet were fractured as a result.[70]

Some months later the Newsreel Collective film crew witnessed the Special Patrol Group wading into pickets at Grunwick and filmed them in action. Chris Thomas, one of the film crew described it as follows: 'For three minutes you can see them wading in, chasing people through gardens, pulling them out of crowds by their hair, thrusting them against walls, with such force that the walls come down!'[71] The film was shown to the ACTT Executive who decided that it should be shown to the TUC General Council and demanded a Home Office inquiry into the SPG. In 1978 the TUC Annual Conference passed a resolution calling for a public inquiry into the activities of the SPG, but this demand was ignored. When questioned in the House of Commons about police conduct at Grunwick, the Labour Home Secretary, Merlyn Rees, gave the following reply:

> It is not my decision and not a decision I would attempt to influence about who should be allowed to be there (on the picket line) at all. It is a matter for the Commissioner of Police. When asked to support the police I support the Commissioner taking his decision.[72]

Thus the elected Minister with responsibility for the police, and in this case for the handling of a strike which had won the support of the entire labour movement, abdicated responsibility to the unelected Commissioner of police. Mrs Jayaben Desai, Treasurer of the Strike

Committee, also experienced at first hand the freedom the police had been given to interpret the law as they wished. When Merlyn Rees himself visited the picket line, she recalls

> I went up to him and complained that the police were denying us the right to talk to the strike breakers in the bus. In front of the police chiefs he replied that I did indeed have such a right. So I asked him to wait for the bus and see the right enforced. But he wouldn't. He left. When the bus came the police refused to let us speak to the strikebreakers.[73]

There is one other conclusion to be drawn from the experiences of that strike. Twenty thousand trade unionists, from across the country, responded to the TUC's call for a mass picket on 11 July. They proved a far more effective force against the SPG than all the resolutions that had been passed, important though these were. Bob Light, a London docker, recalls the scene:[74]

> It was an impressive sight – shop stewards' banners from the four biggest ports in the country lined up across the road. The police made a couple of half hearted attempts to clear the road, but there were just too many pickets. We saw five coaches of the Special Patrol Group making towards us. But 100 yards away the Scabs Protection Group turned round. They obviously didn't fancy the odds. Having failed with that group of animals, the police sent in the cavalry – three dozen mounted police. These horses and riders looked very big in the flesh, especially when they were trotting down a hill right at you. At that moment I thought it was just a matter of time until the line was broken. But as I looked round, the mass of pickets had linked arms to form a wall right across the road about 50 or 60 deep and with thousands more struggling up the road.
>
> The police just could not get through ... It was about the most exhilirating moment I've ever experienced on a demonstration. It took me back to the live electric days of Pentonville in 1972. You could sense the same charge in the air, the same mood of confidence and determination. At that moment the Grunwicks factory was totally blockaded. There was nothing the police could have done to get the scab's bus through.

Lewisham

One month later, in August 1977, there was a major battle on the streets of Lewisham in South East London, caused chiefly by the policies that McNee had adopted in 'dealing' with the Grunwick pickets – a strategy of confronting opposition directly and with the necessary force to break it up. The issue here was whether or not the

National Front should be allowed to march through an area of London with a high proportion of West Indian residents. Although they denied it at the time the police had in the past taken the initiative in re-routing such marches to avoid confrontation. For instance, in Leicester in 1974 the police banned the Front from going anywhere near the main Asian Communities. Yet at Lewisham they ignored calls made by most of the national press, the local press, the local council, the TUC and the Labour Party for the march to be re-routed, or banned altogether. What McNee and his senior officers had effectively set up was a confrontation with the black community, in particular black youth, and anti-National Front demonstrators. The NF march was tiny, demoralized, and was repeatedly attacked by demonstrators breaking through the police line until the police were forced to re-route it, and finally to bring it to an abrupt end. But it was only after the demonstration was over that the police attack was launched, with riot shields and SPG vans driving at top speed towards groups of demonstrators, and repeated on charges on foot and horseback. The violence of those clashes caused a national furore; that and the use of riot shields led some commentators to speculate on the need for a paramilitary force. The riot shields appeared again at the Notting Hill Carnival later that month.

After Lewisham the Police Federation called for a ban on all demonstrations 'likely to lead to public disorder'.[75] McNee opposed this with the equivocal logic that it would draw the police into 'making political judgments outside the framework of the law'[76] since 'My powers under the Public Order Act are limited to imposing controls on, or banning processions', and 'They do not extend to banning other forms of public demonstrations at which widespread disorder could be deliberately provoked'.[77] This was an extraordinary interpretation of the Act, under which McNee was fully equipped with the power to ban any demonstration likely to lead to 'serious public disorder' (See 5.3(1) of the Act).

This tends to give credence to the theory that the police explicitly decided upon a confrontation strategy at Lewisham, the consequence of a political decision by the police, as McNee put it 'to uphold the rule of law on the streets of London – *by the use of lawful force if necessary* ...'[78] It is significant that the Association of Chief Police Officers stated, in September 1977, that 'the police can no longer prevent public disorder in the streets' and called for a 'new Public Order Act giving the police stronger power to control marches and demonstrations, *similar to police powers in Ulster.*' (Author's italics.)[79] It seems that McNee felt some pressure to quash speculation over the role of the police that followed Lewisham. When his first annual report was published, he told the Press 'that the shortcomings of the traditional helmet were evident during the disturbances' (at Lewisham and Notting Hill). Defensive equipment was used reluctantly 'and I stress that it does not mean we have foresaken traditional methods of policing demonstrations.'[80]

The SPG and the Black Community

Yet the police went to Lewisham fully prepared for a riot. Nearly two years later they adopted the same strategy in Southall. In both Lewisham and Southall the black community, West Indian and Asian, took to the streets in opposition to the National Front and found themselves confronted by an aggressive police operation, with the SPG at its centre. It would be naive to accept at face value the police's explanation of why the National Front are permitted to carry out such activities as marches and meetings in the very heart of communities they consistently and viciously insult and attack. The police were fully aware of the level of opposition the National Front would meet in Lewisham and Southall. Were confrontations like these deliberately planned or prepared for in order to train the riot police of the future; and to train them on the most alienated section of society – black youth?

Back in May 1971 the Special Patrol Group raided the Metro a black youth club in Notting Hill, on the pretext that a 'wanted' youth had entered the premises. In the course of the raid sixteen youths were arrested, charged with affray, and all subsequently acquitted. The raid provoked this response from Rudy Nayaran, Vice-Chairman of the Lambeth Council for Community Relations:

> The Special Patrol Group, of course, are the nomad commandos of the Met and move into an area, anywhere, anytime, with no relationship of loyalty themselves to the local community – they therefore descend in a cloud of smoke, do their worst with as much arrogance and contempt as they think fit and leave in their wake the local officers to pick up the pieces. In the Metro Case the SPG descended to seek out, find and destroy one black boy with one piece of stick! The fact that there were no armoured cars or flame throwers owes more to the lack of supplies, than to lack of desire to smoke out the Blacks in what, for waste of police time and manpower and sheer hooligan destruction of community goodwill,

must rank in the Met's history as the greatest monument to arrogance and racialism of all time. The new Commissioner of Police clearly has a role to play in immediately reviewing the function and operational role of the SPG.[81]

The Metro raid followed the pattern of police raids on black clubs and restaurants since the mid-sixties in Notting Hill. In 1972 the National Council for Civil Liberties stated in its evidence to the Parliamentary Select Committee on Race Relations:

We would be failing in our duty if we omitted to convey our considered opinion that the worsening situation between the police and the black community is very serious indeed ... A significant and vocal section of the black community feels it is being harshly treated by the police and that there is little justice when their cases come to court. It feels that more violence is used against black people by policemen than would be used against white people. It feels that their homes are walked into by policemen with a temerity which would not be tried on the white community. It feels that charges preferred against them when they are in trouble are usually of a more serious nature than a white person would receive ... Even if the black community is wrong in these beliefs they are nevertheless widely and sincerely held. Our view is that there is some justification for them ...[82]

It is scarcely surprising that Robert Mark's campaign to recruit Blacks into the police, launched almost immediately he came into office (and on which £25,000 was spent in 1975), met with negligible response. By the beginning of 1978 there were only 199 black policemen in the whole of England and Wales, none of them holding a rank higher than sergeant.[83] Black people were prepared to join the civilian staff of the police but not the uniformed branches, and it is not hard to see the reason why. Mark might claim, as he did in 1972,[84] that 'we have made changes in our training in order to give our officers a better understanding of the complexity of modern urban society and in particular of the position of minority and underprivileged groups within it', but there is no evidence to suggest that this produced any tangible change of attitudes within the police force as a whole; on the contrary the evidence suggests that racism is deeply rooted in the police.

The last few years have seen the police propagandize on the importance of 'good race relations', and at the same time protect the activities of racist organizations. Yet police chiefs seek to blame the left 'extremists' and opponents of racism for the bad relations that now exist between the police and the black community. It is however fanciful to suggest that the white left has 'brainwashed' the black community, principally the youth, into seeing the police as its enemy. The frustration and anger that exploded in the street battles between black youth and the police at the Notting Hill Carnival in 1976, Lewisham and again at Southall are rooted in years of police harassment of black youth.

The recession of the seventies hit black people especially hard. The men and women who had responded to the massive labour recruitment campaign in the West Indies and the Asian subcontinent in the fifties and sixties found, when they arrived in Britain, that their jobs were to be the most menial and the lowest paid; their working conditions the most hazardous; their homes in the declining inner city areas; their once eagerly sought presence in this country the object of racist attack; and their livelihoods the first to be jettisoned in crisis. While total unemployment rose by 65 per cent between 1973 and 1975, the number of Blacks out of work soared by 156 per cent. Worst hit were the sons and daughters of black immigrants. By 1976 at least 60 per cent of black youth in the urban areas were out of work. They drifted onto the streets and the dole queues, from the classrooms where they had been labelled 'educationally sub-normal' and taught more often than not that their culture and their history was worth only scorn.

Any section of young people will tend to come into conflict with the authority of a society that keeps them forcibly unoccupied. The black youth of the seventies have responded to their rejection by white society and the racism within it with a determination to assert their rights and to fight the oppression to which they have been subjected. That response has taken the form of militant anti-racism, of self-organization, and of an attempt to establish their identity and rediscover their own culture.

Because they are 'rebellious' and because they are forced to live in the 'high crime areas' – the police definition of the urban slums – they have become a target for consistent harassment and often brutality. And while the police force as a whole is guilty of this, the Special Patrol Group are past masters at it. The following is the experience of just one area of London, submitted in evidence to the Royal Commission on Criminal Procedure by the Institute of Race Relations in 1979:

Lewisham 1975: In the autumn of 1975 the police commander for the Lewisham area ('P' and 'L' Divisions)* called in the SPG because of what he claimed was a rising crime rate, especially 'mugging' (a term almost exclusively used to describe alleged attacks by black people on Whites). In the course of this operation the SPG stopped 14,000 people on the streets and made 400 arrests (over 20 per cent of the total in that year). The main target of these stops was black people.

One of the worst confrontations occurred when two local policemen tried to enter the Moonshot Club, a centre for young black people, in order, they said, to arrest someone they thought to be in the club. When their entry was resisted, the SPG arrived within minutes, cordoned off the street and prepared to charge into the club. A confrontation was only averted by the intervention of the Club's director, who informed the police that serious injuries would occur on both sides if they carried out their intention – and the police agreed to withdraw. During the period of the SPG presence there were repeated complaints of black people being picked up on the streets and of beatings and interrogations at police stations. A survey carried out by the Deptford West Indian and African Community Association just after the SPG operation showed that black parents were constantly worried whenever their children went out. They were liable to be stopped on the way to school or work, at bus stops and in the underground, not return home when expected and only hours later would parents discover that they were being held in the local police station.

The introduction of the SPG into Lewisham at the request of the police commander was carried out without consulting the local Police Liaison Committee, which had been created on the initiative of the police themselves. This fact, combined with the methods and operations of the SPG, destroyed what little trust existed between the black community and the police.

Brixton 1975: In the summer of 1975, as a result of the activities of the SPG against young black people, the Lambeth Campaign against Police Repression was formed to demand their removal from the area. The campaign reported that they had 'detailed evidence (that) inside Brixton police station youths have been punched, beaten and threatened with dogs to scare them into signing prepared confessions'. The same pattern was followed as in Lewisham – road blocks, early morning raids, random street checks. In one instance a young black boy, 14 years old, was

---

* Randall, Commander of 'P' Division made the following statement to the local press when the first set of 'mugging' figures were released in January 1975. 'Various people have advanced environmental reasons as having helped to create the problem of mugging. But these are lazy, vicious little criminals.'[86] Randall was also head of the Lewisham force when the notorious Operation P.N.H. was launched and resulted in the trial for conspiracy of the Lewisham 21. P.N.H. stands for Police Nigger Hunt.

stopped on the street and a woman cleaning her windows saw the plain clothes police trying to plant something on him. She rushed out, as did lots of other people in the streets, because he was screaming from the beatings he was getting. Within minutes the SPG arrived and a pitched battle ensued, resulting in several arrests.

Peckham 1976: In August the SPG arrested several young black people outside a betting shop. The youths had noticed three or four men – who subsequently turned out to be plainclothes police – opposite. Fifteen minutes later they saw about 13 men coming down the road and, suspecting trouble, the youths went back in the shop. One of them was called outside. He was grabbed, flung through the door, and knocked down. He got onto his knees, and with his arms pinned behind his back, he was punched and kicked. Two girls, C.W. and D.W. were passing and C.W. aged 13, thought her brother was being attacked by a group of local white racists. She dashed over the road and called out to ask if he was all right. She was pushed by the police and told to 'piss off'. Two vans arrived, she was dragged in and hit in the van. Her hair was pulled and later at the station she was stripped naked and searched, and also subjected to verbal abuse. This 13 year old was five foot two inches tall and weighed seven stones. She was accused of assault on three SPG officers.

Brixton 1978: The most recent instance of the SPG's activities occured in November 1978 – and again without prior consultation with the Police Liaison Committee. Over half of the total strength of the Special Patrol Group, 120 officers, supplemented by 30 extra officers from Scotland Yard were drafted into the Lambeth Police area because of its 'high crime' rate. Over 1,000 people were stopped on the streets and 430 people arrested; the *Daily Telegraph* reported after the operation: 'Three-fifths of those arrested were white, the rest coloured. A high percentage of black people live in the area.' In effect 40 per cent of those arrested were black, more than double the estimated black proportion of the local community. The SPG operation was concentrated around four housing estates, all with high black populations. The technique used was described by one black youth: 'I was on my way to the Labour Exchange when four of them suddenly appeared blocking my way. As I moved, they moved and it was clear that they weren't going to let me through. Eventually they said they wanted to search me and after about 15-20 minutes they let me pass. I was lucky to get away. There have been a lot of instances a lot worse.' In another case a young Black was stopped and questioned by almost a dozen SPG as he helped transfer shopping from his mother's car to the family's first floor flat. 'If I hadn't been there they would have arrested him,' his mother said. 'What's happening here in Lambeth is that because we have been able to push the National Front out we have got the police instead.'

On almost the first day of the SPG operation (3 November 1978) ten young Blacks were arrested near Stockwell Manor School, hauled in during their dinner hour and charged under the 'Sus' law. A few days later two groups of four and seven Blacks were arrested on 'Sus' in central Brixton. The grounds on which the SPG stopped and searched people were looking for 'offensive weapons', 'drugs' and 'stolen property'.

After the operation was over Assistant Commissioner Gilbert Kelland of Scotland Yard said that it had been successful and had led to a drastic reduction in crime, although, of course, to a higher number of arrests. In reality the SPG presence in Brixton did not lead to a greater number of police patrolling the streets, but to the systematic harassment and search of the local community in order to demonstrate that the police 'mean business'. Mr Kelland also announced that 'similar operations are planned for Hackney, Dalston and Stoke Newington' (*Daily Telegraph*, 6 December 1978) – all inner city areas with a high proportion of Blacks.[87]

The *Daily Express* reported Kelland's remarks to the press in a rather different tone to the *Telegraph*.

> *The heavy mob were jubilant yesterday. They were sent to Brixton for a month and loved every minute of it. What's more Scotland Yard are tickled pink. The heavies have now been sent to another London area ... where they are fighting crime. The mob, the mobile SPG, backed by Yard detectives, were sent to support local police.* (Author's italics.)[88]

The effects of the SPG operation prompted one of Lambeth's Labour MPs, John Tilley, to write to Commander Adams, head of the local force and other senior officers saying that 'whatever the effect on the immediate crime and/or detection rate of the SPG deployment, the effect on community relations is disastrous'.[89] Lambeth Council also called on the Home Office to set up an official inquiry into relations between the police and the black community in Lambeth. The Home Office refused to do so. As to the crime reduction rate 'achieved' by the SPG, Commander Adam's claim that their presence reduced street crime by 40 per cent 'has to be seen in the light of the statement by Southwark's local police chief, that crime in his borough had increased during November. The same thing might have occurred in other neighbouring boroughs.'[90] In other words when they heard that the SPG were going in people may simply have moved into other areas.

The use of the SPG in the black areas of London is now so commonplace that, according to one black reporter, 'it is scarcely newsworthy. You can guarantee that at any one time they will be in operation against the black community. They seem to travel continuously back and forth between Notting Hill, Stoke Newington, Brixton, Peckham, Islington, Hackney and Tooting.'

The tactics are always the same – road blocks, van 'charges' into trouble spots, violent methods, intimidation and often arrest of anyone who questions SPG actions, or goes to the aid of the 'suspects'. Paul Foot wrote of

> A classic case in January 1973 when three constables from the SPG, Farr, Bloom and Leavers – arrested Errol Tucker and Jewel Princes, for 'loitering with intent to steal' from women's handbags in Grenville Arcade, Brixton. Errol Tucker was grabbed by the neck and held in a vice like grip. Several West Indians gathered round to protest. One of them, a poet, Linton K. Johnson, kept asking Tucker his name. Then Linton Johnson was arrested and charged with assaulting the SPG officers! ... Happily Linton Johnson and Donna Hart, who was arrested with him, were acquitted of assault. The other two young Blacks were acquitted of Sus.[91]

The other method of 'policing' practised by the Special Patrol Group is wholesale random spot searches on the streets. The police have the power to stop, question and search anyone they suspect of being in possession of drugs, or stolen goods, or suspected of having committed a number of minor crimes, of which 'Sus' (Being a 'suspected person' loitering with intent) is most commonly used against black youth. The SPG use this power to its fullest extent. *Of the 18,907 stop searches on pedestrians carried out by the Special Patrol Group in the Greater London area in 1975, some 14,000 took place in Lambeth and Lewisham over a two month period and resulted in 403 arrests. Of the 5,000 or so stop and search incidents in the rest of the Metropolitan area, some 3,700 resulted in arrests.*[92]

Table 1 shows the total numbers of pedestrians and cars stopped by the SPG and the numbers arrested.[93]

Year	Stopped	Arrested	% Arrested
1972	41,980	3,142	7.5
1973	34,534	3,339	9.7
1974	41,304	3,262	7.9
1975	65,628	4,125	6.3
1976	60,898	3,773	6.2

In 1977 the figures ceased to be given separately.

In 1972 the Home Secretary informed the House of Commons that records are kept of all those stopped in the street by the Special Patrol Group.[94] When only one in every fifteen to twenty people stopped searched and questioned by the SPG is actually arrested, and considering that this practice is by far the most commonplace in the black communities, the net result is nothing other than harassment – a legal means of victimization. As a result of their findings the Institute of Race Relations recommended 'that they (the SPG) should at least cease to operate in these (black) areas, at best be altogether disbanded.'[95]

Finally, the experience of one other black area in London puts paid to the claim, first, that the police are not racially biased and, second, to the notion that the Special Patrol Group are just an 'anti-crime' squad, efficient but impartial enforcers of the law.

Brick Lane, in East London is the heart of the Bengali community. It is also surrounded by National Front strongholds – Hoxton, Shoreditch, Newham and Barking – and has suffered nine years of violence and racial intimidation dating back to the Skinhead 'Paki-bashing' in East London in 1971. The East End is traditionally a 'high crime' area, but the assaults and harassment of Bengalis is on a totally different scale to anything else inflicted on the community.

The violence took a far more serious turn in the summer of 1978. Three Bengalis were murdered: Altab Ali was stabbed to death in Whitechapel, Ishaque Ali died after an attack by white youths in Hackney and ten year old Kenneth Singh was found dead on a Newham building site with his skull crushed. Brick Lane and its surrounds was not only a 'high crime' but a serious crime area, with cases of arson, murder, and the use of firearms over and above the almost daily physical assaults on the Asians in the area. Yet the police not only failed to protect the community, they treated requests for help and reports of attacks with, to say the least, an extraordinary lack of concern. For example:

On 11 June 1978, 150 white youths ran down Brick Lane shouting 'Kill the Black Bastards', and smashing the windows of a dozen shops and the car windscreens of Bengali shop keepers. 55-year-old Abdul Monan was knocked unconscious by a hail of rocks and stones hurled through his shop window. He ended up in hospital where he needed five stitches in his face. He lost two of his teeth. This was by far the biggest group to have threatened the Asian community in our area, and heralded a new and frightening escalation of racial incitement. Some Asians and anti-racists fought off the attackers. It was perhaps ten minutes before the police arrived. They held 20 of the 'white youths, but released all except three of them whom they eventually charged only with the minor offence of 'threatening behaviour'. They had actually been phoned half an hour earlier and warned that a crowd of skinheads was gathering in a side street. They later claimed that the incident occured just as they were changing shift and they were not prepared for it.[96]

The Special Patrol Group was posted to the area in June, but failed to stop the dozens of attacks that followed the rampage down Brick Lane. Their presence owed more to the fact that the Anti Nazi League and the Hackney and Tower Hamlets Defence Committee held two mass demonstrations in the area — in mid-June and the beginning of July — than to any intention to stop the attacks. McNee claimed that 'Both the local police and the Special Patrol Group sought to establish a better relationship with the Asian community'[97] Protecting the community appears to have fallen outside the terms of reference of that 'relationship'.

It is one thing to face a hostile and determined crowd and attempt to break it up; harassing individuals in the streets, raiding houses and clubs, breaking up squats is another matter altogether. To succeed in the first instance demands physical strength and training, the right equipment, and sufficient numbers. But it also requires certain mental 'qualities' — aggression, the readiness to use violence, contempt for the opponents, and confidence — in fact all the characteristics of a bully. Bullies, by and large, get their experience and their confidence through attacking those who are physically weaker, and less able to defend themselves. Under the guise of 'fighting crime' that is what the Special Patrol Group has effectively been doing in London's black communities for more than a decade.

There are some police chiefs, like Geoffrey Dear, Chief Constable of Nottingham, who argue:

> they (the SPG) might apparently solve one problem but in its wake create another of aggravated relationships between minority groups and the police in general. It is then in this atmosphere that the permanent beat officer is expected to continue his work, often finding that his task, which was always difficult and delicate, has now been made almost impossible.[98]

Regional Versions of the SPG

But SPG style units are now the rule rather than the exception for regional forces and specifically those covering the main industrial and urban areas. As early as January 1974 the *Sunday Times* reported that a special squad of 800 trained police was on permanent standby in Yorkshire during the miners' strike, and in addition 'a special unit kept watch on known extremists in such areas as Stainforth, near the Hatfield Main Colliery and Cadeby, near Mexborough. Gregory (The Chief Constable) says that he has identified possible trouble areas and a plan of action has been worked out.'[99]

Prior to the decision taken in 1972 that the police should develop and control the nucleus of a para-military force, units similar to the London SPG existed in Hertfordshire, Thames Valley, Northern Ireland, and Derbyshire. Between 1972 and 1974 a further eight units were created – in Avon & Somerset, Essex, Merseyside, Northumbria, North Yorkshire, West Yorkshire, Gwent and Strathclyde.

A total of twenty-three regional forces, in addition to the Metropolitan force, now have SPG-type units. (See *Table 2*, pp 204-205). In August 1979 *State Research* published the results of a survey of all 52 Chief Constables' annual reports in Britain for information on the Special Patrol Groups.[100] They found that

> The key feature that distinguishes SPGs is that they operate over the whole area covered by a police force, are controlled centrally and have an independent chain of command. Like the London SPG, they are drawn from the ranks of the uniformed branch, although some have CID officers attached to them. The SPG units surveyed are generally described as 'mobile support units' and much emphasis is laid on their *anti-crime* role (e.g. backing-up divisional forces, helping in major incidents, and murder hunts). However, nearly all of them are used in public order situations (strikes, demonstrations, and football matches) and most of them have an anti-terrorist capacity (at ports and airports and training in the use of firearms). Training varies from force to force, but most include the use of firearms, riot control (use of batons and shields) and protective clothing (special helmets for example). Finally it should be said some of the units are still more akin to the original concept of a police support anti-crime unit (like those in Norfolk and Lancashire), while others are a carbon-copy of the London para-military model (in Manchester and Strathclyde).

Some of these units have gained national attention as a result of their actions. The Strathclyde Support Unit, in the news in autumn 1979 over the death of James McGeown, became the focus for a campaign for a public inquiry, supported by the Scottish TUC, after it attacked an anti-National Front demonstration in May 1975. In 1973 a large number of organizations and individuals concerned with community relations in Handsworth, wrote to the Chief Constable of Birmingham over a 'further deterioration in the relationships between local police and parts of the black community, which we believe is, in large part, attributable to the policies and attitudes adopted by the police', namely 'Police tactics of using a show of force where trouble is anticipated do not have the effect of preventing violence, but tend to ensure it. The habitual use of such strategy has come to be interpreted by many black people as systematic intimidation ... The activities of the Special Patrol Group reinforce black feeling that they are being specially selected for rough treatment.'[101]

In 1977 the Tactical Aid Group (Greater Manchester) conducted the biggest police-army operation since the SPG-army exercise at Heathrow in January 1974. Five hundred armed police, SAS Units and soldiers sealed off the Collyhurst area of Manchester, diverted buses and searched cars and pedestrians during a 12 hour 'mock' siege. 'The operation was so realistic it was really frightening and no one knew what it was all about until the news this morning,' said one local resident.[102] After the Heathrow exercise it had been suggested that the joint police-army exercise was 'basically a public relations exercise to accustom the public to the reality of troops deploying through the high street.'[103]

The Merseyside unit, Task Force, formed in 1974, has gained the unique distinction of providing the only instance of an SPG-type unit being disbanded. In 1976 'officers were disciplined, two prosecuted and all the personnel re-assigned after a public campaign over the violent and harassing tactics used by the Unit.'[104] Ken Oxford, disbanded the unit when he took over as Chief Constable that year, but immediately formed another – Operational Support Division.

Other units, however, have operated without the hindrance of public scrutiny, a situation that may be changing in Derbyshire, at least judging by the Chief Constable's Report for 1977:

> Changes in operational policy have been brought about during this, the eighth year of the Special Operations Unit. During the early part of the year it was found that the unit was spending some of its time in less productive areas of the country; areas where crime figures were comparatively low and difficulty was being experienced in using the full potential of the unit ... it was more effective to concentrate its efforts and expertise on the densely populated areas where crime, vandalism *and public disorder particularly* were more prevalent ... the Unit has since

spent more of its time in Derby, Chesterfield, Ilkeston and Long Eaton. (Author's italics.)

There is no reason to doubt that the SPG-style units outside London are capable of the same operations and tactics practised by their prototype. Taken together these units could now provide a national force between 700 and 1,000 strong. And since 1972 there has developed a general training in riot control for the police force as a whole in addition to the SPGs.

Riot Control

All police forces in England and Wales now have teams trained in crowd control and anti-riot techniques, and these can be sent to other regions at short notice under a 'mutual aid' scheme. In Devon and Cornwall 'These units of 33 men act very much as a team and have to be taught certain skills for use in disorderly crowds ... seven units underwent a week's training in the college during which time not only were the earlier mentioned (anti-riot) drills taught, but also efforts made to improve general standards of fitness'.[105]

Officers drilled in SPG techniques are used for such training programmes, those 'finishing their three year tour of duty in the Special Patrol Group have gone off to become instructors in the provinces' and 'the expertise of the Met squads is available to provincial forces on demand'.[106] The regional SPG units are also adopting this practice. Thus in Essex members of the Force Support Unit 'have worked in every division of the force throughout the year on a wide variety of tasks' and 'assisted in force retraining in relation to crowd control, drugs searches, and the use of firearms', during 1976 and in the following year 'trained other members of the force in the use of riot shields', while 'senior officers regularly lecture at force training schools.'[107] And the experience and training of SPGs also passed back into the local forces, first, through the high turnover rate – from 1973 a positive initiative was taken to encourage short term service in the SPG in order that more police in London could get special riot training – and, second, through the secondment of local officers to work under the command of the SPGs when on divisional assignments.

Riot control training, of course, goes beyond mere lessons in the use of shields and protective equipment, or special drills or methods of dispersing crowds. It is also a psychological training, designed to develop the aggressive and unhesitating mentality that a unit like the

SPG must have if it is to be effective. As Paul Foot puts it:

> Crack regiments have developed a special heartlessness and ferocity by
> isolating themselves from the world at large. Their troops live together,
> eat, sleep and joke together. They are held together not by the affections
> which bind people in everyday life, but by ceremony, by weird and
> fantastical idols and insignia. They are encouraged not to argue, but to
> obey; not to reason, but to act. Their strength is rooted in their obedience
> and loyalty to their superiors, to God and to the Queen, to anyone who
> orders without expecting their orders to be questioned. Such were the
> values which inspired, for instance, the lunacy of the German Naval
> Command, which prepared to sink its entire fleet in a suicidal battle at the
> end of the First World War: or the crack street troops of Hitler's SA. And
> such – although they are not yet even remotely comparable in bestiality to
> the SA – are the values which inspire the Special Patrol Group.[108]

'Ordinary' policemen trained in riot control will acquire at least
some of such attitudes. The result is that ever increasing numbers of
policemen will view events such as demonstrations and pickets as
provocative, likely to cause 'disorder' and therefore to be *restricted*
and prevented from so doing. Ever increasing numbers of police are
now mobilized with the expectation that they will have to enforce 'law
and order', with their new training, their riot equipment on hand, with
statements from their senior officers about the inevitability of violence,
or the necessity of force in mind, fully prepared to engage in battle
with those they are 'policing'. In such circumstances riot control
becomes a self-fulfilling prophesy – demonstrators or workers on
picket lines, are potential 'rioters', either 'extremists', or in the words
Robert Mark chose to describe the jailed Shrewsbury pickets, people
likely to commit 'the worst of all crimes, worse even than murder the
attempt to achieve an industrial or political objective by criminal
violence'.[109] The result of all this has been seen in action at Lewisham,
Grunwick and Southall. In *The Police in Society*, Ben Whitaker
quotes one 'very senior' but anonymous, officer as saying 'Probably
our major function on these occasions is to control the police.'[110]

How many other senior officers share that view of things?

One month after Southall Paul Middup, Chairman of the
Constables Committee, received a roar of approval from the Police
Constables Conference in Blackpool when he denounced the 'kid
glove treatment' of demonstrators and demanded that the police
should be better equipped for 'riot situations'.[111] And David McNee

redefined the concept of civil liberty with one sentence when he issued the following warning at a press conference in June 1979: 'Keep off the streets of London and behave yourself and you won't have the Special Patrol Group to worry about.'

In their calls for 'law and order' the police have placed themselves firmly on the right of the political spectrum. They have also made the issues on which they themselves take the decisions the major political issues of the day, and 'law and order' is one such. It is also a highly subjective view and quite distinct from the task which the police are said to carry out, that of impartially 'enforcing the law'.

Yet the police have never played an impartial role. They can appear to do so when there is little tension in society. But once tension and dissent rise their role changes accordingly. That is the clear pattern established by developments in the police during the last decade. And it is also clear in the selectivity with which the police enforce some laws but not others. The Special Patrol Group may be mobilized against a picket that threatens to close down a factory to win a strike for better and safer working conditions. It is inconceivable that they would be mobilized to enforce health and safety legislation in that factory. Yet year in and year out hundreds of men and women are poisoned, or maimed and sometimes killed, simply because that legislation is not enforced.

Conclusion

Once the crisis of the early seventies had passed it became possible for the police to change tack – towards a much greater emphasis on the 'community of interests' between police and society (hence the widely publicized attempts to recruit Blacks to the police force, and the consistent public statements about the 'extremist' nature of those who opposed the National Front). At the same time there was a deliberate playing down of the para-military role it had already been decided, *secretly*, that the police should play in the future. The early years of the 1974 Labour Government saw a decline in disputes and strikes, brought about largely by the social contract between government and unions. Whereas industry had lost over 24 million working days through strikes in 1972, four years later the figure had dropped to around 6 million. And the senior police chiefs vigorously and successfully lobbied the new government not to introduce legislation planned to make picketing more effective.*

It was not the case that police methods became less violent, as Red Lion Square showed in 1974, or Lewisham in 1975, or the attack on Right to Work marchers in Hendon in 1976 – all carried out by the Special Patrol Group. Police violence did not become a national political issue because it was not central to the control of society. But in 1977 against a background of growing economic crisis, and opposition to the ever more right wing policies of the Labour government, the police moved towards direct confrontation as a means of dealing with any movement that threatened to become a national focus for protest. The Special Patrol Group could not stop protestors, whether they were black, unemployed, or dockworkers. But it could dole out violence as a deterrent.

Of course confrontation had its risks, the major one being escalation of support for the original movement. Signs of that had already manifested themselves in the black communities, as Commander Marshall, Head of Scotland Yard's Community Relations department, pointed out in evidence to the 1976 Select Committee on Race Relations: 'Recently there has been a growth in the tendency for members of London's West Indian communities to combine against police by interfering with police officers who are effecting the arrest of a black person ... *in the last 12 months, 40 such incidents have been recorded. Each carries a potential for large scale disorder.'* (Author's italics.)[113]

Again, the Grunwick strike became a national political issue *around which trade unionists could be mobilized* only after the SPG onslaught on the first mass picket on 13 June 1977. And again, it was after the police practically route-marched the National Front through

---

* Mark recalls this incident in his autobiography: 'The police know more than anyone about the practical application of the law and whilst their views should not necessarily be given undue weight they ought to be known. One interesting example of the need for this arose, when Michael Foot put his original proposals to amend the law on picketing. The intention was to give pickets the right to stop vehicle drivers or to require the police to do that for them. I told Jimmy Waddell (Sir James Waddell, Deputy Under Secretary, Home Office) in no uncertain terms that if there was any danger of this proposal reaching the statute book I would declare in *The Times* that this was an unjustifiable infringement of individual liberty and an inexcusable requirement for the police to abandon the impartiality in industrial disputes to which they had always been dedicated. We were fortunate indeed in our Home Secretary, Roy Jenkins. He must clearly have shared our feelings to some extent because the Home Office arranged a meeting between representatives of all chief officers and Michael Foot's senior civil servants at which we left them in no doubt that the proposals would be publicly opposed by every chief officer. Happily they were abandoned and no harm was done.'[112]

Lewisham in order to stage a 'show-down' with the left and the black youth, that the Anti Nazi League was launched, and grew into the biggest anti-fascist organization since the thirties, a mass movement that not only put the 'Nazi' stamp once and for all on the National Front, but also radicalized a generation new to political activity just as the Vietnam movement of the sixties, and CND before it, had done.

The police did not abandon confrontation tactics after this. Southall proved that. So did the attacks on picket lines during the bakers', journalists' and other disputes in 1978. But there were no mass pickets on the scale of Grunwick the previous year. The Labour Government in its last throes still had the backing of trade union leaders in the main, and they helped to control their members by agreeing to restrictions on the size and effectiveness of pickets, as well as showing a reluctance to make strikes official.

Within days of taking office in May 1979 the Tories honoured their election promises to 'uphold the rule of law' by granting substantial pay rises to the police and the army. At the same time they prepared new laws to curb the power of the trade union movement – laws which drastically restrict rights to organize, to picket and to strike, first granted to workers more than seventy years ago. These two moves prepared the ground for controlling working class action, which the Tories had every reason to anticipate would be necessary. They came to power during the onset of an economic crisis that threatens to be the most severe since the thirties – far worse than that which ignited the mass struggles of 1972. Then unemployment figures topping one million were unimaginable. Now economists predict that the start of the eighties will see two million workers lining up on the dole queues, and that as many as twelve million people may be living below the poverty line.

Circumstances like these can spark off new levels of resistance – and, in anticipation, the means of control have already been strengthened. In the last five years spending on the courts and the police rose by a third, and no doubt 'contingency plans' are being drawn up in case this proves inadequate. They will be made, as they were in 1972, in secret. Behind closed doors a group of police chiefs, heads of armed forces, top civil servants and counter-insurgency experts will consider the best means of crushing opposition to the interests they represent: the ruling class. The police and the army are above 'democratic' control. The decisions they take will not be discussed or voted on in Parliament, they will simply be implemented, and most of us may not discover what they were until we come up against them in the streets, as did Basharat Hussain, Mohammed Hussain, Kevin Gately and Blair Peach. The reason is simply that such decisions are based on how best to control society and while the government of a capitalist society may be put to the vote, control will never be.

Should the combined effects of economic crisis and the policies of the Tories provoke mass resistance, as they did in 1972, the task of controlling the streets and the factories will still rest with the Police Force. It is a force that has undergone eight years training for that role. In its vanguard are the Special Patrol Groups, ruthless and rigorously trained, and armed with the tools of control, from riot shields to guns. Behind them are the uniformed ranks, now also trained in riot control and many marksmen amongst them too. A riot police force has been developed in Britain during the seventies and the eighties may see them acknowledged in that role.

But while recognizing that, it is also worth recalling once more the experience of Saltley conveyed by Arthur Scargill, because it was after all at Saltley Gates that this chain of events began:

> Here had been displayed all that's good in the working class movement. Here had been displayed what for years had been on a banner but had never been transferred from the banner into reality. You know the words: 'Unity is Strength', 'Workers of the World Unite', 'Man to Man Brother Be.' They're big words. Sometimes they'd been ridiculed. Through all that ridicule, all that sneering, they survived. Here was the living proof that the working class had only to flex its muscles and it could bring governments, employers, society to a total standstill. ...
>
> ... Had they defeated the miners at Saltley, I am absolutely convinced that the Tories would have tried to defy the miners' union and defy the trade union movement – even if it meant the use of troops. But they were scared out of their skins by what took place at Saltley. They could have produced as many troops as they wanted at Saltley and they would have been useless. The mass of the working class and trade union movement decided: this shall be so. In the face of that you cannot have it any other way ... All I can say is that I was privileged to be there.[114]

Epilogue

The following is the tribute paid to Blair Peach by Dick North, a member of the Executive of the National Union of Teachers, of which Blair Peach was a member:

Blair Peach was a gentle man with a great fighting spirit. To the deprived children of Phoenix Delicate School in Bow, East London, he was an exceptionally gifted and patient teacher of reading. To his colleagues in the NUT he was the man whose willingness to take action rather than to talk about it both shamed and inspired those of us who would otherwise have been more cautious.

Blair was a shy man, but he forced himself to speak out because of the strength with which he held his beliefs. He became President of the East London Association of the NUT and was soon a marked man for his unequivocal anti-racist stance. Twice he was beaten up by the National Front and a tendon in his head was completely severed by a vicious bite. He told me that he was terrified to wear his Anti Nazi League badge in the East End – but of course he wore it.

He was one of the leading activists in Teachers Against the Nazis, the first organization to take the fight against racism into the classrooms. He was one of the principal organizers of the demonstration against the use of Loughborough Junior School in Brixton by the National Front – that forced the ILEA to find ways of refusing subsequent bookings to the fascists. He was a founding member of the South Hackney and Shoreditch Anti Nazi League and prominent in the defence of the Asian community in Brick Lane.

In recent weeks he was campaigning for schools not to use the reader *Not Me I'm Workshy*, because of two racialist remarks it contained.

It is not just for his anti-racist activities that Blair will be remembered. He was an active militant within the Rank and File Teachers group in the NUT and a member of the Editorial Board of *Rank and File Teacher*. He was one of the first teachers in the ILEA to face disciplinary charges for taking unofficial action, during the London allowance campaign of 1974. Needless to say, this did not deter him from organizing further strike action.

It was indicative of his commitment that he chose to join the Socialist Workers Party at a time when it was most difficult for socialists to argue for action, and when many with years of experience in the movement opted for an easier course.

He had a phenomenal capacity for hard work – he wasn't the kind of socialist who makes fine speeches and leaves the duplicating and writing of envelopes to others.

Above all, Blair was the kind of man who gave you confidence in the future of socialism. He was a witty and amusing companion who gave us all an appetite for the struggle. His loss will be deeply felt by all his comrades and those who despite their disagreements with him held him in the highest esteem as a fighter for socialism.

It is the task of all of us to provide the memorial that Blair would have most wished for by carrying on his fight against racism and exploitation.

Table 2. Special Patrol Groups in the U.K.

Force	Name of Group	Date Established	Size*
ENGLAND			
Avon & Somerset	Task Force	1973	55
City of London	Special Operations Unit	1977	16
Derbyshire	Special Operations Unit	1970	11 (1976)
Essex	Force Support Unit	1973	32 (1974)
Gloucestershire	Task Force	—	—
Greater Manchester	Tactical Aid Group	1976	70 (1977)
Hertfordshire	Tactical Patrol Group	1965	28
Humberside	Support Group	1978	47
Lancashire	Police Support Unit	1978	—
Merseyside	Task Force	1974-76	68 (1975)
	Operational Support Division	1976	—
Metropolitan Police	Special Patrol Group	1965	204
Norfolk	Police Support Unit	—	—
Northumbria	Special Patrol Group	1974	46 (1977)
North Yorkshire	Task Force	1974	—
Nottinghamshire	Special Operations Unit	—	34 (1976)
Staffordshire	Force Support Unit	1976	23
Thames Valley	Support Unit	1969	41
West Midlands	Special Patrol Group	1970	85
West Yorkshire	Task Forces	1974	—
WALES			
Gwent	Support Group	1972	20
South Wales	Special Patrol Group	1975	54
SCOTLAND			
Central Scotland	Support Group	—	—
Strathclyde	Support Units	1973	145 (1975)
N. IRELAND			
Royal Ulster Constabulary	Special Patrol Group	1970	368

Source: State Research Bulletin (Vol. 2) no 13/August-September 1979, p. 139.
* 1978 figures except where stated.

NOTES

1. Quoted by Raymond Challiner in *Socialist Worker*, 29 June 1974.
2. *Race Today*, August 1975.
3. *Guardian*, 28 June 1979.
4. *Legal Action Bulletin*, June 1979.
5. *Socialist Worker*, 28 May 1979.
6. London *Evening News* and London *Evening Standard*, 24 April 1979.
7. *Evening News*, 7 June 1979.
8. *Daily Telegraph*, 8 June 1979.
9. *Daily Mirror*, 8 June 1979.
10. *Daily Express*, 8 June 1979.
11. *Sunday Express*, 10 June 1979.
12. *Sunday Mirror*, 10 June 1979.
13. Ben Whitaker, *The Police in Society* (Eyre Methuen, 1979), pp. 254-55 and 280-2.
14. Ibid, p. 279.
15. Ibid, p. 279.
16. Ibid, p. 282.
17. *Socialist Worker*, 30 June 1979.
18. Sir Robert Mark, *In the Office of Constable* (Collins, 1978), p. 307.
19. Quoted in J. Harvey and K. Hood, *The British State*, (London 1958), p. 132.
20. Quoted in *State Research Bulletin*, vol. 2, No. 12 (June-July 1979).
21. An advocate of the 'goodwill' approach to government, Gladstone was writing in justification of the Reform Act of 1867/8. See Emil Strauss, *Irish Nationalism and British Democracy* (Methuen, 1951), p. 182.
22. In *A History of the Police in England and Wales*, (1978 revised Edition), and quoted by *State Research Bulletin*, No. 13, (August-September 1979).
23. Quoted by Tom Bowden, *Beyond the Limits of the Law*, (Penguin, Harmondsworth 1978), p. 271.
24. Mark, op. cit. p. 290.
25. Kenneth Sloan, *Public Order and the Police* (Police Review training pamphlet, 1978), p. 25.
26. See Tony Cliff, *The Crisis, Social Contract or Socialism* (Pluto Press, 1975), p. 114.
27. Quoted in Cliff, op. cit., p. 96.

28. Quoted in Tony Bunyan, *The History and Practice of the Political Police in Britain*, (Quartet, 1977), p. 270.
29. *New Left Review*, No 92, (July-August 1975), pp. 15-19.
30. *Observer*, 30 September 1974.
31. See Cliff, op. cit., p. 92.
32. *Observer*, 22 September, 1974.
33. See Bunyan, op. cit., p. 279.
34. *Daily Telegraph*, 28 January 1974.
35. *The Times*, 23 May 1972.
36. See *State Research* Bulletin No 13, August-September 1979, p. 132.
37. Ibid.
38. See Bunyan, op. cit., p. 269 and p. 293.
39. State Research op. cit., p. 133.
40. *Time Out*, 23 April 1973.
41. State Research op. cit., p. 136.
42. Quoted in *Iron Fist and Velvet Glove*, Centre for Research on Criminal Justice, (Berkeley, California, 1975).
43. Mark, op. cit., p. 102.
44. *Guardian*, 1 August 1977.
45. Mark, op. cit., p. 111.
46. *Sunday Times*, 7 February, 1971.
47. Mark, op. cit., p. 224.
48. State Research, op. cit., p. 133.
49. Ibid, p. 165.
50. Report of the Commissioner of Police of the Metropolis, 1972.
51. *Sunday Times*, 25 February 1973.
52. The Home Secretary, Robert Carr, told the House of Commons on 14th June 1973 that the SPG was "doing first class work".
53. Bunyan, op. cit., p. 95.
54. Scotland Yard, Press Release, May 1973.
55. *Socialist Worker*, 5 August 1972.
56. Ibid, 19 August 1972.
57. Ibid, 23 July 1971.
58. Ibid, 22 June 1974.
59. Ibid, 2 July 1974.
60. Ibid.
61. Ibid, 29 June 1974.
62. Mark, op. cit., pp. 167-8.
63. Ibid.
64. *The Times*, 30 June 1977.
65. Mark, op. cit., p. 245.
66. *Grunwick*, a Socialist Worker pamphlet, p. 7.
67. Ibid, p. 9.
68. Ibid.

69. *Socialist Worker*, 19 May 1979.
70. Ibid.
71. *Socialist Worker*, 10 December 1977.
72. *The Times*, 12 July 1977.
73. *Grunwick*, op. cit., p. 10.
74. Ibid, p. 12.
75. *The Guardian*, 16 August 1977.
76. Ibid.
77. Ibid.
78. Ibid.
79. *State Research Bulletin No. 4* (February-March 1978) p. 11.
80. *The Times*, 15 June 1978.
81. *Race Today*, July 1972.
82. Quoted in *Race Today*, July 1972.
83. Whitaker, op. cit., p. 216.
84. *Race Today*, July 1972.
85. See Counter Information Services, *Racism Who Profits*, pp. 18-19.
86. Ibid, p. 10.
87. Race & Class Pamphlet No. 6, *Police Against Black People* (Institute of Race Relations 1978).
88. *Daily Express*, 6 December 1978.
89. Quoted in *Tribune*, 29 July 1979.
90. Ibid.
91. *Socialist Worker*, 19 May 1979.
92. *Tribune*, 29 June 1979.
93. Race & Class, op. cit., p. 11.
94. *Hansard*, 4 July 1972, col. 115, written answers.
95. Race & Class, op. cit., p. 10.
96. *Blood on the Streets* (Bethnal Green and Stepney Trades Council, September 1979) pp. 36-44.
97. Report of the Commissioner of Police of the Metropolis, 1978.
98. Whitaker, op. cit., p. 67.
99. Quoted in Cliff, op. cit., p. 100.
100. *State Research Bulletin*, vol. 2, No. 13 (August-September 1979), pp. 136-9.
101. *Race Today*, February 1973.
102. *Manchester Evening News*, 1 November 1977.
103. *Guardian*, 8 January 1974.
104. State Research, op. cit., p. 138.
105. Chief Constables Report, 1978.
106. *Guardian*, 31 August 1977.
107. Chief Constables Report, 1976, 1977.
108. *Socialist Worker*, 25 May 1979.

109. Mark, op. cit., p. 151.
110. Whitaker, op. cit., p. 57.
111. *Daily Telegraph*, 16 May 1979.
112. Mark, op. cit., p. 151-2.
113. Quoted in *Race Today*, April 1976.
114. *New Left Review*, op. cit., pp. 19 & 20.

Index

Index

Alderson, John, 28, 49-51
Ali, Altab, 193
Ali, Ishaque, 193
Ampex Videofile, 91
Anderton, James, 8, 42-5, 48, 51, 54
Anti-Bloodsports League, 77
Anti Nazi League, 38, 40, 41, 155, 159, 160, 194, 201, 203
Association of Chief Police Officers, 11, 27, 41, 45, 46, 48-9, 93, 185

Balcombe Street siege, 177-8
BBC, agreement with police, 16
Brick Lane, 193-4

'C' Department computer (see 'National Intelligence Computer')
Callaghan, James, 30, 175, 177
Carr, Robert, 168, 177
Cass, Commander, 159, 161
Chagger, Gurdip Singh, 38, 154, 155
Clutterbuck, Richard, 171, 172
collators (see 'police collators')
collators, case of the Wilsons, 129-30
Communist Party, 38
Community Development Projects, 3
community policing, 3-5, 49-51, 65
complaints system, 10, 12, 15
Computers and Privacy, 95-6
Confait case, 19, 20
Cook, Robin, MP, 52-3
Conservative Party, 13, 29-30, 38
Criminal Intelligence Retrieval System, 127
Criminal Intelligence Unit, 97, 98, 103-4
Criminal Justice Act 1967, 17

Criminal Law Revision Committee, 1972 Report of, 17-8, 19, 26, 32
Criminal Records Office(s), 66, 84-5, 86, 94-5, 104
CRS (France), 165, 172

Data Protection Committee, 71, 83, 85, 90, 94, 100, 102, 108, 116, 131, 142
Diplomatic Protection Group, 177
driver number code, 80-1
Drugs Intelligence Unit, 67, 76, 97, 98, 103, 104

fingerprint code, 91
Fisher, Sir Henry, Report by, 19, 20-1, 25
flying pickets, 168-70
Fraud Squad, 67, 97, 103, 104, 106

Gately, Kevin, 36, 178-81, 202
GB 75, 170
Gerrard, John, 175, 176, 179
Gladstone, William, 166
Griffiths, Eldon, MP, 30
Grunwick strike, 3, 14, 38, 58, 181-4, 198, 200, 201

Heathrow Airport manoevres 1974, 33-4, 176, 177, 196
Hunt Saboteurs Association, 77-8

identity cards, 67, 68, 81, 117, 137
Immigration Intelligence Unit, 97, 98, 103, 104, 106
International Marxist Group, 38, 180

India House 1973, 36, 177, 178
Institute of Race Relations, 4, 5, 6, 188-91

Jenkins, Roy, 11, 200
Joint Automatic Data Processing Unit (JADPU), 72, 96, 100, 108, 109, 119, 139
journalists, restrictions on, 15-6
Judges' Rules, 20, 26
jury system, 17, 18, 143
jury vetting, 143

Kelly, Jimmy, 164

Labour Party, 13, 30, 31, 38, 185
Legal Action Group, 156
Lewisham (1977), 181, 184-6, 188, 198, 201

mail interception, 103
Mant, Professor, 160
Mark, Sir Robert, 2, 11-21, 23, 24, 26, 27, 31-2, 33-5, 36-8, 39, 40, 41, 45, 47, 48, 51, 54-5, 67, 167, 175-6, 179, 182, 187, 200
McGeown, James, 163-4, 195
McNee, Sir David, 16, 21, 22, 23-7, 31, 38, 39, 40-1, 42, 48, 51, 57, 67, 182, 184-6, 194, 198-9
military-police relations (see police and the military)
miners strikes, 167, 168-70, 172-3, 195, 202
MI5, 54, 66, 98, 116, 140
MI6, 116
Mobile Automatic Data Experiment (MADE), 135

National Association for Freedom, 181, 182
National Council for Civil Liberties, 14, 97, 119, 130, 143, 187
National Front, 14, 38, 41, 42-3, 57, 154-7, 159, 178-9, 180, 181, 185-6, 190, 193-4, 195, 199, 201, 203
National Intelligence Computer, 'C' Department, 70, 96-109, 116, 139, 140, 145

National Security Committee, 173
National Security Plan, 171-2
neighbourhood councils, 4, 6
Nievens, Peter, 16, 96
Northern Ireland, 42, 66, 70, 109-17, 141, 175, 176, 181, 186, 195
    numbers on army computer, 110, 112, 116

Oluwale, David, 162-3

Parliament and the police (see 'police, and Parliament')
Peach, Blair, 2, 57, 154-65, 202-3
picketing and policing, 3, 13, 45, 200, 201
Police,
    antipathy to socialism, 13, 14
    black policemen, 187
    centralization of, 1, 45-7, 65, 72
    collators, 66-7, 68, 69, 70, 71, 77, 81, 97, 104, 117-31, 134, 137, 139, 141, 143
    complaints system, 10, 12, 15
    computers, 1, 4, 51, 65-150
    and Conservatism, 29-30
    guns, 167
    individuals on file, 104, 131
    and the military, 3, 33-5, 66, 70, 109-17, 132, 172-3, 175, 176, 182, 196
    and Parliament, 2-3, 12, 23, 28, 30, 80, 81, 93, 95, 98, 99-100, 111-2, 140, 177, 201
    pay, 29, 31
    race/racism, 3-5, 9, 44, 155, 178, 184-5, 186-94, 199
    strike (1919), 166
    surveillance by, 1, 4, 57, 65-150
    and trade unions, 3, 13, 14, 22, 34, 46, 52-3, 54, 55, 125, 162, 166, 167-73, 174, 178, 181-4, 195, 199, 200-1, 202
Police Act 1976, 12, 31, 32
Police Federation, 3, 11, 21, 22, 27-30, 31-2, 42, 57, 185
Police National Computer (PNC), 66, 68, 69, 70, 71, 72-96, 110, 111, 112, 116, 117, 121, 127, 128, 131,

132-3, 134, 135, 136, 137, 140, 141, 144
number of transactions on, 92
postcode, 89-90, 113, 124
Post Office data transmission, 116
Powell, Enoch, 28, 32
Prevention of Terrorism Act, 86, 141
Prior, James, 13
Public Order Act, 42, 43, 84, 154, 185-6

racial identity code, 130
Red Lion Square 1974, 14, 33, 36-8, 39, 157, 178-81, 182, 200
Rees, Merlyn, 37, 52-3, 99-100, 111, 183, 184
Reiner, Robert, 27, 30
Royal Commission on Criminal Procedure, 21-7, 56, 57, 188
Royal Ulster Constabulary, 53, 70, 109, 110, 116, 175, 176

Saltley picket, 3, 168-70, 172-3, 202
Scargill, Arthur, 168-70, 182, 202
Scarman, Sir Leslie (now Lord), 14, 33, 36-7, 179, 180, 182
Shrewsbury pickets, 3, 198
socialism, antipathy of police to, 13, 14
Socialist Workers Party, 38, 154, 203
SOUNDEX, 87-90, 109
Southall, 38, 40, 51, 57, 58, 154-65, 186, 188, 198, 201
Special Air Services (SAS), 111, 170, 173, 175, 196

Special Branch, 52-6, 64, 66, 67, 70, 71, 76, 78, 85, 97, 98, 99, 100, 102, 103, 104, 106, 109, 116, 122, 125, 130, 143, 176, 178
Special Patrol Group, 1, 2, 3, 4, 36, 130, 153-205
State Research group, 52, 53, 54, 146, 165, 173, 195
STATUS, 108, 139
Stirling, Col. David, 170-1
Strathclyde Support Unit, 163, 182, 195
Superintendents' Association, 11, 21-2, 31

telephone tapping, 103
Thames Valley Police,
computer, 66, 70, 113, 115, 119-31
number on record, 121
'third force' concept, 165-6, 171-3
Towers, Liddle, 163
trade unions (see 'police, and trade unions')
Trades Union Congress, 159, 165, 183, 184, 185, 195

Ulsternet, 110, 113
Unison, 170
Unit beat policing, 66, 117, 118
urban aid programme, 3

Walker, Gen. Sir Walter, 170-1
Whitelaw, William, 37, 155, 166
Wilson, Harold, 61n, 111, 112

Contributors

DUNCAN CAMPBELL
is a journalist on the staff of the *New Statesman*. He has also written extensively about the technology of surveillance for *New Scientist*, the *Sunday Times, Time Out* and computer magazines. In September 1978 he was one of three defendants in the ABC Official Secrets trial, which resulted in a conviction and conditional discharge for breaching the notorious Section 2 of the Act by interviewing a former soldier in the Intelligence Corps. He has been writing an account of the ABC case and the secret intelligence agencies which it involved, and has also submitted evidence to the Royal Commission on Criminal Procedure concerning police intelligence gathering and the use of computers.

PETER HAIN
is an anti-racist campaigner and socialist activist. He has written *Mistaken Identity* (1976), *Radical Regeneration* (1975), and *Don't Play with Apartheid* (1971), and has edited *Community Politics* (1976) and *Policing the Police* Volume 1 (1979). He joined the Labour Party in 1977, having previously been a prominent Young Liberal and, since 1976, has worked as a research officer at the Union of Post Office Workers.

MARTIN KETTLE
is home affairs correspondent of *New Society*. He was born and educated at Leeds and read modern history at Oxford University. From 1974 to 1979 he was research officer of the Cobden Trust. He is a member of the *State Research* group which monitors developments in policing, the military and emergency planning.

JOANNA ROLLO
is a journalist on *Socialist Worker*. Previously she has worked in the international department of the National Union of Students, the Committee for Freedom in Mozambique, Angola and Guinea, and also Counter Information Services.

58
180